HOPE FOR FILM

HOPE FOR FILM

From the Frontlines of the Independent Cinema Revolutions

Ted Hope

with Anthony Kaufman

SOFT SKULL PRESS
An imprint of Counterpoint
Berkeley

Library of Congress Cataloging-in-Publication Data
Hope, Ted.
Hope for film : from the frontline of the independent cinema revolutions / Ted Hope.
pages cm
ISBN 978-1-61902-332-1 (hardback)
1. Hope, Ted. 2. Motion picture producers and directors—United States—Biography. 3. Independent filmmakers—United States—Biography. I. Title.
PN1998.3.H6865A3 2014
791.4302'33092—dc23
[B]
2014014012
Cover design and illustration by Jonathan Bennett
Interior design by Sabrina Plomitallo-González, Neuwirth & Associates

SOFT SKULL PRESS
An imprint of Counterpoint
www.softskull.com

Printed in the United States of America
Distributed by Publishers Group West

10 9 8 7 6 5 4 3 2 1

To Vanessa,

You are my hope and partner in all things. May we forever continue to help each other reach higher, deeper, and truer.

To my son Michael,

May you too find a path that allows your passion to sustain both itself and you, while never losing sight of the privilege such a gift is.

Contents

Acknowledgments

When people think about film producers, they don't normally recognize a "body of work" and how the films fit together. That's usually reserved for directors. But the films I make and love all have a powerful and personal story at their center. And the vision for those stories has a singularity largely driven by the director, but not the director alone. The fact that I had partners all along, directors who were generally willing to listen, and an environment where everyone was willing to figure things out and make things better is the most fortunate aspect of my professional life so far.

If I hadn't arrived in New York City when I did, gotten caught up in the indie film tide that was then rising and lifted so many, and happened to be in the same class that Anne Carey was taking, who knows how things might have gone? Drinking beers on the lift gate of a grip truck with Rich Ludwig led me to Hal Hartley, and riffing on Godard and aliens led me to James Schamus. Good friends and collaborators spoke well of me to Vanessa Guest, not yet suspecting she'd become Vanessa Hope, a collaborator in the greatest of ways—including filmmaking.

For all filmmakers, collaboration with the producer and the whole creative team is essential. Collaboration is a class that film schools should add to their curricula now that they finally have producing departments. I can't help but think about how fortunate I was to have Anne Carey, James Schamus, Christine Vachon, Hal Hartley, Anthony Bregman, Ang Lee, Mary Jane Skalski, and particularly my wife, Vanessa Hope, along with everyone else, from the executives who initially supported us, to the unions and the crews that backed us when we had little but our passion, and later David Linde, without whom James Schamus and I could never have built our film company, Good Machine. I could never have done it alone.

Chapter 1

Inspiration

It was January 1991 and bitter cold. Why in the hell were we out on the streets of New York City shooting a movie? The U.S. military had just launched its massive air campaign in Iraq. The nightly infrared news images of the bombing of Baghdad looked a bit like the high-contrast black-and-white film stock we were using on the film that had brought us together, a short called *Keep It for Yourself.* Directed by French filmmaker Claire Denis, it was my first project for the film company Good Machine, which I had just cofounded with James Schamus.

Our office was above one of the strip clubs on Warren Street in Tribeca. My longtime girlfriend and I had split up, and I was through with silly things like romance. There was only one thing I wanted to do: work, work, work. I should have been in heaven, but the production was going horribly wrong. The film crew didn't trust Claire or her cinematographer Agnès Godard—they were insisting on shooting in chronological script order to help the nonprofessional actors reach a level of emotional truth. Even as a newbie producer, I knew this was not the most efficient way to shoot a movie, but I wanted to make directors' movies, and I felt I had to trust them. Meanwhile, members of the crew were saying, "Who are these European rank amateurs?" They were threatening mutiny. Then, light streaks kept mysteriously showing up on the exposed film stock—unbeknownst to us at the time, the already-sensitive celluloid was conducting excessive amounts of static electricity as a result of the low humidity in the freezing temperatures. In order to continue, the camera crew were nestling the film stock in down jackets or putting hot water bottles around the film magazines.

Despite the troubles on the movie, we finished it and it turned out well. Each day required the confidence to solve what looked to be an impossible challenge. I've learned that a producer cannot lose faith in his or her director, the crew, or the project. You may need to discuss uncomfortable realities in private with a sympathetic (and hopefully wise) ear, but in public, you must demonstrate that you know (and not just believe) that there is something special about the project.

Claire would often tease me by saying, "Today is not a good day to film." She had been an assistant director to the French New Wave maverick Jean-Luc Godard, who would often show up on a set, evaluate what was going on, and declare, "Today is not a good day to film"—and then go home. Claire knew such pronouncements were the opposite of how American indie films work. The first time she said it, I felt my temperature rise, but then I realized it was a joke. Today, I see it as a cruel truism of what I do—producing requires mounting a campaign to barrel forward, even when it's not "a good day to film."

Claire Denis has gone on to become one of the masters of world cinema (e.g., *Beau Travail*), and our company, Good Machine, turned out to be a success, producing some of the most acclaimed American independent films of the last two decades (*The Ice Storm*, *The Brothers McMullen*, *In the Bedroom*, and *Crouching Tiger, Hidden Dragon*, to name just a few).

The world keeps changing rapidly, even if some things don't. The United States will likely be in Baghdad, in some capacity, forever, but the independent-film community and the whole entertainment industry is altogether different from what it was when I first began watching films.

I got started with a few advantages that not everyone has. I am male, and white and was born into the middle class to parents who valued education, art, and political engagement. These were colossal head starts allowing me to advance in ways others only dream of. It's comforting to think the film business, or America for that matter, is a land of opportunity, that hard work and talent can take you to the top. George Carlin pointed out that it's called the American Dream because you have to be asleep to believe it. To be able to walk into a room and be the person others are accustomed to doing business with is a great advantage. I wish I could say I earned my place and the opportunity to make the films I did, but the truth is, I just took advantage of the place I was in—one that I was born into. Most people are not so fortunate to even be let in the door.

Fortunately, I have never been short on ideas or the belief that big things could be accomplished. I was raised to think we could change the world. And I received a last name, Hope, that helps keep me out of the depths of despair, even when it becomes clear how arduous that task really is.

I was also fueled with the fire of urgency. I learned the fragility of life when I was only six years old and my dad died. I had a hard time understanding what death really meant, but as I grew into a young man, I began to appreciate how random life and death can be. And I was able to recognize life, like privilege, as an incredible gift, one that could motivate me to work harder and reach for things I wasn't sure I could ever obtain.

Movies became a touchstone fairly early on for me in several ways. When my dad was in the hospital, *Planet of the Apes* was about to come out. Although my father was a college English professor, I remember watching *Batman* on TV with him and loving the silly fun of it. I bought *Planet of the Apes* trading cards and brought them to the hospital to plan our trip to the film when it opened. He died before that happened, but my mom took me to the first three installments knowing what it symbolized for me—despite the fact she couldn't stand them. Movies were about unspoken connections.

Mom would truck me and my sisters into Cambridge, Massachusetts, to go see Charlie Chaplin and Buster Keaton films. Initially I would try to do the Little Tramp's shuffle for my friends, thinking it was hilarious. Not getting the reference, they just thought I was weird. Having to hide my love of films only made it more precious, something that became part of my secret identity.

One of my dad's dying wishes was for my sisters and me to have a great education, ideally at one of the country's leading boarding schools, like Phillips Exeter or Andover. He knew the advantages that the prestige and exposure such institutions could offer. My mom, made a widow with three kids at age thirty-three, began to teach at the local community college. It was not easy. She remarried about a decade later to another teacher at her college. But with what they were paid, she got more emotional than financial support. We were middle class, but we didn't aspire for material goods or fancy things. My mom and dad, and then she and my stepfather, were committed to living within their means.

Despite their financial limitations, my mom and stepdad were able to send one of my sisters and me to Exeter. Education was what money could buy. For years, I kept the prep school aspect of my education under wraps. Places like Exeter signify privilege. And early on, I wanted everyone to believe I fought for everything I got.

Now, there is no question that both the education and the reputation of Exeter gave me a tremendous advantage. Exeter trained us students to think that we could rule or run the world. Most people enter adulthood already beaten down, unable to access stories of success. Exeter offered U.S. presidents as role models, and every presidential candidate stopped by the school (it being located in New Hampshire, home of the first primary in the country). It was such a gift to be there.

Exeter was a tremendously politicizing experience for me, too. My New England town was working class, best known for being where the Hells Angels summered and where everyone's father seemed to be an employee at General Electric.

Now I was watching my new classmates arrive at school in limos. Many of the Exeter kids expected to take over their dads' businesses; at first I thought this meant that they had it made—and I was a bit jealous. I didn't see until later that it was also a trap. They were encouraged to do what was expected of them. At fifteen years old, the idea that you are going to end up mirroring your parents can be discouraging. Recognizing this, I was determined from a young age to do something different from what was expected of me.

On my first day at Exeter, my mom noticed that Jean Renoir's *Grand Illusion*, one of the greatest movies of all time, was screening at the school's Wednesday film series. I made sure to go. To me, it was like watching amazing literature. After that, I made sure to go every week I could. That's where I first got to see some of the all-time American greats—provocative, bold, and groundbreaking movies such as *A Clockwork Orange*, *Taxi Driver*, and *Midnight Cowboy*. And in high school and on a gigantic screen. It seems virtually impossible now. As you sit alone in a big room with towering images, films sear into your mind in a way that today's young viewers, watching in the comfort of their own homes, will never have.

I will never forget the year that Woody Allen's *Annie Hall* was competing in the Oscars. I was a teenager then, but felt like I did when I was just a little kid. I stayed up all night, riveted to the awards show, as if I were watching the Stanley Cup hockey championships, rooting for Woody Allen's film as I had for Bobby Orr, Derek Sanderson, and the Boston Bruins a few years prior. *Annie Hall* felt like my movie. The characters were people that I thought I might get to know one day. The situations were real; no one had a superpower beyond wit and intelligence. And it was so playful with the form; it was making its own rules.

Following rules has never been my strong suit. When I was a kid, I was fascinated by power and what I could get away with. I was fascinated by the difference between how we were perceived and how things actually were.

At Exeter, I couldn't resist getting into a little mischief. Mostly this meant executing pranks with my friends, but the authorities seemed to think I was up to something more severe. One of my friends broke down in tears when she confessed to me that the faculty asked her to spy on me. My drive to ridicule the establishment was, in part, the fuel that pushed me to advance my career later in life. My "I'll show them" attitude simply yielded dozens and dozens of movies.

Even today, I can feel that rage, to tear it down, to *show the motherfuckers*, to yell, and lash out. It's comforting in its own strange way. The Clash sang, "Anger can be power; let fury have its hour." It is a song of my youth, but it captures the drive I needed to make it happen. It carried me into and out of college—and after.

I wasn't a star student or an impressive leader by any means. But I started organizing events, some legal, some not. It was enough that one of my friends told me that I was going to make a great film producer; I would forget this comment, but found it written in my high school yearbook some twenty-five years later. My friend went on to become a neuroscientist, so someone that intelligent must have known what she was talking about.

In 1980, when I was a freshman at Lewis & Clark College and was home for Thanksgiving break, my creative energies were further sparked. The Clash's *Sandinista!* came out on import and Martin Scorsese's *Raging Bull* and Godard's *Every Man for Himself* opened at the same time—and these were the worlds I wanted to inhabit and be a part of. I wanted to be in that realm where art met politics—where culture could help reveal our world, connect us to people different from ourselves, and, even beyond this, make us feel part of something fun, meaningful, original, and authentic. These films felt like a rallying cry. Exciting. Urgent. Vital. And very much "of the moment."

During college, politics was my first love. Politics felt like the only responsible choice if I wanted to make a positive impact in the world; filmmaking seemed self-indulgent. On summer vacations and later, when I was between colleges, I canvassed door-to-door for Ralph Nader's community-organizing and citizen-lobby operations. The work trained me for hundred-hour workweeks and helped me recognize that so much taken for granted in life is actually a privilege. The use of our labor is one of the key ways that we can define ourselves and the world we desire. Many of the lessons I learned from citizen-led politics would eventually find their way into my career as a filmmaker.

Several lessons I mention in this book are derived from the key tactics I gathered during my time knocking on doors in Oregon and Massachusetts: listen to your audience; use hard work to inspire others; engineer serendipity; maintain enthusiasm; strengthen the bonds of community; and, above all else, never forget the human side of the equation in the creation of both art and business.

Nevertheless, during my brief immersion into organized politics, I quickly became frustrated by how difficult it was to bring about change in either the political process or the cultural mind-set. I imagined that with movies, I could do more, and do it far more quickly. Although I grew up in a small town in Massachusetts, I was fortunate to have a mother originally from New York City who introduced me to incredible films. I consider myself quite fortunate that I formed an early movie-going habit. After a long day of canvassing work, seeing a movie each night would carry me through to the next day (without the aid of the more popular, self-destructive diversions consumed by many of my contemporaries).

There were so many films that inspired me to make movies myself: Godard's *Breathless* and *Masculine/Feminine*, François Truffaut's *The 400 Blows*, Scorsese's *Taxi Driver*, Francis Coppola's *Apocalypse Now*, Spike Lee's *She's Gotta Have It*, Jim Jarmusch's *Stranger Than Paradise*, Susan Seidelman's *Smithereens*. I began to dream about the transformative, myth-making power of film and considered how deeply it connects diverse audiences—and not just locally but also around the world. These were more than great works of art; these films brought people together, taught them to talk, to think differently. Through film, we could unite and achieve solidarity. Those dreams are even more real for me today than back then.

Eventually, I moved from political organizing to New York University film school, a leap made easier by a scholarship I received. It quickly became apparent that directing was the most coveted position at NYU, because it was the job that presumably brought glory and recognition. Not only were few people choosing to become producers, but there wasn't even a producing department at the school yet. Besides the conventional belief that Hollywood, in all its glitz and glamour, was the only filmmaking path, producing was then and still is largely misunderstood. I met one of my longtime business partners, Anne Carey, on the first day that we both transferred into school, and our shared affinity for helping to facilitate works of cinematic art helped us through those dark ages when "indie" didn't quite yet seem like an option. There was no place for those scrappy, emotionally raw, formally adventurous, or remotely transgressive subjects. It just wasn't being done yet.

When I observed the work of directors at that time, I found it prohibitively intimidating because of the large number of rapid-fire decisions that rest on an auteur's shoulders. But I now realize that independent producers who produce the way I do not only make just as many decisions with as much speed and consideration as their directors, but we're also who the director—and everyone else—turns to in a crisis. And we producers must see the film project through from its earliest incarnation to its theatrical release and beyond. Our role requires us to go well beyond the details of each project or the concerns of any one position. Our responsibilities are numerous: to take care of the well-being of our entire industry and its ability to support, both creatively and financially, a diverse body of work and artists, and to ethically shape the way projects are born, nurtured, executed, delivered and distributed. Producers must look at the big picture even as they concentrate on specific projects. We are also small business owners, committed to having a sustainable company that can both initiate projects and manage them after they are completed. We are cheerleaders and shoulders to cry on, the force that allows other artists to dream and sustains them when the dream may not be obtained. All of which goes far beyond any individual film.

Likewise, when I got a scholarship to attend NYU, I saw a bunch of students who thought it would be neat to make movies, but none seemed to recognize what a privilege it was. It wasn't *necessary*. The school and the faculty seemed like yes men, embracing anything that anyone said or made. I did not believe that everything was good or deserved to be made. I wanted to understand how to go deeper, how to make things that cut harder and unlocked the wonderful. I carried with me the feelings I had when I first saw those movies at the Exeter film series. I was awestruck by those films and felt that somehow, a path would let me into the mystery of such creations. If NYU didn't have that yet, l was going to find the path myself. I needed someone or something to rally against, something I could prove was wrong. Those chips on one's shoulder can act like rocket fuel.

If I knew then all the tumultuous responsibilities that producing required—the fragility of the creative process, the complications of investor management, the lack of transparency and clarity in the way films are distributed—I might not have become a producer. But producing is as much about process as it is about execution. Producing well is not only an obtainable skill, but also a methodology that can enhance your life. My focus may be filmmaking, but the rules I follow have also given me something far beyond just a satisfying existence. I often say to students and audiences that indie producing is a horrible job, but a wonderful life.

Producing, at its core, is also a creative act. I have been both the originator and the generator of many films, the individual who has had to nurse them along, enticing and inspiring others to join along the way. From films like *American Splendor*, which I had dreamed of making for almost a decade, to filmmakers who I championed for years before the industry took notice—people like Hal Hartley and Ang Lee—it is the producer's passion that drives so much of the creative activity that goes on in the film business. The satisfaction of getting movies made, seen, and enjoyed, however, is often a private pleasure, while the failure to get it done or done well is a private suffering. Producers are unsung heroes, a class that is misunderstood and barely recognized.

When I came to New York in the early 1980s, the American independent-film movement didn't exist. At the time, I was living on less than ten dollars a day. I'd never eaten sushi, my shirts were all torn, and yes, the frames of my glasses were taped. All I knew was that I wanted to make the equivalent of European art films from an American perspective—personal films about what it was really like to live in this world. Slowly, that hope of uniting the Clash with Godard's radical sensibility, Truffaut's respect for humanity, and Scorsese's visceral intensity was coming within my reach.

When I saw Jarmusch's *Stranger Than Paradise* during its opening weekend run in 1984, there was a guy outside the theater, harassing people with flyers and saying, "Come see my movie; come see my movie." And when I sat down, a trailer began, and there was the same guy from outside the theater, on the screen selling tube socks. It was Spike Lee, hawking *She's Gotta Have It*. And literally, that same week, when I got off the subway, I saw Jim Jarmusch on the platform, and I remember thinking, "These people's lives are like mine: They're making movies in New York and getting it done. Why can't I?"

The second wave of punk rock and do-it-yourself aesthetics were in the air: that notion that if I have something to say and can say it with a whole lot of passion, maybe someone will connect to it. So I wondered, Can you take those two sensibilities—European art film and DIY punk—and apply it to American independent movies?

One of my first jobs on a set was for Alex Cox's *Sid & Nancy*, the story of punk icon Sid Vicious of the Sex Pistols. I learned a lot from the experience, but perhaps the greatest lesson was "Don't ask for permission." So much would never have happened if we always followed the rules. I had read all the Sid Vicious scripts circulating at the time, and Alex Cox and Abbe Wool's was by far the best. When I heard they were going to shoot in New York City, I wanted to get hired. The production assistants were hiring all the coolest kids in town, and I didn't seem to qualify. I stopped by the office and dropped off my resume. I called. I mailed. But I was getting no traction. Desperate, one day I showed up at the office at 7 am, with two cups of coffee. The production office coordinator showed up soon after, and asked if I was there to work. I told her yes, gave her the coffee, and jumped inside as soon as she opened the door. I emptied the trash, washed the desks, reloaded the copier, and stocked the refrigerator. I made sure I was always the hardest working person in the room. At the end of the day, the coordinator asked me if she could do anything for me. I asked to speak to the production manager. She asked why. "To be hired," I replied. She laughed and told me not to worry about it. And I was.

There was so much chaos and drug use on the shoot that it gave production assistants like me the opportunity to step up and fill in for areas that weren't being covered. The first time I ever stepped in for the assistant director to call "Roll" and "Cut" was a shot when Sid falls down the stairs at the Chelsea Hotel. I thought the movie was going to be a disaster, but miraculously, when I finally saw the finished movie at the New York Film Festival, all the mistakes and all the other things I thought were fucked up looked gorgeous, transcendent, and emotional. I thought to myself, "You don't know anything yet."

One afternoon, I dropped off my résumé at the Continental Film Group. It sounded like an important company since it had such a generic name—even if it only had one person working with the company. I told the guy (now a longtime close friend, Peter Hawkins) that I wanted to do product placement. "I could do what Spielberg did with Reese's Pieces in *E. T.* for independent films, too, you know?" I said. They were making a film titled *Once Again*, and even though I'd never done it before, I made a proposal that I'd raise a hundred thousand dollars' worth of product placement before the company started shooting or it wouldn't have to pay me a single cent. (Which I eventually succeeded in doing on the film.) Eventually, I worked my way up and became a production and development executive for Continental. I was the company's first year-round employee.

For Continental, I found a script that I liked called *Tiger Warsaw*: the story of a son who returns home to seek forgiveness from his father. Roy London, the acting coach who led Geena Davis and Sharon Stone to their Oscars, wrote the script.

During the preproduction on that film, I had the only panic attack of my entire career. I was in charge of putting together all the actor deals, hiring the crew, and securing the principle location. I needed money to lock everything down, but my financier wouldn't put the initial funds into the bank until I closed all the key actor deals. I had never dealt with agents before. And they were pushing to close. I was juggling calls from one agent to the next. When I had secured Patrick Swayze, I was trying to get other actors like Mary McDonnell and Piper Laurie to all sign on, but I didn't have enough time in the day to get it all done. When one of the agents asked me, "Was this 'a most-favored nations' deal?" I didn't know what it meant, but it sounds like a fair term, and I said yes. He said "Great. Done deal." And we closed it. I wasn't sure what I agreed to, but if it was that easy, I was going to use it again.

What *most-favored nations* means is that everyone is treated equally. We weren't paying Patrick very much, despite his just coming off *Dirty Dancing*, so as a result, I had closed all of the actors' deals and the film was going ahead. But before I had said yes to that agent, I literally broke out in hives. Luckily, I found the cure in this term, *most-favored nations*. And since then, I've continued to learn the benefits of treating people fairly and equally.

We got the film made, but the whole experience taught me—at the ripe age of twenty-three—that the industry was filled with self-indulgent, misanthropic, power-obsessed, narcissistic adolescents masquerading as grown-ups. Everyone was fighting each other on that movie: The director-producer locked the line producer out of the office, the cinematographer refused to talk to the director, Patrick Swayze was swearing at the other actors, vehicles were rolled regularly, and key crew members were junkies. It was all absolutely insane. What with the tremendous amount of drug use, both legal and illegal, I said to myself, "The last thing people need is more movies. What they need is serious counseling."

On the positive side, the experience made me want to change the way films were produced. When I started working as a production assistant, there was always a lot of drug abuse on sets. But whether people were using or not, a frenetic quality on the set made everyone seem cocaine-fueled. It was not about building a creative atmosphere. No one could ever take advantage of serendipity; it was just about going forward with blinders. It all made me question whether I really wanted to remain in the film business.

So after *Tiger Warsaw*, I quit. I decided I would go back to school either to become a drug counselor or to design sustainable ecosystems for developing nations (by the way, not unlike my responsibilities in the developing film business to this day). But after further thought, I couldn't foresee spending another few years back in school.

Then I got a phone call from another company, this one called Films Around the World. The company rep told me, "We have to come up with a movie we can complete within ten days: Find a location we can shoot it in, and find people that we don't have to pay much. We don't have a script, we don't have a cast, but we're going to shoot it in four weeks from now regardless, and we'll pay you three hundred a week to be the production manager." Since I was broke and without any idea what I was capable of doing next, I took the proposal as an offer I couldn't refuse.

We found an abandoned tuberculosis ward in a New Jersey hospital, where apparently the first lobotomy in the state was performed. We quickly came up with the story of a haunted insane asylum where eight teenagers (four good, four bad) go to play and get into trouble. Basically, we were just running people up and down the halls. The film was eventually called *Doom Asylum*. The company credited me as associate producer, but embarrassed and unsure whether I had even earned it, I hid it from my résumé for years. (If one of the movie's stars, Kristin Davis, from *Sex and the City*, hadn't had it listed on her own credits, I might never have owned up to it). But the film used many techniques that my directors and I applied to many of our first passion projects and still use today: Find a core location that could serve as a base for the entire story and production; write scenes for different times of day, so that the sun is your main lighting instrument; cast friends and acquaintances who want to be there as much as you; and make sure that people enjoyed being there despite horrible conditions. *Doom Asylum* was an exercise in how to get a movie made with as little available as possible. If I ran a film school, I would require the students to make a feature film for just a thousand dollars. They'd learn tricks that they could apply for the rest of their lives, no matter how poorly the movie turned out.

After making *Doom Asylum*, I had eight or nine movies that I actually wanted to make. But I didn't exactly know what the process was, except for trying to get the scripts better and meet people with money who could fund them. One of those scripts was *Bad Hero*, a romantic drama about an undependable guy who was often in the wrong place at the wrong time—and who a certain type of woman was cursed to fall for over and over again. I was impressed with the ambition of it and the rhythm of the dialogue, which sounded like Sam Shepard meets David Mamet. But I had no idea how I would get the money to make it.

At the time, I was living with a bunch of friends in a massive three-bedroom apartment on 111th Street for nine hundred dollars per month all in—this was the early 1990s. The building was trying to go co-op and recruit people to buy their apartments for cheap. But we organized and all signed a no-buy pledge. The landlords pushed us hard, and finally, we all agreed to move out if they paid us thirty thousand dollars each. It was enough money to pay off a year of college loans, and for the first time in my life, I had five thousand dollars left over to do something important with. I tried buying the movie rights to books by Philip K. Dick and Jim Thompson, and although these authors were still relatively unknown in film circles at the time, no one would license the material to a fledgling producer. So I reached out to the writer of *Bad Hero*, a thin-as-a-pencil son of a Long Island iron worker. Hal Hartley and I met at a bar, drank a lot of beer and agreed to work on the script together.

But after a couple of years of our trying to get *Bad Hero* made, Hal called me one day and said, "Meet me at Grand Central Station. I want to show you something." It was a big mystery. But I met him there, and we boarded a Long Island Railroad commuter train. Hal then told me he wanted to show me where he had grown up. It was a puzzling invite. He didn't say anything more at first. Finally, I had to ask him why. What was the big deal about his hometown? "We are going to shoot this script there," he said, and he handed me a new screenplay.

"We're not going to shop it around," he said. "We're going to make it now. I took out a loan; my brother took a loan out, and my cousin did too. We have forty-five thousand dollars. You have to tell me how to make a movie for this amount of money."

The film was called *The Unbelievable Truth*; it was about girl who was obsessed with nuclear destruction and who was about to go off to college. She falls in love with an ex-con who is rumored to have murdered, many years before, the father of his high school sweetheart. We shot for ten days in Lindenhurst, Long Island, and stayed in a scary motel, four to a room, where we could hear the drug addicts fighting over their last fix and the prostitutes letting out an extra yelp to let their tricks get their money's worth. We did our call sheets on a mimeograph machine that printed on heat-sensitive paper. The paper would only hold the ink for twelve hours; by morning, we needed to print a new version so people could see the plan that day. It was as scrappy and gritty and exhausting as possible.

I remember shooting a scene on the doorsteps of the house where Hal grew up. Actress Adrienne Shelly, with smeared lipstick on her face, was talking to actor Robert John Burke about the importance of doing what you love. But I couldn't keep my eyes open. Every time we rolled camera, my eyelids started to close. I was going on three hours' sleep. The days did not hold enough hours to get all of our work done, and I couldn't figure out how to map out the rest of the production. The sun was setting in twenty minutes, but we needed hours of daylight to finish. We were doomed. I drifted off into another three-second nap of despair. But then, suddenly, I became alert to the actors in the scene. Adrienne looked desperate, awkward, and eager, and Burke's character was mesmerizing. And they were so fresh and natural and deeply connected to each other that my eyes widened, and I abruptly felt alive and into it. Hal loved the take. Cut. Everyone picked up the equipment and moved on to the next sequence. Then Hal got this glow about him, and we could see that the sun was casting this perfect light. What we had scheduled for three hours and multiple camera setups, Hal now saw that he could capture in a single, continuous take. He held the camera in a two-shot, and fifteen minutes later, three takes later, we had it "in the can"; we were back on schedule. Suddenly, it was all working. The impossible became possible.

I still felt very much like an amateur, but when Hal not only completed *The Unbelievable Truth*, but also brought it to the 1989 Toronto International Film Festival, and it was picked up for distribution by Miramax, we were no longer just a bunch of people making movies for a hobby. During the premiere party, there were all these girls coming up to him. I felt as if I were standing next to a rock star. People were swarming around Hal, and I could hear people murmuring, "He made the movie." It was the first time I thought that maybe it was possible, that maybe I, and others like me—people without connections or money—could not only make movies for our living, but also get them seen. And maybe we could change the world a little bit by what we made.

When James Schamus and I formed Good Machine in 1991, one of the core questions was, Did we want to make *radical* films—in both form and content—like one of our common favorite auteurs at the time, Chilean director Raúl Ruiz? His films were wildly experimental, yet unpretentious, expansive, and playful. But dreams are one thing; practicalities are always another. James and I wanted to survive and make more than just one film. We decided that we wanted to make films that were influenced by filmmakers like Ruiz, but that appealed to a larger audience. I wanted to reach people, to bring about the change of mind that I believed politics had a difficult time achieving. And we wanted to bring pleasure to significant numbers of people—all those different groups hungry for substantive cinema and unsatisfied with mainstream movies.

The name of the company, Good Machine, came from Jon Amiel's first feature, *Queen of Hearts*, the story of an Italian family who moved to London in World War II and underwent much hardship and suffering, until they inherited a great cappuccino machine, the *bella machina*—and a café culture was born. We felt we could serve up the same sense of intellectual and visceral satisfaction. James had the forethought to realize that if we kept the Italian term, there was a good chance that those unfamiliar with the language would butcher the name. So we went with the simple English.

With a bow tie and rimmed glasses, James was the quintessential egghead who, I don't believe, had ever spent a day on a professional film set. But that limitation was not going to stop him.

We first met while I was working as one of New Line's first paid script readers. The company had just struck it rich with *Nightmare on Elm Street*, and it was offering twenty-five dollars per script to me and a few others in exchange for our opinion on the scripts' creative and commercial merits. I read screenplays during the entire time that I also worked as a production assistant. Reading scripts was a great way to get my foot in the door, meet executives, and find the sort of material the film companies were looking for and why. Most importantly, it exposed me to the common failures of most screenplays and what separated superior work from the merely mediocre.

In my coverage of a weird alien abduction memoir, I suggested they hire someone like Godard to do it as a sci-fi thriller—someone who could visualize how bad writing could be transformed into something truthful. Upon hearing my suggestion, Janet Grillo, the development executive, told me I should meet an aspiring writer and producer who had come in the day before and had pitched a black-and-white, silent version of *The Hunchback of Notre Dame*, starring Willem Dafoe. It seemed like we might be kindred spirits.

I took Janet's suggestion and met the man at DeRobertis Pasticceria and Caffe, the Italian pastry shop featured in Alexander Rockwell's 1992 indie film *In the Soup*. Seeing James reading some obscure French novel, I felt like I was walking onto the set of *Stranger Than Paradise*. I had never met somebody around my age who could talk in such depth, with such spontaneity, connecting all the cultural dots, and I was mesmerized by his intelligence and wit. Although I had been slogging my way through the gutters of production and was not as schooled in semiotics as James, we had read enough of the same books—Jon Berger's *Ways of Seeing*; Robin Wood's *Hitchcock's Films*—and shared the same generosity of spirit to know we could get along and collaborate.

At this early point in our careers, both of us felt free to dream big, to believe that we could make the kind of films we aspired to and actually support ourselves. We also didn't really fathom all that was involved. Ignorance is the bliss that launches many a first movie or film company.

※

We dreamed of art fueled by a love of cinema. And believed that this would be enough to sustain ourselves, both financially and creatively. But all of us in the industry were in for a big surprise. Entertainment industries across the board were about to face their most disruptive era, and few of us were truly prepared for it. To the degree that any of us are still thriving is a testament to flexibility and tenacity.

More keenly than ever, I recognize that the new era we live in requires everyone to help each other build a community, demystify the mainstream entertainment industry's creative process, and innovate. One of the perils and pleasures of being an independent-film producer is that the job description has continued to expand yearly. For a while, production seemed to be primarily about creative guidance and management—getting the job done well: A producer was there to deliver the director's vision. Then it became about sourcing the material—script, book, idea—often just getting there first. Then the job expanded further to involve acquiring participants and talent and managing them as fully as possible. Soon after that, producers needed to do even more: put together the money, find the distribution partners, and arrange complex financial structures. If that wasn't enough, it became the producer's responsibility to initiate financial modeling and marketing plans and to execute these with as little deviation from the initial idea as possible. Today, film producing also requires being a community organizer—aggregating audiences and moving them forward. This role happens to suit me well, since community organizing was one of the first skills I acquired before my film career. Organizing is a process of collaboration, where the end is not always in sight and power is held and defined by the constituency.

To make art, survive independently, and make a living that is tied to modest financial gain, you have to be driven. Success is not as important to you as the pleasure of what you're doing, the love and respect for what you're creating, and the ambition to take culture *further*. That's always been the case, both then and certainly now.

Though it may be one my favorite aspects of the movies, the pleasure of sitting in a darkened theater with hundreds of strangers appears increasingly archaic. That image—rows of seats, the beam of the projector shining through a small window in the rear of a large room, a screen alive with moving images—is what most people imagine when they think of the movies. But for me, the definition falls short of what cinema is now. If we fail to acknowledge that film—like all art forms—has grown into a continuous experience, a running conversation between the form, the artists, and the audience, we place ourselves forever in a passive role, one that will contribute to the withering of culture.

Some folks resist changing what they've always done. A filmmaker's priority is always to make another movie; a distributor's priority is always to distribute another movie. But it's just not that simple. Some people in the business don't seem to notice the drastic change or want to admit that it happened. We deserve a culture predicated on today's realities, not yesterday's routine. As an independent-film producer and an avid fan of ambitious and diverse work in all forms—and as a citizen of the world—I am always excited to keep up with the changing times. But nothing has prepared me for the onslaught of the last few years.

Back in 1991, cell phones were the size of a small suitcase and looked like something out of *The Flintstones*. The primary use for our oversized desktop computers was accounting. To operate them, you had to know DOS command language, which might as well have been a Martian code for most people. I learned it. I kept up with it and promoted the fact that I had a power that others were slow to embrace—that knowledge got me jobs. Years later, James Schamus and I wired our office machines so they could talk to one other, but we were terrified when we finally dared to plug a phone line into them and accept a message from the outside world. We were sure all of our precious knowledge would be stolen, never to be returned again.

Those advances seem cute compared with recent changes. The Internet has transformed the business of the arts and how we connect with each other, well beyond our imagination. If Hollywood suits and corporate media higher-ups once determined the majority of our choices (simply by limiting them), we—the audience—are now the curators and the programmers, recommending films and other cultural pleasures to our friends, exchanging playlists, and sharing our opinions on social networks. We can now reach out online and mobilize others to vote both with their feet and their dollars, to act not on impulse, but on the knowledge and experience that comes with a highly connected, digital universe.

As audiences and creators, we are more sophisticated than ever. Innovation is happening so rapidly, the old guard can no longer keep up. Audiences are more accepting of a wide range of styles; people come together and collaborate, becoming something far more generative and influential—a community—and the tools of organizing and educating that community are accessible and ubiquitous. Low-cost digital cameras as well as distribution avenues like YouTube and iTunes are available to nearly everyone, and you can be exposed to the history of cinema or music or just about any art form at any time you want—all for free, or virtually so. So why aren't we making better creative work? And why can't we come up with better ways to support the work and help it progress? We can. And by doing it together, we can build it better.

With fewer barriers, fewer rules, and fewer conventions, filmmakers—and creators of all sorts—are freer to focus on developing new art forms, expanding beyond current modes, and discovering new ways of accessing and sharing content. We are on the verge of opening up *which* stories can be told, *how* they are told, and to *whom* and *where* we deliver them. Our ability to interact with films in different environments and in new social multi-user ways keeps changing. Cinema is not a single form or experience, but almost as varied as the artists who create it.

We can now usher in a new kind of cultural democracy and, as both creators and audiences, determine our own futures. And while certain qualities continue to hold value—ambition, discipline, passion, respect for your collaborators—others have taken on greater importance and relevance: making do with fewer resources and using the strength of community empowered by the Internet and social media. Be it true cross-platform transmedia or simply a new way of configuring old models of entertainment, there are several new ways forward—ones that for the first time in our history have the potential to exist mostly outside corporate control.

Even though I have depended on corporate power over the years, I've always operated largely outside its ultimate influence. Independence is the only choice when you're not necessarily interested in a mass audience, and for the first time ever, we can effectively work outside that structure and specifically address the niches. We are right around the corner of an incredible blossoming of a new and vibrant cinema.

And the important thing is that we the creators and the audience are all in it together. Thinking through what I did right or wrong over the years comes down to whether I knew enough to ask or offer help. I know I am fortunate. I know success is fragile. And I know that if not for all those people who held out their hands at a critical time, I could not have gotten it done. Filmmaking is about partnerships. There is no single rule governing them, but the truer we are to these partnerships, the greater the opportunities born from them. With every movie comes a new partnership and a new company; the lessons gained from them allow us to further improve our craft. You can't produce if you don't partner well. If you don't love the group, then producing isn't for you.

Timing is such a tricky thing. Often, it may not be "a good day to film," but you can't let that stop you. Your team may not be the best or even up to the task, but in the group, there is probably someone who you are going to work with again. You need to find a way to be in the right place at the right time, and when you show up too early or too late, you also need to make sure you know how to make the most of that situation.

Early on, during my three years working as a production assistant, I learned that I would never get bored if I used the time to figure out how I could make things better. Was there an accident waiting to happen that I could thwart? Could I bring more organization to the project? Could something be done now that might save time later? Does someone nearby need me, or I could learn something from someone? Thinking in these ways not only kept me from being bored, but also made me a producer. We produce opportunities. We generate good fortune. But we never do it alone.

What follows are the lessons I've learned during my very fortunate career as an indie film producer from some of the most talented directors and artists in the business. It was a privilege to work with them, and the lessons they taught me continue to serve me well in life, as well as in my career.

Chapter 2

Patience

"Let me take a minute to think about it."

The phrase seems innocuous enough. But for Ang Lee, perhaps the most commercially successful and critically regarded director whom we ever worked with at Good Machine, the comment was far more than a simple request to ponder.

Ang *really* took a minute to think about things—often far longer. You'd say something to him, and he'd nod and take it in, and you'd move on, maybe have lunch, and then go on to something else. And then he'd finally answer the question that you asked him hours before—often without acknowledging that time had passed or that other events had intervened. Ang would just start back in, expecting you to be right there with him. We learned to give him this time, as he frequently had some critical, important, and sometimes brilliant points to add.

Many times on the sets of his early films, *Pushing Hands* and *The Wedding Banquet*, the assistant director or another crew member would come up to me concerned and saying, "Ang is going into that zone again." I would then look out on to the set, and there Ang would be, with either a scowl or a thoughtful look on his face, almost still, taking a moment to think about it—and many of his collaborators just standing there staring at *him*.

It's very easy to fall into assumptions when you're making a film and to think that all filmmakers do things in a standard and specific way. This one-size-fits-all mentality corrupts productions, but Ang helped me recognize that every director—just like the crew and cast—is unique. The director has his or her own pace, style, and sensibility, and it's the producers' job (all the collaborators, really) to understand their director's unique way of working and protect it. We can't apply a template, but instead have to custom-fit each production around the vision at the center. For Ang, some of his distinctive qualities might well be cultural. He was born in Taiwan and only moved to the United States to attend the University of Illinois at Urbana-Champaign in the late 1970s and then NYU's Tisch School of the Arts for graduate film school. But it was more than just his upbringing; you must pay attention to what is truly unique about everyone as an individual.

When I was an undergrad at NYU, I was fortunate to see Ang's thesis film *Fine Line*, and I thought it was one of the best shorts to come out of NYU. Starring Chazz Palminteri in his first role, it was a very kinetic and visceral film, shot handheld, about a Caucasian guy from Little Italy who falls in love with a girl from Chinatown. Even back then, Ang clearly knew how to use the camera to capture emotion, but I didn't know anything else about him. Because Ang Lee went to NYU (like Martin Scorsese) and the film was set in Little Italy, I just assumed Ang was Italian. I even convinced myself that his name must be a pseudonym—another Italian American using a name like "Angle-E"? It was the age of graffiti and tags, and what can I say, I like wild guesses.

Early in my producing career, I drew up a list of directors whom I wanted to work with. The list included Ang Lee, Nicole Holofcener, Kelly Reichardt, Phil Morrison, Jem Cohen, and Mark Friedberg (Friedberg would soon became a successful production designer, working on many of Ang's films). Later, when I actually started pursuing directors, Ang was my first call. And when I pitched the idea of a producer-led, director-driven film company to potential partners, like James Schamus, Ang was always on the list. It was just a matter of finding him—and I hadn't. I had scoured the New York phone book (this was before the Internet), I had called his agent, but he didn't want anything to do with me.

Eventually Ang found me.

So much is serendipity. I would never have met Ang if it weren't for my ignorance in choosing to forgo Sundance in 1990, the year that James had been executive producer for Todd Haynes's *Poison* and I had line produced Hal Hartley's *Trust*. These were the days before accounting software, and someone had to stay behind and do the books. And at the time, nobody knew Sundance was a big deal. So I had thought, "Why would I ever want to go to a film festival? Particularly one all the way out in Utah? I'm a producer."

I was sitting in a tiny little office, above a strip joint called the Babydoll Lounge in what was then a semirough section of Tribeca (yes, there once were semirough sections of Tribeca), trying to do the accounting for our first year in business, when a humble-looking Asian man wearing a windbreaker and holding a plastic bag walked in and said, "Excuse me." I didn't know who he was or why he was there. And then he said, "I'm Ang Lee. And if I don't make a film soon, I'm going to die."

He dropped the plastic bag down on my desk. Inside the bag were two scripts, *Pushing Hands* and *The Wedding Banquet*. He had entered both screenplays in a script contest in Taiwan and had won some prize money. A mutual friend, David Lasserson, had told him that I was the only guy in New York who could make a movie well for a budget that low.

It was a gift to have money for one movie and the promise of more for the next, but it wasn't enough to get things done "right." It was going to be an exercise in cutting corners and discovering solutions. Ang was eager to move forward. He'd do whatever was necessary to get his movie made, and if this was all the money he was going to get, he was committed to finding a way. Once we began collaborating, it quickly became apparent that even with the right attitude, making a movie with Ang wasn't going to be easy. He had his own idiosyncratic, culturally and individually specific ways of doing things.

We made Ang's first film, *Pushing Hands*, for around $350,000, shooting on 35 mm film in eighteen days. Each day was long and felt longer than the day preceding it. But because of a union dispute with the studios at the time, film people in New York weren't working, so everyone on our crew felt that it was a privilege just to have a job. And because *Pushing Hands* was partly in Chinese, no one thought the film would ever be a big deal. Back then, American films, particularly indie ones, weren't selling for millions at Sundance and never seemed to make waves overseas. Other than the fact that people had a job, there didn't seem to be an upside for anyone. Everyone was just there to work. But because the budget was extremely tight, it seemed as if our money was disappearing into an abyss with every passing hour. I had to make the production function better and more efficiently.

Decisions weren't getting made, and we were squandering resources. In low-budget production, it rarely seems you get a moment to think about things; you have to act and solve problems every second. Instead of thinking three steps ahead, we were falling behind. In my production-centric view, I believed that if we didn't replace the assistant director and instill careful planning in mornings and evenings, we would never finish the film on time. It took me another couple of days to act—that often-disastrous gulf between thought and action—but sensing greater danger, I finally fired the assistant director and imposed a schedule and an order on the production. Bam. We got serious.

We didn't have the funds to hire a replacement, so I stepped in as assistant director. Things started to change. Ang needed rigid instructions to get the film done, and having an authoritative leader on set actually worked best for him. We needed to review the shot list and shooting schedule at the beginning of every day and go over the next day's plans at the end of the day and regularly throughout the day; we also needed to remind Ang whether we were ahead or behind and what would come next. If we didn't get on him and his director of photography to make decisions and commitments and not deviate from the plan, the production would drift. But when Ang and the director of photography did act decisively, we flew. The crew responded to decisiveness. But then, the crew *always* responds to decisiveness. (Ironically, I think the rigidity of those first two productions created a desire in Ang to find a way to build greater creative flexibility and spontaneity in his later films.)

I became intimately acquainted with Ang in those days, because, as a result of the film being so financially challenged, I took on the job of not only producer and assistant director, but also Ang's personal driver. While chauffeuring Ang back and forth from the set to his home in White Plains, we planned our shooting days. But after a fifteen-hour day, it's hard for anyone to stay focused on the road, and it's even harder when your director is so tired that he frequently forgets where he lives. I thought I had learned the route to his home, but again and again, we would drive by the house, or make a wrong turn, or take the wrong exit off the highway. Often we'd be a mile or two past the turn, and Ang would all of a sudden say, "Hey, you missed the turn!"—a fitting meta-phor for many movie productions.

Eight years after he graduated from NYU, Ang often stayed at home writing, cooking, and taking care of his son. Clearly, Ang was a gifted artist. His short films proved it. But because he wasn't the sort who knew how to sell himself to people with power, he wasn't at a level commensu-rate with his abilities. For all that time between his first feature and his fourth, *Sense and Sensibility*, none of the other tenants in his apartment building knew that their neighbor was one of the great filmmakers of our era.

When we finally finished *The Ice Storm*, we told Ang he had to move and get an actual house for his family (which he finally did). By then, he had earned a substantial amount of money, after all. You could misinter-pret Ang's willingness to stay put as spaciness, but he was just extremely focused on what he was creating.

While looking at Ang, you often feel as if he is "taking a moment to think about it." It may be *several* moments he's taking, but he isn't taking decisions lightly. Ang has a unique ability to see his entire movie and completely hold it in his mind: how the shots fit together or comment upon each other; how the scenes shape our expectations; how the char-acters evolve or not. It must be hard to think of something else when your thoughts are filled with the challenges of creating an entire world. And Ang not only seems to be doing it with the movie he's shooting, but also appears to be thinking how the work will prepare him for the next world he might get to build. It's not surprising he misses a few turns in the road or stays put a bit longer than others.

It wasn't just me who learned how to think differently in those days. If one role of a producer is to inspire a filmmaker to realize his or her dream and find the big vision that everyone will get behind, then the next role is to knock this dream back down to reality by helping the director understand what can be accomplished within the limits of what he or she can obtain. The third role of the producer is to help the director recognize how those chains can be a blessing. With those initial films, Ang came to understand how limitations benefit the process. Ang became conscious of the time one has to make a movie and how to use it wisely, and when is the right time to take a moment to think about things—and to protect the necessity of doing things in the way only he knows how.

In those early days before his reputation grew, I always needed to find people who could accept Ang. But it wasn't easy. Ang is a wonderful, sweet man, but he's also perplexing and can sometimes require you to work very hard to figure out what he wants. I needed to find people who wouldn't be put off by this quality or wouldn't misread Ang's indirect communication as his not having an opinion. Americans are trained to want decisive leadership, and I think there's a bias in the film business against anyone who doesn't subscribe to that template. On sets, this bias can sometimes hamper non-American and women directors, who often work in a different mode. But unless we learn how to be open to different sorts of leadership, we risk losing out on working with and being led and inspired by many excellent artists.

But sometimes it felt like we were speaking a different language. On Ang's next film, *The Wedding Banquet*, we were looking at the wardrobe for the young female lead's character, and everything had been settled. Ang had signed off. We were completely prepared—or so I thought. On the day we were ready to shoot a scene with May Chin, the actress came out with the selected dress on, and Ang looked miserable. I needed to understand why.

"Ang, what's the matter?"

He didn't respond.

"Ang, you're not happy with something. Tell me what you're not happy with."

"Everything's fine," he said, but he was scowling all the while.

"It's one of those dresses, right?"

Ang just shrugged.

"Which dress did you not like?" I asked.

"All the dresses were great," he said.

"It was one of those last dresses, right?"

He didn't bite. But I persisted. "Was it the brown dress?"

"The brown dress is lovely," he said.

"It's lovely, okay," I said, "but did you not like it?"

"I liked the brown dress," he said.

"But you're upset, Ang. Did you like the blue dress better?"

No response. A long moment passed.

"Yes," he said, finally. "I liked the blue dress better."

In that moment, it suddenly dawned on me that Ang would never come out and say he didn't like something. So one of the first steps in producing for Ang was learning how to provide questions, like, "Is there something that could be improved?" It wasn't enough to say, "Did you like that take?" You had to say, "Would you like to shoot again?" It was about finding out what questions worked. And along the way, Ang became accustomed to how to make sure he got what was needed to make an "Ang Lee Film."

When I talked to crew people on *Crouching Tiger*, *The Hulk*, or *Brokeback Mountain*, they frequently told me about similar situations. And it didn't stop in production, but continued throughout the post-production as well. Ang would say, "I need some sheep to run down the mountain." And the response would be, "Why? Weren't you happy with the sheep? Did you want more sheep?" "Yes," he would say finally after a barrage of questions, "I want more sheep."

Everyone has a strategy for getting what he or she wants. And the producer is often trying to get consensus: to find the thing that everyone agrees on and that is within reach. Many directors explain to me the process of compromise, and how what starts out as a fair compromise eventually leads to a subsequent compromise, and then another compromise and another and another, until they've strayed far from what was the core idea that made them want to do the film in the first place. (This process is often described as the fear they have with Hollywood-based development.)

When I started out at NYU film school, I compromised, too. It was on my thesis film, *Crest of a Hill*, when I realized that, for this very reason, I wasn't cut out to be a director. Originally, it was a more experimental film—I had previously made shorts where I dressed up as a baby and poured chocolate pudding over myself and dragged a taxidermied scowling dog with me around downtown. But not everyone got to make his or her movie; only a few were chosen by the school. So to get my project chosen, I changed it to become more of a naturalistic coming-of-age story. After I shot it, I got into the edit room and quickly realized what an idiot I had been: My compromises disconnected me from the material and I was so disgusted with myself for not standing up to the gatekeepers—in this case, my professor—that I never finished the movie. I sold out. This was the opposite of directing. If I had someone to help me in my initial decision, I might have been more true to myself. The experience taught me that this is what the film world needed: not another director, but someone who could be the director's ally.

Ang's "Let me take a minute to think about it" might initially look like the absent-minded professor or the artist whose head is in the clouds, but Ang used this method as a way to preserve the things that he wanted and to stay committed to his vision. He didn't compromise.

Pushing Hands was the perfect film to have started with Ang Lee, because I had to learn how to achieve a balance with another person. As with the tai chi exercise the film is named for, I had to use the momentum of another person's force to determine where to go. It's a philosophy that embodies Ang as a director, but it can be applied to working with different collaborators, who have different ways of doing things. I am an Ang Lee–trained producer in that I now recognize the balance of equal and opposite reactions that the whole system embodies: places where you need to push, times that you need to give.

On *The Wedding Banquet*, we were moving into production with a $1.5 million budget, to be shot in Connecticut. We had $700,000 coming from CFP, a Taiwanese film studio, and we were expected to match that. But we couldn't find any other funders, so we soon realized it was going to have to be made for just $700,000. Looking for ways to cut costs, our location manager John Rath said, "Ted, why is it set in Connecticut? We can save travel time and housing costs if we shoot right here in New York." And so we did. In hindsight, I think one of the reasons the movie did so well was that it was a love letter to New York City. I don't think it would have had the impact and value had we made it a suburban story. While a budget decision led us to a house on Twelfth Street in downtown New York, it was also easier to believe that these characters lived in Manhattan.

When we tried to find sales agents for the film, everyone said it had zero marketability. It was gay, it was Chinese, and it resembled movies made in the 1940s—except that it was gay and Chinese. All the agents said, "This is not sellable." At that point, we had two options with the $2,000 we had in our bank account: We could pay our staffers, Mary Jane Skalski and Anthony Bregman, or we could take that money and buy plane tickets to the Berlin International Film Festival and try to sell the movie ourselves. With Mary Jane and Anthony's blessing, we flew to Germany, armed with nothing but backpacks and our laptops. The first time we saw the film projected on the big screen was at the press screening. People were literally standing on their chairs applauding the film. Over the next ten days, we were doing meetings in hotel lobbies and bars, and we made $3 million worth of international sales on this "unsellable" film. And we had only charged a 10 percent sales fee, as opposed to the 30 percent sales fee that would have been standard for an outside sales agent. The result: We had our first hit and our investors had money in their pockets.

International sales was the business to be in. My producing fee on *The Wedding Banquet* was under $25,000—5 percent of the budget—which I split with James. But we made $300,000 selling the film overseas. At the time, the industry didn't see that there was real business in American independents internationally. There were no producers who had foreign-sales companies. It was really only Harvey Weinstein who had a fully integrated company, Miramax, which developed, produced, and distributed independent films and had an international sales arm.

We were at a crucial turning point where the art and the means of producing that art had changed. So when the industry began to recognize Good Machine for the consistent quality of our films, I began pursuing David Linde, who was working in international sales at Miramax. It took me two years to land him, but it changed us for the better. Good Machine's international sales arm became a key to the success and growth of the company. We made close to forty-five features, without ever having direct financing, largely due to the foreign-sales business. Without it, there would have been no *Crouching Tiger, Hidden Dragon*.

If Good Machine got its first solid footing with *The Wedding Banquet*, we hit our stride with *The Ice Storm*, another Ang Lee film. Based on

Rick Moody's best-selling book, it was the biggest movie we had ever done—with a $15 million budget. The opportunity to work on such a scale and level of production, with a professional crew and actors, was partly responsible for giving me the confidence to get married—which I did ten days after we wrapped.

We had compiled a fantastic crew, which straddled the line between our indie past and our more established future. The production designer, Mark Friedberg, had been the art director on the very first Good Machine movie, the short film directed by Claire Denis. The cinematographer was Frederick Elmes, who had shot David Lynch's *Blue Velvet*; the music supervisor, Alex Steyermark, had worked on a number of Spike Lee's movies; and the editor, Tim Squyres, had worked on all of Ang's previous films and would work on most of his subsequent ones as well.

I had always felt that our weak link was our costumes. One of the challenges of filmmaking is never to judge your characters or their actions overtly. I felt that our costumes commented on the time rather than existed within the time. And fashion is one of the easiest tools of ridicule. Here, I believe we crossed the line and went overly bold. (It was also the only department to go over budget.)

Despite my opinion of the costuming, we ultimately had strong, creative collaborators. And it showed me that the shooting schedule, the budget, the script, and Ang's meticulous preparations (he had devised an elaborate chart, scene by scene, character by character, on what their point of references would be for art, fashion, politics, paintings, books) weren't everything. What elevated the movie was the people involved. We were very fortunate in how we put together that team. And everyone on that show loved Ang.

Making *The Ice Storm* taught me a lot about trust and confidence, the benefits of intense preparation, and the importance of continued relationships and the collaborative process. When making movies, people often fear that they are making separate movies, with different agendas because of each department's own pursuit of excellence. A consistent tone and a common pursuit are both difficult goals to deliver over the extended schedule of a feature film shoot. But this wasn't the case on that film.

The Ice Storm was also the first time I worked with stars. (We had the French actress Isabelle Huppert on Hal Hartley's *Simple Men*; she was a big deal to me, but she wasn't recognized as a big star to hardly anyone else in America.) Fox Searchlight approved Sigourney Weaver right away, but it had us chase some other actors for the rest of the cast. When Kevin Kline was approved, the first thing I noticed about both Sigourney and Kevin was that they were real people who communicated an enthusiasm for the project right away. There was no hassle about their deal or about accommodations—the things I had been trained to think mattered the most to stars of their stature. They spoiled me. Kline was a great cheerleader on the set, and he treated everybody with respect. Not only did he deliver on screen during every take, but he delivered off screen, too, making everyone happy to be there during production.

One day, Sigourney had come in with some notes on the script. I thought, "That's not what we do in indie-film-land," but she had notes on just one scene: When her character comes back from having sex with a young man the night of the ice storm, she felt that the character, who has been treating people horribly throughout the whole movie, needs a break. So she was responsible for writing the scene where the character curls up in a fetal position in the bed. It may be one of the best scenes in the movie.

If Kevin and Sigourney showed enormous generosity, Joan Allen reflected a genuine professionalism that I had never before witnessed. During one of the toughest nights of shooting, there was a scene in which Joan's character comes back from having extramarital sex and finds Kevin Kline in the bathroom. We must have shot the sequence eighteen times. It was a precise dolly move that required several points of focus. And each time, Joan was exact; it was like witnessing the human body as the perfect instrument. Previously, I may have been a little jaded about the nature of acting and what actors contribute, but after that experience, my view changed.

One of the things that is so remarkable about Ang—and you could see this early on—is his incredible mental capacity. Not only could he hold the entire movie in his head, but he was also prepping another movie while he was making the one at hand. From the beginning, Ang was a director trying to learn and improve his filmmaking skills with each movie. It wasn't an accident that he brought actors from one film to another. He progressed, and through those first three movies (the third was *Eat Drink Man Woman*), Ang would always be thinking hard about what was still to come. I remember trying to understand why certain action sequences were so important to him in his sixth feature, *Ride with the Devil*. It was because he wanted to make a big-budget action film like he would eventually do with *The Hulk*, and he was trying to improve his skills and help connect the dots from one movie to another.

Ride with the Devil, Ang's Civil War–era epic romance, is another story unto itself. Making that movie literally became a ride with the devil. Ang once said to me that he did not respond to most Hollywood scripts because they did not need directors—the direction was written all over the pages. The writing might suggest where there was a close-up or what a character might be feeling—things that might be better left for the director to interpret. As the film industry came to understand what an Ang Lee film was, he demanded that his scripts be written in the minimalist fashion he preferred. Since Ang's screenwriter, James Schamus, was generally also one of Ang's producers, the director often got what he wanted. The industry went with it, too, as Ang's films became increasingly recognized for their emotional truth, complexity, and depth of detail. He didn't need anyone to spell those things out for him on the page.

On *Ride With the Devil*, also written by James Schamus, my producing partner at Good Machine, the centerpiece was always the legendary raid on the city of Lawrence, Kansas. In the script, James wrote something like, "As the Bushwhackers ride into Lawrence, it creates havoc"—the equivalent of *Gone with the Wind*'s "Atlanta burns." These were the only words written on the page to describe the action: less than ten words. Ang knew what he wanted, and there was the room to direct.

As his producers, James and I knew that the Lawrence raid was important, and we had scheduled four or five days of shooting for the sequence. We had worked up a series of vignettes based on factual tales we had researched. And the vignettes would come and go in development, based on both what Ang wanted and what was feasible at the time. Different sequences would get killed as we tried to make the budget work. It's tough to destroy a city on horseback; it takes time and a whole lot of money. Our location manager and line producer, Declan Baldwin and Robert Colesberry, found a town that had been wiped out by a recent flood. FEMA (Federal Emergency Management Agency) wanted the town destroyed. They had relocated everyone up the hill, building new schools and facilities, but they had gone through their budget and could not complete the high school's gym. By providing the additional funding, we were able to dictate how the town would be demolished, building the perfect back lot for Ang in the process.

As we prepped, we cut scenes, only to discover during meetings with the production designer and the costume designer that Ang had told them those same scenes were back in. Ang's efforts to sort things out—efforts that had us constantly juggling—helped him figure out the chaos in the Lawrence sequence. He designed the movie's chaos by creating a production atmosphere that mirrored it. One reason I accepted and embraced this chaotic process was Ang's personality: He was a humble, appreciative, and funny collaborator. His past work also earned him this privilege. On his first three films, *Pushing Hands, The Wedding Banquet*, and *Eat Drink Man Woman*, he might have yearned for additional creative chaos, but he had the common sense to recognize that he wasn't there yet.

Ride with the Devil was a colossal financial disaster. In 1999, it earned about $635,000 on a budget of roughly $32 million. A handful of things went wrong, not the least of which was that the film studios changed during the production and the release of the movie. What's more, the company that acquired the film in the end (USA Films) was bought and sold by another company (Universal Studios). Consequently, the movie became the bastard stepchild that nobody wanted. It was also precisely the kind of film that was neither here nor there in the eyes of marketing departments. It starred a young cast, but was about a historical subject. It was about war, but its primary subject and theme was emotion and conscience. It had tons of gunplay, but the characters spoke in a funny, poetic vernacular. With a cast that included the singer Jewel and Johnny Depp's lookalike Skeet Ulrich, the film would make the traditional art-house audience look at it askew. Every aspect that might have been attractive to a particular audience had another opposing element that turned that audience off.

What were we thinking?

I don't think Jewel was a case of bad casting; she's really good in the film. One of the things that Ang wanted to do from the very beginning was capture the authenticity of the times, and it plagued him that all young actors have perfect teeth, when nobody from the period would have had perfect teeth. And when he saw a picture of Jewel and she had these crooked teeth, he said, 'That's what I want.' The fact is, according to film industry experts, nobody in her young age bracket is worth real sales value to overseas buyers or distributors. But someone who is a pop star—and who can act, and who is very attractive—can be exciting to the marketplace. We had done a screen test with Jewel and Leonardo DiCaprio, who at that point in time wanted to be in the film. And she really delivered. (Leo, of course, eventually dropped out. Ang actually felt good about it, because the character was supposed to be a virgin, and Ang felt that Leo wouldn't seem like a virgin to anyone. Not that Tobey Maguire necessarily did, either, but he did have those big eyes.)

Filmmaking is a collaborative process, and to get things right, you sometime have to take on certain responsibilities, while other people take on other responsibilities. While I was responsible for the production, James was responsible for the script, which was based on Daniel Woodrell's book *Woe to Live On*. He would also handle the studio relationship and the marketing. When then Fox chief Tom Rothman, whom we knew from his New York indie days, agreed that we could develop the book, it was on one condition: that we wouldn't make a movie with the word *woe* in the title. So we were going forward with the title *To Live On*, which I thought was a great title. But that same year, Zhang Yimou's *To Live* came out, and Ang, as a Chinese filmmaker, couldn't come out with a film that had a title so close to another world-famous Chinese filmmaker's. So we had to find a new title. We employed a marketing company to help us come up with a title. The titles it delivered were dreadful. *Ride with the Devil* is a terrible title for an Ang Lee western. A generic title that belongs to a biker movie, it would only appeal to eighteen-year-old kids. A title like that is a great way to distance the traditional art-house audience. As producer, I fought against it. But I didn't win the battle. The studio seized upon this title, and it stuck.

But the real question about the film's success or failure revolves around economies of scale. How did we raise $32 million to make a Civil War film that doesn't satisfy the audience's need for bloodlust and that pivots on the choice not to kill?

One challenge in studio producing is the balance between raising enough money for the story your filmmaker wants to tell and making films that are profitable. When you're making a studio film, it's the studio's decision as to whether the film will be profitable. Studios are looking after the business, and you are looking after the art and craft. As the producer, not the studio, you're trying to make the best movie possible. And when Ang decided to tell that story, I signed up to get it made. Given the chance, I would do it again. Would I recommend this approach as a profit-making venture? No. But I wasn't looking at it in that way. I was there to make an Ang Lee film.

Filmmakers often ask themselves if they'll ever make a great movie— and here they often mean *great* in terms of an epic quality. The sweeping, large-scale movie is harder and harder to do in today's world. Yet it's still the draw for lots of aspiring directors. So I asked myself, "Why shouldn't we be making a $32 million film if we got the chance?"

I can look back now and think about the conversations we had about the script: how hard it was that this movie was about restrained emotions and didn't have the sweeping passion of a typical period epic. How the movie was, moreover, about the challenge and struggle of coming into your own. I remember discussing it with James and Ang, and what we specifically admired in it was just that restraint. But now, I don't know whether a movie of that scale can afford such restraint. Restraint is a luxury that Ang enjoyed on his lower-budget films, but as his projects have grown in size—from *The Hulk* to his 3-D adventure *Life of Pi*—he has to be a lot more aware of the audience's expectations, as well as his own.

The penultimate film we did with Ang at Good Machine was *Crouching Tiger, Hidden Dragon*, both his—and our company's—biggest success. I was not deeply involved in *Crouching Tiger*, but I watched the struggles to get it made at this crucial point in the history of Ang's career, Good Machine, and the independent-film business.

We set out to make *Crouching Tiger* because *Ride with the Devil* was such a flop. Ang didn't think he was going to be offered another film in the United States. There was the perception that he had squandered his chance. It was reaffirmed by his agency Creative Artists (CAA), which initially said it wasn't even going to take the standard 10 percent commission of Ang's directing fee for *Crouching Tiger*. Agents rarely forgo an opportunity to make money, but they're also in the business of relationships, and an arty Chinese-language martial arts movie seemed the furthest thing from a profitable venture. When Ang offered to defer a large part of his own salary, CAA said it would let him go make his little movie in China, but the agency would not get involved with it. Later, of course, success changed everything.

While we were trying to make *Crouching Tiger*, it became clear that unless we had guaranteed U.S. distribution, we were going to get screwed. The reason is that the value of a film had come to rely on a U.S. sale. Without it, you couldn't be confident in closing international sales, which are crucial for an independent film to recoup its budget. The sales potential for a film without U.S. distribution is far less than a film with this distribution. For a long time in the history of indies, all that we needed was the perception of the ability to secure a U.S. sale. So it was more about the faith in getting, than actually having, a deal. There were enough distributors around, and we were regularly producing quality films. What's more, buyers believed that our films would always find their way into the American market. We weren't funding our movies with cash; they were funded on faith. But as those U.S. release slots started to narrow in number, and as American distributors became more savvy about evaluating a film's international potential, both licensing fees and sales commissions were dropping, and consequently, making money became more challenging.

When we made *Crouching Tiger*, we were working with new financier Bill Kong, who would go onto become one of the most important Chinese producers. Although it was his first film, he thought he could raise $15 million for the film. But as we got close to the shoot, it was clear that between what he could bring in and foreign sales, we'd be up to about $10 million. So we had to do things to reduce the budget as much as possible, to $12 million. Ang and all the lead actors, for instance, deferred a substantial amount of their salaries in exchange for net profit participation. It turned out that this move was very lucrative for them. But we were still $2 million short. How were we going to get there?

To get the film made, we made a deal with Sony. To acquire both the requisite American distributor and that crucial last bit of $2 million financing—just 17 percent of the total budget—we gave Sony 65 percent of the film's world rights, including U.S. distribution. It was a great deal for Sony, but a terrible deal for us—although that's what it took to get the film made. Frequently, you find that last 15 percent of the budget makes all the difference in the world in independent film. People can demand so much for it. Years later, when James started Focus Features at Universal, he told me that his group had a very simple business plan:

he wanted 75 percent of the world rights on a film for 25 percent of the cost. He had learned his lesson.

Our experience making and selling *Crouching Tiger* pointed to the impracticality of single film financing and sales. Good Machine was not unique. With U.S. distribution less secure and a reduced ability to avoid that 15 percent trap, you'd often have to give up most of the financial upside to get your film made. It's a passion business, which means it's great for hard-nosed business folks and terrible for the passionate ones. Even when you succeed, you're often likely not to see much profit.

Against this backdrop of difficult financial arrangements, our experience with *Crouching Tiger* was frustrating. Although the film made a lot of money (over $213 million worldwide), little went back to us and to the company. As a business venture, our potential was clear, but as it currently stood, we were not exploiting the opportunity.

It soon became clear that James and David wanted a bigger sandbox to play in. I and my fellow Good Machine producers Anne Carey and Anthony Bregman, as well as our in-house lawyer and director of business affairs, Diana Victor, were all interested in coming up with a new model that wasn't so revenue-driven. We wanted to focus instead on delivering quality movies that were motivated more by passion than dollar signs.

A couple of things along the way set in motion the split between James and David and the rest of us. First, just when we were getting ready to make Todd Field's *In the Bedroom*, we were pitched Michael Bay's remake of *The Texas Chainsaw Massacre*. We'd be getting a much bigger fee if we did the latter, of course, but I'd have to abandon *In the Bedroom*, and it wasn't something I wanted to do. Our corporate overhead was going up, and paying the bills was a constant concern. The most responsible thing would have been to suck it up and take the cash.

Second, one individual at the company had a history of losing their shit on underlings and horribly mistreating subordinates. I made an ultimatum to James and David: This person had to be fired, because the behavior was unforgivable. Keeping the person on represented the opposite of what I valued, and I didn't want to have a company if it had to have someone like that in it.

I lost that battle. James and David defended the person's money-making abilities. Their compromise was that the person would go into therapy for anger-management issues. But I thought it wasn't good for the company to have this person on board; I didn't want to have a company so focused on profit that it would treat employees that way. The incident showed me where we were as a company, and I didn't like it.

There were other human resource issues at Good Machine, some poor record-keeping, substance-abuse problems among the midlevel management, and above all, a struggle to balance what was good for the company and what was personally satisfying for each of us. These challenges were frustrating because all of us just wanted to make good movies. Fortunately, James was diligent about staying incredibly focused on the micro details of the company and making sure all of the legal and financial stuff was in place. Production and budgets may have been my initial expertise, but the business was changing. For me at that time, the corporate equivalent wasn't fun. It wasn't making a movie.

My experience with Ang, James, and David taught me a lot about what I wanted to take from, and give back to, this business. I always felt there was a wealth of visionary artists who needed the support, collaboration, and dedication that we were able to give to Ang. Anyone can point to a host of successful filmmakers who came out of the indie trenches, but I am confident that there are far more directors that never, or barely ever, got the chance. For Ang, it took three films. And it was a huge act of courage for Emma Thompson and producer Lindsay Doran to bring him on *Sense and Sensibility*. James's commitment to Ang was a courageous act, too. And James's focus on Ang helped build not only Ang, but also Good Machine.

I don't really believe this is an auteur industry, where a sole creative genius is cultivated in film school and held in high esteem by film criticism. Yes, there are great filmmakers to be found, but they don't just pop up out of thin air. Often, a friend or brother or committed producer or visionary executive takes a chance and stays with the filmmaker. A team of collaborators needs to commit to learning new languages and ways of working, helping to make sure that an emerging artist's vision makes it to the screen. An enterprise is driven by more than just money, even though it does need money in the first place. But passion often allows luck and opportunity to strike.

For every *Ride with the Devil*, there's a *Crouching Tiger* to follow it (and maybe a *The Hulk* to come next). It's wonderful to see success for the few people who may not have found it a decade before, but with each passing year, the system fails many more people. And our culture and our industry suffer for it. One of the joys of producing comes when we are a fortunate enough to recognize the gift before us and can prevent someone from being overlooked. And our culture and industry sing because of it. Just look at Ang Lee. He took time because he needed time, and his career needed more than just one experiment to thrive.

Ironically, if there's one gene that I lack, it's patience, and if there's one thing the industry rewards, it's the opposite: decisiveness and action. But Ang helped me learn the value of patience. When someone looks like he or she is being indecisive or doesn't give you an answer right away, sometimes it's best to just sit back, wait, and go have lunch. And when you return, you discover that what you thought was hesitancy was actually the alchemy required to transform the commonplace into something marvelous.

Chapter 3

Joyfulness

"There's this cute guy with a funny voice who came by the office," Mary Jane Skalski said to me one day, during the early years of Good Machine. "I promised him that I'd get you to watch his movie."

I wasn't interested. I wanted to go home. I put the videotape in my backpack, and I don't think I ever would have watched it, except for the fact that just before I left, the phone rang and it was Tom Rothman. Tom had just started Fox Searchlight, the specialty arm of 20th Century Fox, but it had not released or acquired any films yet. We knew Tom because he had distributed Ang Lee's films *The Wedding Banquet* and *Eat Drink Man Woman* when he was at the Samuel Goldwyn Company.

"Have you heard of this guy, Eddie Burns, in New York?" he asked. I told him that Eddie's film *The Brothers McMullen* was in my backpack. "If you think his movie is worth finishing," he told me, "Fox Searchlight will put in fifty thousand dollars for a first and last offer on the film"—which means they get first dibs on the project, but if anyone else makes a better offer, they have the opportunity to trump it.

That night, I watched the tape and I enjoyed it—for the most part.

Shot at his parents' home in Valley Stream, New York, with a crew of three and a cast that included his girlfriend, Maxine Bahns, the cut was thirty to forty-five minutes longer than what it should have been. And it wasn't a comedy—yet. In one sad scene, Burns's character Finbar McMullen drinks whiskey and plays chess by himself. The scene went too far. Eddie and I later joked that it was like something out of Swedish filmmaker Ingmar Bergman's grave art-film classic *The Seventh Seal*. However, I saw something special in the film: I could personally relate to all of the characters and all of the stories; you could feel who these people were. And with a little less angst, there could be plenty of laugh-out-loud moments to make it a fun and rewarding story.

That very same week, I had also broken up with my filmmaker girlfriend Tamara Jenkins and had begun a whirlwind courtship that would inevitably yield a failed marriage. So it made perfect sense that I'd get caught up with all the romance and anxiety in Eddie's film.

Very soon after watching it, I sat down with Eddie, and we began talking about what cuts he could make to the film. I remember hearing the surprise in Eddie's voice: "Oh, I can cut out on the joke?" He had thought that he needed to continue scenes through to when characters leave the room, and not just simply end at the strongest moment. Most of what was done was simply that: If it wasn't funny, it got cut out of the movie.

For two and a half weeks, after his day job as a production assistant on *Entertainment Tonight*, Eddie reedited the film, starting at 8 PM and going to the wee hours of the morning. When he wasn't sleeping in his car, he was cutting the film, and he eventually took out an entire thirty minutes. And once he did, you saw what the movie wanted to be: honest emotions and good laughs, from one scene to the next. When we finished the cut, we screened it for Sundance Film Festival director Geoff

Gilmore. We may have been the last film submitted that year, but he immediately welcomed it to the festival.

In 1994, the relationship between Sundance and the indie business was beginning to take off in a big way. Disney had just bought Harvey and Bob Weinstein's Miramax, and the newly cash-infused moguls were more aggressive than ever, buying Kevin Smith's *Clerks* at the festival in January and preparing to launch Quentin Tarantino's *Pulp Fiction* into the box-office stratosphere that October. We thought our invite to the festival might just be our ticket to success. But there was one problem with our Sundance plans: Eddie had accepted a slot in the Independents Night screening series at the Independent Filmmaker Project (IFP), a nonprofit devoted to supporting independent filmmakers. He never thought he'd get into Sundance, so screening his feature in December in New York prior to showing it to the world in Park City in January didn't seem to Eddie like the bad idea it was.

We had to find a way out of the IFP screening. It would totally undermine our distribution chances at Sundance.

But Eddie was an incredibly loyal guy. We had encouraged him to drop the IFP screening, but the organization had originally accepted it after everyone else had rejected him—he had a collection of over one hundred rejection letters that he had framed—so he was going to do the IFP screening no matter what. He thought he owed it to IFP. But we had a plan.

At the IFP screening, all the distributors were there to get a jump on the film, because word was now out about its upcoming official Sundance premiere. Luckily, these were the days of the videotape. We put in the tape, and at the eleven-minute mark, after a particularly funny scene where Eddie's character cuts his banana into his corn-flakes—meant to echo the effect that some relationships have on men—the tape stopped. Was it a glitch? Everyone was still laughing when we announced that the screening was over due to technical problems. Unbeknownst to the industry audience, it was a very carefully orchestrated teaser, and it set us up to sell big at Sundance in January. Always leave them wanting more.

Then the challenge was finishing the film. With the $50,000 from Searchlight, we still didn't have enough money to get it ready for Sundance. Eddie and his father, Edward J. Burns, who was a police sergeant for the New York Police Department, asked me if I could raise finishing funds. We figured it would cost a total of $250,000 to complete and blow it up from 16 mm to 35 mm film, do a professional sound mix, and have all we needed to officially "deliver" the film. We found a company that would give us the money, but it wanted half ownership. Wisely, the Burns family didn't want to give that up. We strategized about the lowest amount we could pay to get the film blown up and receive a proper mix and score. We figured we needed another $50,000, but that was just going to be for a festival print. So the Burnses took out another mortgage on their house and gambled everything. If no one bought the film, they'd be screwed. It was a risky decision.

We were fortunate enough to get our first screening of *The Brothers McMullen* at the Egyptian Theater at Sundance. A lot of people didn't like the Egyptian in those days, because if anyone shifted around, you heard it. But I thought it was noisy in the best possible way, particularly for a comedy, because if someone laughed, it would spread infectiously throughout the house. Right before the screening, I got a call from our entertainment attorney John Sloss. He couldn't make the screening, because his brother had been in a skiing accident and John was en route to the hospital. Was it a bad omen? John was well on his way to becoming an indie film legend for his savvy ways of extracting top value for the films and filmmakers he represented, and we had hoped to have had him by our side for the full ride.

Fortunately, the screening went great. Tom Rothman, from Fox Searchlight, had watched the whole movie standing up in the aisle. Immediately after the lights came up, he took advantage of his first "option" on the project and said to me, "Let's go out and talk."

We went to the Italian restaurant Cisero's on Main Street and sat in a booth. I found a pay phone to call Sloss—several cell-phone carriers didn't yet work in the mountains of Park City—but I couldn't reach him. Tom knew it was to his advantage to make a deal early, and particularly without a tough negotiator like Sloss around, because the CEO didn't want to spend too much money up front. But if the film succeeded, Rothman's plan ensured that everyone would share significantly in the proceeds. I believe the contract stated that we would start getting bonuses when the film reached the $3 million box-office mark and then the $5 million mark, and so on. We knew it was rare that an indie would do that well, but we decided to sign with Rothman. He had always treated us well; he truly loved the movie; and as the "new kid on the block," his upstart company Searchlight had more to prove with our film than just good judgment. When I told Sloss later, he was upset because he understandably wanted a larger up-front fee. But my gut told me that the value of having a new outfit with deep pockets launch its corporate brand with our film was invaluable. Searchlight also went one step further.

Eddie was very prolific, and by the time he got to Sundance, he had finished the first draft of his next project, *She's the One*. Shortly after the festival, we closed a deal to make Eddie's next picture with Searchlight—a shrewd and protective move on its part. That same year, executives at New Line were upset because they had put a lot of money behind first-time filmmaker David O. Russell's *Spanking the Monkey* in the hopes of establishing Russell's name as a director and launching his next bigger project *Flirting with Disaster*. But Miramax ended up with *Flirting*, leaving New Line in the lurch for all the initial support. The incident had come up in conversations about *She's the One*; Searchlight recognized that promoting the first film was also helping to promote the next one.

We did not anticipate how much love *The Brothers McMullen* would receive. The film won Sundance's Grand Jury Prize, garnered some enthusiastic reviews, and earned more than $10 million at the domestic box office. What's more, we had a deal for a second film. Eddie's life seemed blessed.

We made Eddie's follow-up, *She's the One*, in 1996 for $3 million. We cast still relatively unknown actresses Jennifer Aniston and Cameron Diaz (as well as unknowns Amanda Peet and Leslie Mann). In order to get the movie made under the union's low-budget agreement, we gave half of the back end to the union crew. It was an unprecedented arrangement. And this sort of generosity and team playing is what Eddie always stood for. The film made about $9.5 million and went into net profits and paid out. To this day, I run into crew people who say it was one of the only films where they ever got money on the back end, meaning money received if the film earned a profit.

Eddie never forgot that he was once a production assistant who lived in his car. That kind of awareness infected his personality and manifested itself in different ways: He knew the names of everyone on his crew, and he loved nothing more than going out and drinking with them and engaging with them in an honest and authentic way. Some films you look at and can feel the pleasure the team took in making it—or you simply *perceive* it as pleasure, because it may very well have been anything but fun getting the movie done. But on certain films—like Eddie's—there is an acknowledgment of the privilege of making films and the pleasure that comes with exercising that privilege. When a filmmaker projects this attitude up on the screen, it is as if he or she is inviting the audience to a party.

Eddie and I worked together on one more film, 1998's *No Looking Back*, originally titled *Long Time Nothing New*. Both of us wanted to take a creative leap, but we hadn't really agreed on a common direction. It's what we in the business often call "creative differences," a euphemism for people not getting along. But Eddie and I liked and respected each other and were getting along fine. It's just that we were butting heads over a number of issues related to the project: the script, the casting, and the budget.

We met often, and I would give him notes on each new draft of the script. I don't think it was something that either of us was enjoying; we tried to raise the script to a new level, but could never specifically define what we were aiming for. He wanted to do something other than a comedy and make something with more "weight," but we weren't finding the right tone. Moreover, our story wasn't that unique. The lack of uniqueness was okay for Eddie, who said it would be easy for audiences to relate to the film. But I always believed that the one way indies succeed is to distinguish themselves in the marketplace. You have to keep the story fresh. But our story was three familiar tales rolled into one: We had the prodigal son returning; the small-town girl with dreams of the big city; and a woman stuck between two guys, one good and one bad, or maybe one good who first appears bad and one bad who first appears good. Audiences had seen it all before; we just had mashed it all together. I also kept fighting some of the casting decisions. I didn't feel that rock star Jon Bon Jovi and Lauren Holley, who was coming off

Dumb and Dumber, were what the indie audience was looking for. But Eddie was trying to reach a wider audience.

Eddie was also hoping to get a budget of over ten million dollars. To my eyes, this seemed not only unrealistic, but also a little unbelievable. I understood where Eddie was coming from. He had two films that did well. *She's the One* wasn't a huge box-office success, but it had made a profit, and people were happy with it. And as a filmmaker looking to grow within an industry that often evaluates filmmakers on the type of budget they can command, it was natural that he wanted to go higher.

Eddie's agent Bart Walker had also made a name for himself finding financing for his clients. He definitely deserves props for garnering funds from overseas banks and foreign companies for a range of independent filmmakers, from Mira Nair to Jim Jarmusch, along with an unprecedented level of creative control. But this was a relatively new business development; many of the directors we worked with in the 1990s had no agents or managers or lawyers. Early on, we, the producers, were the only people who looked after the interests of the directors. When agents came into the picture, there were sometimes clashes over scale and budget; agents would never tell their clients they were overreaching or setting themselves up for failure. (After all, the bigger the budget, the bigger the agent's fee.)

When, years later, I finally signed with the United Talent Agency, the representatives asked me what I wanted from them, and I said that I wanted an agency that would always tell its directors honestly when the final cut wasn't ready or the budget was too high. They told me that this would never happen; agents would never deflate their talents' egos in that way. For those same reasons, none of Eddie's advisors would tell him that his budget was unrealistic.

So unlike his advisors, I expressed my uncertainty about the budget and these new funding sources. The conversation went something like this:

"Who are these new financiers?" I asked.

"One of them is an old-time movie actor's son," Eddie said.

"Have they done anything before?"

"No, but they're going to be doing a lot."

"But we don't have big movie stars," I argued. "We don't have any stunts or violence, and there's a woman at the center of the film, and it's not an Oscar movie. Nobody funds a film like ours at that level."

"Yeah," he said, "but these guys say they want to."

"How do we check them out?" I asked.

"My agent says they're okay."

And so it went.

When you're making a movie, you want to believe, with all your heart, that the movie you're making is worth all the money in the world. And you don't want to be the stupid fool who took seven million dollars when you could have taken ten. Together with your need to believe and the industry's need to make money, you're always forced to think bigger. But you're not encouraged to think practically. And when you do think bigger and not practically, there are going to be conflicts. My relationships with directors have often been challenged by the phrase "This may not be realistic." It sounds like a violation of faith. It's not exactly "I don't believe in God," but sometimes it feels pretty damn close to that.

Despite my reluctance, Eddie's representatives told him he'd get everything he had asked for. And for a moment, it seemed like it would happen. We entered into negotiations for a dream financing deal. But there's an adage for such scenarios—*too good to be true*—and the deal collapsed, though not before Eddie had put in some of his own money to jump-start preproduction. Now we were in too deep to stop. We needed to find a deal, or Eddie would lose it all.

As so often happens in independent production, we were able to make the film by cutting down our budget as much as possible. Eventually, Eddie got half of the seven-million budget from Polygram, the music company, which had recently gotten into the film business, and the other half from our friend Tom Rothman, who took international rights. But this amount totaled less than half of the budget we had originally sought.

Rothman turned out to be a truly loyal guy. Here was a domestic drama, with apparently little foreign value, but he persevered. And while the production went smoothly, the distributor, Polygram's Gramercy unit, didn't support the film when it was released in theaters. Plus, the reviews weren't good (Roger Ebert wrote "the movie bogs down in earnestness"). The story wasn't fresh, and the actors were not what the art houses were looking for. The movie only played for about a week and half and earned just over $222,000. The entire venture seemed like a complete disaster. After the creative differences we had, and what looked like a financial failure, Eddie and I decided we had better not work together on his next movie. There is only so much any business, creative, or personal relationship can endure, and with *She's the One*, we had reached our limit. Best to end with the friendship intact.

Surprisingly, about three years later, I got a sizable check in the mail with a statement that the film had gone into net profit. I never would have believed it. In fact, I didn't at first, calling Michael Nozick, my producing partner on the film, just to make sure it wasn't some sort of a prank. But it shows you why Eddie was right that Jon Bon Jovi was an incredible choice for the film. Sure, the singer was good in the film, and he's a rock star in the United States, but he's even bigger in Europe, an outright phenomenon, and the movie played far better overseas than could have been expected. Turns out that in 1998, Bon Jovi was all you needed to get into the black—and Rothman was a shrewder businessmen than we foresaw. We had always thought Rothman was only helping because of his relationship with Eddie, but the future Fox CEO knew the value of what we had, and his company had built a global system to exploit it, with remarkably lucrative foreign deals in place.

Good looks go far in the film business. A lot of people parlay those qualities into a career in TV. And while he has certainly explored television, it has never been his first love. He was seduced by midperiod Woody Allen classics like *Manhattan, Annie Hall,* and *Hannah and Her Sisters.* And I respected that. It was always a pleasure to work with Eddie, and it wasn't simply because every one of the movies we made together had a happy ending, financially, too.

There are the movies that you think are going to change cinema, and then there are those that are a joy to make. And from Eddie I learned that both types are valuable. Eddie's total respect for his crew and his collaborators are the marks of a decent guy. And sometimes, working with a decent guy can be as inspiring as working with a director whose creative reach exceeds his or her grasp. At that time in New York, it was very easy to get stuck in a semipretentious rut. And Eddie's passion for making movies taught me a lesson: Not every project needed to revolutionize the cinema or the planet. Sometimes, it's okay just to have fun, particularly when you've done all the right things to make sure you have friends and family who will always be loyal to you.

Eddie wasn't afraid to try new things, either. When traditional distribution didn't work out for his 2007 film *Purple Violets,* he tried out a new platform: iTunes. He was the first filmmaker to distribute a feature directly via iTunes, and the venture gave him incredible access to this digital service. Apple also saw the value of having Eddie on board and used his notoriety to help launch its platform as a place to sell films. It was a win-win situation, and for Eddie, it was a remarkable feat to end up on *The Today Show* with a film that didn't have conventional theatrical distribution. He did, however, have Apple in his court. A couple years later, Eddie embraced social media in ways that few filmmakers were beginning to recognize, ratcheting up friends and followers in the tens of thousands. It was a logical extension of what he had been doing all along. Eddie's success in the world of new media gratifies me too, as Eddie has always been quick to credit me with encouraging him to reach out and engage with his fan base.

There are many pleasures to be found in American microbudget cinema, but here are two: You can recognize the people on the screen as the same people who live on your block, and second, they give off the idea that anyone can make a movie. Of course, it may not be as easy as it looks, but the way that Eddie now lets fans have access to his projects—asking them to contribute poster designs and songs for closing credits via Twitter—helps instill the dream that they can make movies, too, while also making them feel like a part of each movie.

What Eddie had, above all else, was a close-knit New York family, a family that believed in him and taught him about hard work, staying grounded, appreciating people around you, and following your dreams. (To this day, I find that many people's best lessons come from their families; when I interview people for a job, I often ask them what lessons they learned from those close to them.) Eddie found a way to make a film for twenty-five thousand dollars and didn't give up even after receiving a hundred rejections. And he never let his dream go. Even when his film-directing career temporarily stalled, it gave him something to fall back on, and he found a new model that he thought was exciting and he made it exciting for the whole community. He said, "I don't need a million dollars. I don't even need a quarter of a million. But I can still make a movie and I can even distribute it, and that's a remarkable thing." A lot of filmmakers out there think they got where they are because they're so damn special and they think they don't owe anyone for it. But Eddie never forgot who he was and those who helped him.

In independent film, there is an expectation that you always have to work your ass off—that art isn't real unless you suffer. That you have to sacrifice your personal relationships and your financial credit score to get your movie made. That all that matters is getting the final shot of the day on schedule and that you capture it exactly as you always intended to. But like Eddie Burns, I've continued to make films with filmmakers who have taught me that success doesn't always have to be a struggle. Sometimes, it can be pure joy.

For another example, Nicole Holofcener always made it clear to me that she would not destroy her life to make her debut feature, *Walking and Talking*.

"There's no way you can get this movie made in twenty-five days and not work fifteen hours a day," I told her.

But she went back to her cinematographer, Michael Spiller, and they came up with a list of shots for the entire film, designing a visual style that would also keep the days at a sane length of around twelve hours. Not every day turned out to be that short, but you could see the planning that went into it. Originally, I saw it as a weakness. I thought, "We're not maximizing our schedule." But Nicole planned out exactly what she wanted and how she would communicate it. She could see the bigger picture, what was best for her team and, ultimately, for her and her film.

Sometimes, while making movies, finishing movies, or selling movies, people find it very easy to focus on the details and lose sight of what's more important.

I first learned about Nicole through Mary Weisgerber, who was a location manager and a friend of mine. Mary had given me Nicole's student film, an acclaimed short called *It's Richard I Love*. It was a neurotic love story, starring Cynthia Nixon (later from *Sex and the City*) and Keith Gordon (who became a director in his own right). I was coming off my second production with director Hal Hartley, and although he and I had made two movies in two years (*Simple Men* and *Trust*), I was not yet able to support myself just producing, so I had to find a few more directors damn quick if I was going to survive as a producer.

Nicole, however, did not have an agent yet, and I had Mary, who, as I said, introduced us. I met with Nicole on a sweltering day in New York City, where I had just come from my first meeting with an agent at William Morris, so I was wearing a tie for the first time since high school. The heat was uncomfortable, and the tie made me even more so, but I think the "professional look" impressed Nicole somehow, or at least camouflaged my own nervousness at meeting a new director.

Nicole had just completed a first draft of *Walking and Talking* the day before. I thought the script was absolutely perfect for me to produce. It was set close to where I lived. It was a character-focused, situation-based, dialogue-driven humanist film that was informed by the best of independent cinema—from Woody Allen to Eric Rohmer to television. It had a joke every five lines, was told from a woman's perspective, and was about female friends—something that remains underserved in cinema to this day. We would also be able to draw on the incredible pool of actors living in New York at that time—people who could deliver both freshness and familiarity. We didn't need stars. We ended up casting Catherine Keener,

Anne Heche, and Liev Schrieber, all of whom, of course, would later become far more recognizable names.

Walking and Talking was also a story about young adulthood. Because I was then in my twenties, I identified with the characters in the story. It celebrated and captured what we were living and what we loved. As much as independent film in the 1990s was about delivering stories to underserved audiences—based on race, gender, sexual orientation, class, and creed—there was another great underserved audience: mainstream young adults, who were only being served idealized representations of themselves. Hollywood was not focusing on the everyday, middle-class existence of most young adults, the small moments, like when your cat dies or you are losing your best friend. This kind of story hadn't played out in mainstream movies very regularly. And this was Nicole's specialty.

So we developed the script, which meant constant rewriting—she went through approximately twenty-five drafts. And the work I did with Nicole on the *Walking and Talking* script would set the template for my standard development process with dozens of filmmakers later. In large part, it starts with a series of questions: How do you find the theme? What do you want the big takeaway from the movie to be for the audience? What do you want them to remember intellectually, and what do you want them to feel emotionally? At a certain point, Nicole came up with this image in her mind: The character Amelia (played in the film by Keener) is holding her friend Laura (played by Heche), who is getting married and starting a new way of life, afloat in the water. That, to me, was a baptismal moment of surrender and passage. It was about loving someone so much that you let her go. And that was the big takeaway of the movie in a single visual and heartfelt instant.

But it was a process to get there. Once we found this telling scene, and once the theme of love as loss emerged, we had to make sure that the theme emerged elsewhere in the script. After we were sure that the script captured the theme, we wanted to look back at the characters to see how the idea was reflected in their identities and internal conflicts. Then we looked at how the notion was revealed in the relationships between the characters. Expanding further, we asked how this idea exists in the world of the film, in general. The script for *Walking and Talking* answered all those questions. And it felt natural and organic, and funny and emotionally true.

Walking and Talking became Good Machine's first project when we incorporated in December 1989, though we had gotten other movies in production sooner. (Some months later, on a single day, we were shooting three films, Dani Levy's *I Was on Mars*, Ang Lee's *Pushing Hands*, and Hal Hartley's *Ambition*.)

We decided that we needed to make another short to raise industry awareness for *Walking and Talking*, because *It's Richard I Love* was getting old. So Nicole wrote a five-minute film called *Angry*, which was originally titled something more accurate like *Mom, I Am Breaking Up with You*. We shot it in two days: I was the producer, the first assistant director, as well as the caterer, and I made a frittata with sausage and peppers to boost morale on the set. If everyone sees that the producer is so dedicated that he's serving the food, the crew is more likely to put their heart and soul into it, too. As we had hoped, *Angry* got into Sundance, where we planned to use it to promote the feature script we hoped to make the following year.

But Nicole can actually thank Hal Hartley—not Sundance—for helping her get the film made. Hartley's *Simple Men* was headed to the prestigious competition section at Cannes, and I learned that Dorothy Berwin, who headed up business affairs for Zenith, the company that helped finance both that movie and Hartley's *Trust*, wanted to get a movie going herself. I told her the story of *Walking and Talking*, of two female friends and their fears that one woman's marriage will break up their friendship. Dorothy recognized a universal story, one that was messy and funny and unafraid to say how things were. It would be a perfect project for her to launch her own producing career.

Even before I got back from Cannes, I called and asked one of our assistants to put all 120 pages in an envelope and send it overseas— this was before the Internet. I was always cutting costs and the fact I was willing to call overseas indicated how urgent I thought it all was. A couple weeks later, Dorothy called and said she loved it, especially the scene with the cat suicide. Midway through the film, the main character's cat, which appeared mopey all along, jumps out a window. As far as I was concerned, the scene didn't advance the story and it didn't reveal the character, and I had actually convinced Nicole to cut the cat-suicide scene a few drafts before. Turns out the assistant had sent the wrong draft, so *Walking and Talking* ended up getting financed because of a scene that had been cut out of the script! It is the sort of beautiful mistake that you've got to love and embrace when it comes. Nicole's patience, loyalty, and commitment paid off—we received a million dollars, and we got to make our movie.

Walking and Talking was right after *Brothers McMullen*, and it all came together as we just received the financing for Eddie's follow-up, *She's the One*. Our company had found a building in Tribeca to use as office space, and on one side of the wall, we were prepping *Walking and Talking*, while on the other, we were producing *She's the One*. At the time, I remember asking both directors who they wanted to score their film. Nicole's favorite musician was Billy Bragg, and Eddie worshipped Bruce Springsteen. We didn't have enough money to pay Bragg, but we knew from his songs that he was a liberal guy with an ethical bent.

When I finally got in touch with him, I told him I'd make my entire budget transparent. And we'd give him whatever we possibly could and make sure he'd get something on the back end, too. And he agreed, no contract, no hassle, no lawyers. When he passed through New York and performed his sketches for Nicole, she was like a teenage girl, giddily anticipating her own private concert. He sat her down on a bar stool and serenaded her with an acoustic guitar. "The Boss" did not do the same for Eddie, but we did get Tom Petty for *She's the One*—still pretty incredible for a low-budget film.

Walking and Talking was a fun shoot. Although it was her first feature, Nicole valued the process as much as the product. She wanted to enjoy herself while she made the movie. She was disciplined, but she also made sure there was a huge quotient of joyousness. For many guys coming out of film school, their filmmaking bible is *The Art of War*. In contrast, Nicole embraced the realist young-adult novels of Judy Blume as her influence. She explained her outlook: The crew is the family that I'm a part of for five-plus weeks; let's enjoy our time together. At one point, we had to shoot a love scene, and Nicole needed a stand-in. She got me to simulate a sex act—everyone giggled as they watched me wriggling my hips. Nicole wasn't even beyond making fun of the producer to provoke some laughs from the crew. And I didn't mind occasionally looking the fool if it meant keeping the team in high spirits.

We barely finished *Walking and Talking* in time for its Sundance premiere. And what happened to get there was one of the craziest twenty-four hours of my life.

Coming off *The Brothers McMullen* sale, I had convinced our sales agent to inform the industry that we would be selling *Walking and Talking* within twenty-four hours of its Sundance premiere. As I said, we barely finished the film on time. When I picked up the print at DuArt the night before our screening, it was literally still wet from coming out of the film printer.

Arriving at JFK for our 6 AM flight to Salt Lake City, we faced a huge line at the airport, snaking through the terminal. The film was all 35mm (digital wasn't even a dream yet), and the reels were in big metal cans with thin metal handles—not the kind of thing you want to hike all over the airport with. The heavy film print canisters were cutting into my hands every step of the way.

When we finally got on our plane and started taxiing down the runway, the captain said the plane had to turn back—there was a man on board who had bitten his nails to the point where blood was dribbling from his mouth. Even though this was well before 9/11, his hysterics had the flight team wondering if he had put a bomb on the plane. We exited the plane—again, my sore hands lugging the film cans—so the flight team could search the plane for explosives, and then we reboarded it. We took off again. But a few minutes into the flight, the captain said we had to turn back yet once more. As I filed off the plane for the second time, hands still aching, I looked into the cockpit and saw that the window had been shattered. Evidently, a bird had hit the windshield and the whole thing looked like a spider web, full of cracks. Another bad omen?

The airport was complete mayhem. Blizzard conditions were approaching; everyone was trying to rebook his or her flight. We didn't know what to do. Then James Schamus, who was also on the flight, showed me that he had what it takes to run a studio. "We're going to have to rent a jet," he said.

This was beyond my imagination. We didn't have money. We were broke indie producers. But James called veteran New York power agent Sam Cohn, who gave us a number to call. For the low price of seventeen thousand dollars, we could charter a private plane. My entire fee on the film was twenty-five thousand. Fortunately, the charter company took Visa.

It took hours to locate a pilot who could fly the plane—and he had already flown twenty-two hours that day (twenty-four was the legal limit, and Salt Lake City was more than two hours away, but no one said anything). We were most likely putting our lives on the line to make sure we arrived at our festival premiere on time.

The plane we rented was supposedly an eleven-seater, but we had fourteen people. Smart guy that he is, James took a pass. Two others had to stay behind with all the luggage. Eleven of us climbed aboard, but we saw only ten seats. Turned out the other seat was the toilet—not the most comfortable seat for a cross-country ride—so I sat up by the pilot. When we got up in the air, he asked for my Visa card. As he went to swipe it, he let go of the controls and the plane started to dive. Not only was I losing my entire bank account, but I was probably going to lose my life.

By the time we finally landed to refuel two hours short of Salt Lake City, half of my crew was drunk and I was calling Sundance director Geoff Gilmore, assuring him that we'd make it into town for the 8 PM screening. Gilmore wanted to cancel it, but I told him that we'd make it. When we finally got to Salt Lake City, we had ninety minutes to get the film print on the platters that were used for projecting films. The snow was already a foot deep, and we had to drive through the mountains. It was normally a ninety-minute drive, but surely it now was going to be longer. Only one lane was plowed, but we had an SUV and I instructed the driver to forge a new path the whole way there. We couldn't fail now.

We were late, but fortunately for us, Veit Helmer, the filmmaker whose short movie preceded us, was telling jokes and keeping the audience entertained when we finally arrived. Nobody cared that our screening was twenty minutes late.

The screening went great. Harvey Weinstein muscled in to make a deal. After six hours of negotiations, we sold the North American rights for $1.2 million. The deal closed at 2:45 AM, and I was overjoyed. We had rented a house for our whole filmmaker group, and I woke up Nicole and told her we sold it to Miramax. She wasn't pleased. Harvey had already gained the moniker "Harvey Scissorhands." But as it turned out, he and his team believed in the film and didn't touch a frame.

It took eight years for Nicole to make another movie, and *Lovely and Amazing*, her next film, was made on the same budget as her first. The arrangements were somewhat heartbreaking for me, because to make the movie for one million and to make it the way she wanted, they had to shoot in Los Angeles. With the budget so low, I could not justify making a move to L.A., so my colleague Anthony Bregman went out there and made it happen.

On average, directors take about eight years between first and second film projects, so Nicole was on schedule; however, roughly 80 percent of women filmmakers take this much time between all projects—and I don't suspect it is by choice. But the time lag is a shame. In the narrative-feature world, only 6 percent of directors are female. Coincidentally, eight years is also about how long it takes people to raise young kids. And Nicole had twin boys. Most filmmakers would begrudge that time off, but sometimes, it's nice to remember that movies aren't everything.

For John Waters, art is his life. But the two are so inextricably related and filled with fun that neither takes away from the other.

I don't think we would have independent film as we think of it now if it weren't for John Waters. When I wanted to lead a political revolution in small-town Massachusetts, I read John's memoir *Shock Value: A Tasteful Book About Bad Taste*. Filled with such joy and punk attitude, it was liberating and inspiring. More than anyone I had ever read before, John Waters represented a fuck-you celebratory attitude— I'll tell whatever story I want, and you'll come to love it, too. It was akin to Emma Goldberg's famous line "I don't want a revolution I can't dance to." John's movies were highly radical and tremendously enjoyable to make and to watch.

I never thought I'd make a movie with John Waters, but one day, his agent called and asked if I wanted to hear his pitch. When John came in to tell us about *A Dirty Shame*, it was like having our own private nightclub performance. With his pencil-thin moustache, pointed sneakers, and beanpole stature, John was instantly recognizable and his delivery was impeccable. What I saw in the pages of *Shock Value*, I could see during his twenty-minute summation of *A Dirty Shame*. He was coming off a handful of tamer movies like *Hairspray* and *Serial Mom*, and he clearly no longer wanted to play it safe; he wanted to return to his *Pink Flamingos* bad-taste roots. When many filmmakers pitch their stories, they're still working on them. But John's pitch was a well-thought-out performance, exuberantly conveying the pleasures he had for his story of sexual deviance and family values. There was no way I was going to let him leave our office without my signing on to do the movie.

It turned out that John had also pitched the project to my friend Christine Vachon, at Killer Films. We had worked together on Todd Solondz's *Happiness*, and I saw no reason to compete with her for the project. I was happy to share producing duties with her again, and John was happy for us to team up.

But we quickly learned that John's manner of working reflected his unique character. His hometown of Baltimore, for instance, is not the most cost-effective place to shoot a movie, but it's so much a part of his identity that he always demands shooting there. He also wanted to work with the people he wanted to work with, even though they might only have experience working on a John Waters film. He liked to surround himself with the people who made him most comfortable.

Frequently, one thing that producers look for when working with an experienced director is ways to highlight and bring efficiencies to their craft. We pushed John to use some new people and brought in a new director of photography, Steve Gainer (who had shot Larry Clark's *Bully*). And because the budget was so much tighter, we encouraged John to shot-list and storyboard the film, something that John had never done previously. As both money and time were going to be tight, we needed him to embrace the prep so that we could have a more organized and cost-effective production. We also hired an experienced prosthetics designer to construct the gigantic breasts Selma Blair wears in the film. But that was about it in terms of the limits of our success. John was John, and a John Waters film is a John Waters film—nothing any producer was going to change, thankfully.

The thing that you quickly learn about John is his love for every aspect of the story: the character, the actors, the creative collaborators, the locations, the music—every little thing makes him excited. I think this enthusiasm may be informed by his awareness that his life could have gone a different way. By his own admission, his delinquent tendencies could have ended him up in jail just as easily as leading him to be a film director. This self-awareness informs every aspect of his filmmaking. And his enthusiasm was contagious; being on his set was a delight. During production, John would have set visits from local policemen, bikers, transvestites, beauty parlor addicts with big bouffant hairstyles, city councilmen, and art-world celebrities. It was all John's family, and we were now part of it, too. Making movies or leading any other sort of creative life is a privilege, and few directors I've worked with have taken this privilege to heart as much as John.

Early on, we didn't have money to make John's movie. We were stalled because of some insurance issues involving our star Johnny Knoxville, of *Jackass* fame. Frankly, we were concerned that Johnny lived his life in a way that was not conducive to our obtaining affordable insurance. It came down to a Mexican standoff with our financiers: Would they demand prohibitively expensive yet highly protective "essential element" insurance? Or would they allow us to go forward with standard coverage? Eventually, they backed down, and we managed to push on.

I decided to front my own personal funds to keep us on schedule and staff up, acquire props, and figure out how to house the actors and out-of-town crew. Doing so is a big no-no: Everyone knows the biggest mistake you can make in producing movies is to put in your own money. And it wasn't like I ever had money I could afford to lose, but I saw no other way to make things happen. It was a necessary gamble. And I wasn't alone. The whole city of Baltimore seemed to be chipping in. Equipment was loaned, hotel rooms provided, cars leased, and all without a dime being spent beyond my limited funds. But we did it, because people love John Waters and they trust John Waters and they know that John Waters will protect them.

Ultimately, we had no problem prepping *A Dirty Shame* even though we didn't have a penny yet from financiers. For me, the community's generosity was a lesson about how this kind of love and appreciation can help you. The admiration was not just an act. Just a couple weeks before production, New Line's art-house division, Fine Line Features, another member of Water's extended family, having released his earlier movies, finally closed a deal for worldwide rights, giving us the cash to make the whole movie. It shouldn't have surprised us: John is friends with everyone. He is the Pope of Trash and the King of Baltimore, and people of all stripes come to shake his hand.

John had cultivated a close-knit cadre of fellow characters in Baltimore, whether it was actors like Mink Stole, Ricki Lake, and the real-life Patty Hearst or faithful crew members like his salty, quick-witted casting director Pat Moran and his Dumpster-diving costume designer Van Smith, who created the notorious wardrobes for Divine. Seeing all of them enjoy each other's company and take pleasure in their collaboration helped me to be true to myself and stop conforming to how others may have perceived me.

During production, John didn't want the days to be brutal, which meant that sometimes, we would only do two takes to keep it sane. As an independent-film producer, I have frequently found that my role has been not only to push people to move faster, but just as often to give permission for filmmakers to take their time. Many indie directors are so aware of their budget limitations that they compromise before they get what they want. But it's my job to say whether I think it's worth the multiple takes and risk losing the momentum for something greater. With John, we quickly discovered that his rhythm was getting shots done quickly and moving on. At times, we definitely said, "Do we want to try this line a bit differently?" But he often saw that he had what he needed and he pushed forward. John is very aware of who he is, his own aesthetic, and what he wants to achieve. Oftentimes, I throw suggestions to a director to help fine-tune his or her vision. But John Waters's brand and style didn't need me. It had already been fully formed, and pushing it further might have forced the entire ship to capsize. Producers need to know both when to step in and when to step away. Leaving well enough alone is an art form unto itself.

Up until I worked with John, I'm not sure I had been close to anyone who had built for himself a life that was so purely motivated by joy. So much of the independent-film life is about what's missing, about striving for something more, about angst and constant irritation with the way things are. But working with John, I saw a much different approach. I saw somebody who had found a way to express who he was in various media. He has several careers—books, artwork, criticism, acting, directing, all of them going strong. How did it happen? Because he was true to himself.

When we shot *A Dirty Shame*—it was 2003 and one of my first productions under my new company, This is that, after Good Machine sold to Universal—I was returning to my own roots. I didn't aspire to be a Hollywood producer. I wanted to continue working with the filmmakers who were experiencing a similar process of discovery. The business encourages you to build an empire and expand upon that, and I was compelled at different times to think that I should do this, too. But I needed the antidote that tells you, "Love what you do. Love who you work with. Love the tales that you collaborate on." And that will be the big payoff, not millions of dollars. That's the story of being true to yourself. And that's the story of Eddie, Nicole, and John. At certain points in their lives, they all could have gone the other way, but they decided, "This is what I want to do, and I'm going to do it in a way that doesn't sacrifice who I am."

Chapter 4

Commitment

Never make a film with your ex.

While that advice might sound obvious, it was hard for me to heed it during my years working with filmmaker Tamara Jenkins. She is a very dynamic person, with a fantastic sense of humor, a unique eye, a great work ethic, and tremendous energy—one of the funniest and most emotionally open people I have ever met. Every time I was with her when we were a couple, I was in the thrall of her storytelling and couldn't think straight. After we had broken up, I still wanted to prove I could help her and earn the loyalty I never felt I had. I've gotten over all that now. But I couldn't then.

Tamara had won both the student Academy Award and NYU's top award for her short thesis film, *Fugitive Love*. In those days, student filmmakers could win every award and festival and still not get an ounce of attention from either Hollywood or any entertainment attorneys. I spoke at Tamara's class at NYU when she was a grad student, and I dug her film. Later, she sought me out for some advice. Another producer had offered her a "deal": no money down, and she was expected to deliver her next project to him free and clear. We met at a bar. I told her that it didn't sound like much of a deal. After a whiskey or three, well, one thing led to another, and we were soon a couple. This was the early 1990s, after all.

After the success of her first film, my business partner James Schamus was asked by PBS's then recently launched Independent Television Service to supervise a series of short films. The series became a compilation of movies titled *TV Families*. Among them were Todd Haynes's *Dottie Gets Spanked*, Ayoka Chenzira's *My Own TV*, Jon Moritsugu's *Terminal, USA*, and Tamara's *Family Remains*. Tamara's offering went on to win a Special Jury Prize for Excellence in Short Filmmaking at Sundance. Because *Family Remains* came soon after *Fugitive Love*, people in the business finally took notice of her. Funders started to inquire when she would make her first feature film.

But Tamara's process was anything but standard. She did not develop her scripts from outlines, but instead generated various scenes more intuitively. She had great stuff, but it was unclear how it would fit together—or if it ever would. The Sundance Labs invited her to develop what would be the script for *Slums of Beverly Hills*.

I felt I couldn't produce a feature-length film with Tamara, because we were too close. We started dating during the making of Ang Lee's *The Wedding Banquet*, and one night during production, we broke up. Two days later, we got back together again. It seemed like this was our pattern: break up, make up, repeat. We couldn't end it, and we couldn't keep it together. My guess now is that we were drawn together by the work and our ambition—and not the romance—but couldn't admit it. Whatever the reason, it would not make for good chemistry on a movie set.

Ironically, Tamara's company was called Boyfriend Productions. Her previous boyfriend was Peter Himmelstein, whom I had met at the beginning of our relationship when he came into Tamara's apartment with the key he still had and I was wearing some clothes he had left behind. He was taller and thinner than I, but we had the same shoe size and could wear the same shirts—he had good taste in shirts. Nice fabric. Good colors, and costlier that what an indie producer could afford. I was looking sharp as well as a bit shocked when he walked in. Peter was an architect, but he was also schooled in film and graphic design, and designed the title sequences for Tamara's movies, including, later, *Slums of Beverly Hills*. We hired him later on to do titles on Eddie Burns's *She's the One*.

Before I go on about Tamara, let me digress a little about Peter. My producing partner Anne Carey and I later adopted Peter for our development slate, because he wanted to write and direct, and he was one smart, clever, and funny guy. We developed a thriller with him called *The Key Man* and another project about real-life left-handed baseball pitcher and hipster-swinger Bo Belinsky, who married a Playboy bunny and who was also a drummer in singer-actress Joey Heatherton's Las Vegas act. Neither of those projects got made while I was working on them, but at the time, I gave Peter my "formula" for the perfect Sundance acquisition film.

My Formula for the Perfect Sundance Film

1. *The protagonist:* Center the story around an everyday person, someone the audience can identify with (not a wealthy or an evil type).

2. *The plot:* The protagonist needs to go through a serious arc, suffer hardship, and then come to some understanding that the audience didn't expect.

3. *Be bold:* Show risk-taking in the filmmaking. Make it feel like it may all fall apart, but then save it at the last moment: People should say, "It's bold."

4. *Be disciplined:* If you can't be bold, be disciplined. If it doesn't fit the form, cut it out.

5. *Own your aesthetic:* Embrace, even flaunt, your aesthetic and the *limits* of your aesthetic. Don't be ashamed of your limitations. Own your choices.

6. *Engage bigger issues:* The story has to be bigger than the movie itself and should deal with issues of either class conflict, gender conflict, sexual conflict, or other political issues. How do you comment on the world at large while still examining the minute and particular?

7. *Cast:* You need to cast a few stars or soon-to-be stars, so it should be an ensemble piece that covers generational conflict. You have the old-name actor you're bringing back and the up-and-comer whom no one had seen yet, along with actors who can move from TV into feature films.

8. *Shock value:* It needs some moment of audacity, the kind of thing that people will talk about and that might even shock the uninitiated.

9. *The right mix:* Have a sense of humor about great tragedy— or find the tragedy in the hilarious. Embrace the cocktail; make it at least *feel* fresh.

10. *Leave them wanting more:* Shorter is better; 90 minutes is the new 120 (today, 80 is the new 90). No one ever says, "I wish it had been longer" when they leave the theater.

After I shared my formula with him, Peter wrote a script called *Peep World*, which sort of followed these rules, and it became a hit at the script stage. It was a good piece of work, and script readers were digging it. After we developed the script, John Lesher, who was then at the Endeavor Talent Agency (and would later both launch and run, up to its demise, Paramount's specialized arm Vantage), read it and promised Peter to make him not just a paid writer but a star director.

Some promises may sound like a dream come true for a director, but they can be a nightmare for the producer. When you go to the marketplace with a script and an unsigned director, it gives the project a certain amount of cachet. Agents want to sign the director. And signing is a big deal, because the signing agent gets a cut of all the projects the director is later involved in. We wanted to use this bait of an unsigned director to elevate the casting of *Peep World*. We made our strategy clear to Peter and explained we wanted to hold the project until such a time when we could use the various interests to lock in the best cast. But without telling us, Peter signed with Lesher. After we learned about it, we abandoned Peter and the project. It's understandable he wanted to sign with a hotshot agent like Lesher. But making movies—like life—rarely goes well when partners have different agendas. If your collaborators display different values or methods of working than yours early on, it will only get worse once the going gets tough.

In the end, Lesher didn't get Peter's film made and Peter did not become the star director he was told he would be. (About eight or nine years later, Barry Blaustein, a former *Saturday Night Live* writer who wrote *The Nutty Professor* and its sequel, *The Klumps*, eventually directed *Peep World* for the indie production company Occupant Films.) Peter, however, did end up directing *The Key Man* and perhaps got another shot to prove Lesher right.

As all dramatists have been taught, the gun introduced in the first act has to go off in the third. My story with Peter and Tamara had plenty of drama, but I was never quite sure what would constitute the gun, the bullet, and the explosion in the third act.

By 2002, Tamara and I had worked out our troubles caused by our prior personal relationship, and I was pleased and excited to be invited to her wedding to Jim Taylor (who is director and Oscar-winning screenwriter Alexander Payne's writing-producing partner). Peter was also a guest, and as much as I thought I was over our disagreements, my body must have betrayed me. Peter and I laughed about our initial meeting and our shared legacy of Tamara's Boyfriend Productions. We relived some of our hardships and mistakes. As we kept talking on and on, I did not know how to stop. I laughed harder and harder and a little too hard until my hand shook and jerked, and the next thing I knew, a big glop of wine had leaped from my glass. Peter's shirts were still as elegant as when I first wore one after my first date with Tamara. But no matter how crisp and cool they were, nothing looks good drenched in red wine. I offered to pick up the laundry bill, but it would take more than a trip to the dry cleaner's to make that mess go away.

Tamara's first film, *The Slums of Beverly Hills*, opened the Cannes 1998 Directors Fortnight, a parallel, but still highly distinguished alternative to the main festival. The film played well in the United States, receiving positive reviews and launching Tamara's career—kind of. It is much debated in the industry why American women directors struggle to sustain a film career. Like Nicole Holofcener, Tamara didn't get a chance to make another film for a long time after directing an impressive and successful first feature. When Tamara and I ran into each other periodically, it seemed like the past was behind us. Things were going well with my company Good Machine; we were getting a lot of movies made. And Tamara was eager to get behind the camera again.

One day, I had phone calls from both the producer Ed Pressman and Tamara, both of whom were collaborating on a project about famed photographer Diane Arbus. Ed had consistently produced provocative films by some of the top auteurs in the business. Tamara had a long fascination with Arbus. Her short films are virtual homages to Arbus's work. As perfect as the relationship seemed, Ed and Tamara were stuck. Both liked and respected each other, but they weren't solving the script problems. Nor were they able to plan a film that would fit the budget that Tamara was likely to command.

Tamara's concept for the Diane Arbus story was about a young filmmaker named "Tamara Jenkins" who was obsessed with a photographer named "Diane Arbus" and lived to make a movie about her. "Tamara" was eventually hired to make a movie by a producer named "Ed Pressman," who didn't have the rights to the legendary Diane Arbus photos. So the fictional Tamara's assignment was to make a movie that wouldn't feature the photos. But there was another major challenge: "Ed" wanted someone like Nicole Kidman to play Diane Arbus. But "Tamara" didn't think "Nicole" was right, because "Diane" shouldn't look like a movie star. In the script, when "Tamara" can't get "Nicole," she gets "Cate Blanchett."

We sent the script to the real Cate Blanchett, who we thought was perfect to play the character "Cate Blanchett." Cate passed, and her agent asked if we'd kindly remove the character "Cate Blanchett" from the script itself. I've often found that if people in the film business can take something too seriously, they will.

Coincidentally, we were given Tamara's Arbus script literally the same day that we were given Charlie Kaufman's *Adaptation*. Due to Tamara's and Charlie's shared celebration of the postmodern metanarrative, *Adaptation* threatened to upstage Tamara's project. But beyond this challenge, there was always going to be major casting problems for Tamara's script. We wanted the lead actress to be someone like Jane Adams (from Todd Solondz's *Happiness* and the HBO series *Hung*) who looked a bit like Arbus and felt like a real person. At the same time, though, we needed a star to play the lead. And even if we got Cate or Nicole, they wouldn't be the protagonist in the film, and salespeople can't sell cameos. Another problem was that to make the movie that Tamara envisioned, we were looking at an eleven-million-dollar budget, but we felt it needed to be closer to seven million for the project to be viable. We tried to find places to trim, but the best we could do was eight or nine million—still too much for a postmodern art film that could not support a star in the lead role.

The whole ordeal of not getting Tamara's metanarrative, industry-reflexive, eccentric personal biopic made coincided with the sale of Good Machine. When Good Machine was absorbed into Universal, one thing I negotiated was a deal with James and David's new company, Focus Features, for a discretionary development fund that we could spend "anyway that we wanted," which meant projects that they approved. As part of the deal, Focus and my new company, This is that, would cofinance two projects "blind"—no pitch or treatment needed, only the selection of the director. We chose one by Nicole Holofcener and one by Tamara Jenkins under very specific parameters: The projects would be contemporary, would be made for under eight million dollars, would have highly castable parts, and wouldn't be depressing.

Choosing to work with Tamara yet again may not have been the best idea, but I knew that she didn't have a great experience on *Slums*, and I thought I could fix this and give her a good experience. I thought I was now emotionally mature enough not to allow the past to affect the present or the future. Yeah, right.

By the time Nicole had finished editing her movie *Friends with Money*, Tamara had still only delivered her script. But we all move at the speed that's best for us. I've always liked the phrase *personal velocity*, and you see it manifest itself clearly in different directors' development process. Some take decades to make a film; others, months. Ironically, neither project was financed or distributed by Focus, which put both films into turnaround because they did not fit the company's foreign-sales-driven structure at the time. (Note that *turnaround* doesn't simply mean that a studio is abandoning a project and granting the producer the right to shop it around. There are other caveats: Producers have a limited amount of time to find other backers and must reimburse the studio for any previously agreed-upon terms—sometimes, turnaround costs can be pricey.)

Most problems in the film business come from the misconception that all adults are capable of good behavior. I like to think that people who share creative ambitions form a tight bond. There's the sense that no one is going to come between you and making good work. But experience has demonstrated otherwise. There are many ways that things can come undone. I was not at all prepared for what I would face producing Tamara's second film, *The Savages*.

Born from that blind deal with Focus, *The Savages* started with a colossal script based on Tamara's relationship with her brother as their father began suffering from dementia. Tamara initially delivered something like three hundred pages. She knew she had to bring the script down to size and that such a lengthy first draft couldn't be submitted to the studio. But when people remark on the depth of character in *The Savages*, it's because Tamara knew these characters cold, their every thought and choice. And her process was warranted—all the investment she made in the detailed nature of the screenplay paid off creatively. But from a producer's standpoint, you can feel panicked when you're given a three-inch script to read. The sound of such a beast hitting your desk should always be cause for alarm.

When *The Savages* was set up at Focus, I frequently found myself making apologies to the studio: "Sorry it's going down this way," I'd say, "but it's not ready." Then Tamara would go to Focus, and because she can talk and pitch and she's great in a room, her visit would buy us another six months.

When she finally pared the script to an acceptable length, we delivered it to Focus, which loved it. But the company admitted there were challenges for foreign sales. Relationship- and character-based comedies are more of a domestic phenomenon. And comedies about old men with dementia walking through death's door don't have the strongest track record. But hey, you couldn't say it wasn't fresh. John Lyons, head of production at Focus at the time, really liked Tamara and the project, and the script got a tremendous amount of love from the agents. The characters were real and heartfelt; it wasn't like the usual dreck. Reese Witherspoon's agent loved it, and it was exactly what Reese was looking for in her transition to a woman's role (versus the young, spunky type she was known for with *Election* and *Legally Blonde*). But she was still far too young for the part. No one would think she was going through the midlife crisis of that character. But for a while, we wondered whether the interest of this stellar talent who had generated a lot of box-office receipts meant the script should change to accommodate her.

Ultimately, Tamara decided there was no way she could make the movie with any actress of Reese's age. The Focus people regretted not having a Reese Witherspoon movie, but they understood Tamara and said we could cast Laura Linney. Everyone knows Laura is an incredible actress who will one day win an Oscar, but unless you're Meryl Streep or Angelina Jolie, an actress over the age of thirty won't be able to help get a movie financed. So if we were going to go with a great actor like Laura in the female role, we would need to cast a name that meant something for international sales in the male role. Tamara always had Philip Seymour Hoffman in mind to play the brother. In contrast, Focus tried to come up with actors who would work for them, like Mike Myers, who would balance out the international value of not having Reese. We were continents apart.

Tamara was willing to consider whatever Focus suggested, but we also needed to protect her movie and all the things that made this the story she wanted to tell. Focus listened and wanted to be supportive, and eventually said, okay, cast Philip. But then about three days later, we heard, "There's no way we can make this movie." We countered, "But you told us to cast Laura and Phil!" And they countered, "That's the movie you want to make, and we don't want to stand in your way." And we replied, "What budget can you make this for? We'll do it for any budget under the sun." And Focus got back to us in a week or two and told us, "There's no budget you can make this movie for, with Laura and Phil and us, on the subject of an old man dying." The response was frustrating, particularly because it was coming from my former partner James Schamus.

When James and I split up and he went on to start Focus, he remained a friend and an ally, but we were never particularly close. Maybe it is a guy thing or a former-partner thing. We have periodic dinners together, sure, but we're not exchanging photos of our kids. Although business often may give us a reason to talk to each other, it's also a barrier to real friendship—hopefully that won't always be the case. I love to listen to James talk. I'd pay a ticket for it. He's both funny and delightfully pompous, and he always presents a solid argument, and generally, it is very hard to argue with his logic. Yet, with *The Savages*, I wished certain decisions could have come quicker.

There's a myth in the indie film business that studio corporations are evil. But on the movies I've made, the studio's goals have been the same as my goals, which are the same as the filmmaker's goals: to make the best movie possible. And the studios have always known that the best way to market these films is with the complete support of the filmmaker, and they try to win it along the way. I've never been in a situation where the director didn't get his or her cut of the movie, except for Jesse Peretz's *The Ex*. And in that case, Harvey Weinstein allowed Jesse's version to survive as the definitive version on DVD. (I never figured out why Ang Lee wanted a director's cut of *Ride with the Devil*, because I thought we gave him the cut he wanted the first time around.)

When we weren't reaching a deal on *The Savages* with Focus, we started to test the waters with independent equity investors. Equity can often be helpful, even though it seemed that Focus would never need outside money. It was commonly believed that Focus had the most-accessible money in the world, because the company obtained funds through General Electric, Universal's parent at the time, and GE had an incredibly low borrowing rate.

We came upon a former agent named Fred Westheimer, who had evidently made an alliance with a mysterious and incredibly wealthy man, and together they formed a new fund to make movies. We sent a script of *The Savages* to Fred; then Tamara met Fred and his daughter, Erika Westheimer, who helped run the company, and it was a love fest: Erika and her group loved the script, they loved Tamara, and we loved that they said they had money that they wanted to put into our movie. Early in the process, Focus wasn't interested in the Westheimers' money, but when we traveled out on our own later, we sure were glad we had the Westheimers in our back pockets as a financing option.

Now, I've been around long enough to know that there are a lot of new funds for producing movies that don't really exist at all beyond their *Variety* announcement. But I also know that sometimes, the best thing you can say is that you have someone who will put up half the money. Generally speaking, in the film business, no one wants anything until someone else has said he or she wants it. So we have to manufacture desire. As a rule, I don't close deals with investors I don't know if I can trust, but I *can* use their interest to foster more interest elsewhere. I felt a little bit more secure with Fred, because he came from an industry background. He couldn't be total bullshit. But I wasn't going to cry if his group went away, either. So when the Westheimers said they'd put up half the budget, whether it was six million dollars or ten million, that's all we needed from a partner at that point. Even if they dropped out before *The Savages* ultimately came together, they would be a possible magnet for other financiers who might come on board. Money likes money, and the first commitment is always the most difficult and thus the most valuable (even when it's not real). However, as I discovered, once you make your bed, you have to lie in it, and the partners you want at the start of the journey may not be the kind you need later on.

With the Westheimers' new venture Lone Star supposedly backing us, we went out searching for a new home, starting with the top. Tamara pitched Peter Rice, then head honcho at Fox Searchlight; he wasted no time and quickly passed on it. Tamara's ever-tenacious agent, Bart Walker, suggested we keep pushing and got us a follow-up meeting with

Searchlight. I was nervous, as I take "no" as a no. Because Peter had clearly passed once already, I didn't understand what we were doing. But Bart said we had to try again, so we did. I wasn't the only one who was confused; during the meeting, Peter got upset, rejected our project, and said to me, "Look me in the eye, Ted: I. Will. Not. Make. This. Movie. Don't pitch it again." He was pretty damn clear: Searchlight was passing a second and final time.

Despite this setback, a number of factors quickly helped us gain momentum. I had seen the trailer for *Capote*, and you could tell that Philip Seymour Hoffman had done something extraordinary. I started telling people that he was going to win the Oscar (I am sure I wasn't the only one, but it was still early). Jim Taylor, Tamara's husband, came onboard *The Savages* as an executive producer along with his writing partner Alexander Payne. They shared their experiences making *About Schmidt*, Payne's movie that starred Jack Nicholson. Everyone would read the script and think it was completely tragic, and Alexander would say, "No, it's a really funny movie, but with a lot of soul." Fox Searchlight, which had later made Payne's *Sideways* such a hit, didn't buy *About Schmidt*, so Taylor and Payne made the movie with New Line. Consequently, Searchlight, like many others, regretted its decision.

So Jim and Alexander, who, courtesy of *Sideways*, now had a deal with Searchlight, met with Peter Rice, where they reminded him of *About Schmidt* and its similarity to Tamara's project. Nothing concrete came out of the meeting. But it was the Friday before the Golden Globe Awards. On Sunday, Phil won the Golden Globe for Best Actor. On Monday, Peter called me up and said that despite everything he had said before, Searchlight would love to finance our movie. His final "no" was not so final after all. Soon, we were all headed off to Sundance, and we, Searchlight, and Tamara's agent all got together to go over a few deal points and shake hands: Project green-lit. I guess the third time *is* a charm.

When Searchlight finally said yes, the company also told me that it didn't want Fred and his daughter involved. Even if there was no contract with Lone Star, I didn't want to toss the Westheimers away. Despite not knowing if their money was real, I felt the need to protect Fred; he had stood by us, even if it did not take very much to do so. I insisted that Searchlight meet with Lone Star. The people at Searchlight, however, made it very clear to me that they wanted us to make *The Savages* for six million and they wanted to control it fully. Eventually, the Searchlight folks agreed to do the meeting for me, but they vowed they would not get involved with Lone Star.

When we realized that Phil was probably going to win the Oscar, and Linney, because of the "most favored nations" contractual clause, would need to be paid the same as Phil, we all recognized that the budget for *The Savages* would have to increase—the actors couldn't be expected to work just for scale (the Screen Actors Guild's specified minimum) anymore. So strategically, Searchlight might have a good reason to keep an equity partner on board.

And sure enough, once it became clear that the movie was reaching a price point that Searchlight wasn't comfortable with, the company agreed to have Lone Star involved. Those with good business sense learn to pivot rapidly. For this reason, it is not at all surprising that Peter Rice continued to rise up the ranks at Fox, long after our movie was just another piece of annual accounting.

The negotiations appeared to be going smoothly. I was even told that Searchlight had embarked on a bigger deal with Lone Star—why have someone fund just one movie when you can insist they fund several? I don't know how much of this was true, but I had to be wary. My partners were quickly becoming more wedded to each other than they were to us. From Searchlight's point of view—or any distributor's, for that matter—they wanted the money, any money, to be subservient to them. But it put me in a difficult situation because my partners on each side had multiple agendas and were not just concerned with our movie.

We moved ahead. We had the Westheimers. We had Searchlight. We entered preproduction.

The independent-film business is always about putting the money you have up on the screen, so productions are invariably based in the ugly sections of town, where the rents are cheap. My New York City office for *The Savages* had no windows, but I didn't need to look at the auto-parts stores and stumbling drunks on the sidewalk below. It must have been day two of prep. My phone rang. It was Fred. He said his daughter—who had been a wardrobe supervisor professionally—was going to produce the movie with us and share our producing credit.

Now, I don't mind giving credit where credit is due, but Anne Carey and I had been working on the film with Tamara for a long, long time. If I'm going to agree to give someone credit, I want the person to work hard for it and truly deserve it. Otherwise, it denigrates everything every producer has ever done. But Fred said that regardless of what I had done to get us this far or what Anne or I would do in the future, if we didn't give Erika a producer credit equal to ours, Lone Star would pull out of the movie and the entire film would collapse. The Westheimers may not have been our partner contractually, but if we wanted to make it, we now needed them. It wasn't a negotiation; it was an all-or-nothing proposition.

At first, I said no, thinking I was calling his bluff. He said fine, but he wasn't going to fund the movie. Six hours later, I backed down. What else could I do? I couldn't call up Fox and tell it the movie is going to collapse because of my desire to preserve an appropriate credit for the work I had done. This was the film business, after all.

Then came another major wrinkle.

Tamara's agent Bart had been at the Sundance meeting where Searchlight had come aboard and gone through the deal points. Among the terms, we had agreed not to make the movie under a Directors Guild of America contract. Such a contract would have locked in higher rates, union staffing, and residual payments to directors, assistant directors, and line producers. Going DGA gives you a more experienced level of crew, but at a substantially higher cost. Tamara was not a member of the DGA, and guild terms were an expense that neither the studio nor I saw as necessary. We needed every penny up on that screen.

Sometime after Sundance, Bart went on vacation. And when he came back, he threw a wrench in the entire works. We needed to close Tamara's deal to move the film forward. But presumably to try to sweeten his client's deal, Bart disputed my version of events and claimed that he had never agreed to make a non-DGA film. The Searchlight people knew otherwise, but for them, this was a standard negotiating ploy. For me, my integrity was being questioned and my relationship with my main creative collaborator was being jeopardized—all for the sake of a few minor deal points.

I don't know what Tamara felt at the time. She and I had a complex relationship, to say the least, and she had an apparently loyal supporter in her agent, who had never broken up with her. I don't know if she wanted to take sides, but I'm sure she wanted what was best for her and her movie.

Bart and I got into an angry pissing match via email. Fox Searchlight's head legal chief Joe DeMarco and Searchlight's Claudia Lewis, who were copied on the emails, eventually told us to stop arguing and act like adults. Beyond being intensely embarrassing, the episode seemed endemic of an increasing sentiment in the industry, in which concerns for ethics and truth were put aside at every step for the betterment of the deal.

Finally, Bart and I stopped yelling at each other and then stopped talking to each other, and Tamara won some extra rights in her contract. Usually, when deal points like this are resolved, core relationships aren't sacrificed. But this was different; this was yet another crack in the foundation of the producer-director relationship that was already fairly shaky. We had to prep the movie in six weeks, which is a very short amount of time, and it was a pressure-cooker way to work. And it didn't help that the director was told by her agent that her producer was willing to hire a lower-quality (i.e., nonunion) production staff just so the movie could be made for less. A director and a producer must share a common agenda, trust and believe it, and never doubt it. Tamara and I started that film with a trust deficit.

I don't like having bad blood with anyone in the independent industry—we're all in it together, and it's not constructive to hold grudges—and I believe that Bart and I will find ways to do business together again. Bad situations reveal a lot about the nature of the business and what precautions you have to take. Any difficult contractual point is not something you leave to a conversation; I now always get the points immediately in writing, and as I would later come to learn, sometimes even that is not enough.

During the production of *The Savages*, we were also having problems with the crew. I hired someone who I thought was an excellent assistant director, Chip Signore. Jim Taylor wanted to make sure that his wife had the best support, and he wanted to make sure that the film would be as good as the film could be, so he saw it as his job to challenge

Chip's shooting schedule. But it's one thing to question the hiring of an assistant director in order to have the strongest directorial support; it's another to saw one leg off the table just to prove it can't stand on three legs. The intentions may have been good, but the results were far from it. From my side, by defending Chip, I felt I was protecting Tamara, but that meant I was battling Jim. I found myself in a situation where everyone was questioning everyone else's decisions. It was making a challenging movie even more difficult to make.

We also had a problem with the actor whom we had cast as the father. It took a long time to cast an actor who would be willing to play the dad with dementia (it's death for an actor's career to be thought of as a dying old man). But we finally found our actor in Philip Bosco, a known agoraphobic—he won't fly in planes, ride in elevators, or generally be in other small spaces. We wanted to film in Arizona; it was a big part of the film. But we didn't know how to make it work: Could we drive Philip out in a Winnebago? Or do we build a set in New York? And if we do, how do we make it match the rest of the set that is actually in Arizona? We needed to shoot on a stage in order to receive the New York State tax credit rebate, but we ended up building sets of both a house and a plane, which the tax credit makes no demands for. We ended up having to build more sets than necessary, at an expense that was way too great.

Our production designer was Jane Ann Stewart, who worked closely with Alexander Payne and came on the film as "a favor to him." Another thing I learned is not to take favors. It quickly became clear to me that she was not making the same movie that I was and refused to recognize it. By now, the set construction was out of control, and as a result, instead of Tamara thinking about what she could do within our budget, she believed that we had to do much more. So Jane and Tamara and the distributor were miles apart from each other. The question of trust had been undermined repeatedly. And because of my history with Tamara, she had to be thinking, Is Ted working in my best interests? I knew I was, but I sensed she doubted me.

If there are warning bells with a particular crew person—if the person has an attitude or is not up to the standards you need—you must act on it immediately. The hassle of firing someone is far less painful than the trouble caused by an ineffective or disruptive collaborator. Yet department heads, in particular, are difficult to let go. They often hold unique knowledge of the production; they may have formed important bonds with the cast or other department heads; and it requires time to get a replacement up to speed. Any change of plans is always costly. But on *The Savages*, maintaining the status quo was eating into our budget and hindering what we could achieve. But in a war with many battles, this felt like one where I needed to surrender and just work with the crew we originally hired.

If there's any element in the movie that I think is wrong, it's Laura Linney's wig. It's the worst possible wig I've ever had in a movie. I wanted to fire the hair stylist, and this is where Erika Westheimer, the producer who had been forced on me by her father, wanted to take control. Because the hairdresser was going to be working specifically with Laura, Erika wanted to resolve the issue in a way that wouldn't upset Laura. So I let her. But Erika never fired our hair person.

As a result, I feel I let Laura down. When I see my failure as a producer in that movie, I see it all in that wig. It pulls me out of the film. It distracts me. No one else complained to me about it. But Tamara and I had plenty of conversations about it. And here was a political issue that became an aesthetic issue, and I regret the decision to this day. I should have stepped in and replaced the hair person, but I had given up that authority.

Each director makes movies in his or her own way. There is no right way or uniform template. Tamara may be a supertalented director, but on set, she is not a decisive person. Like Ang Lee, she was forced to grapple with an industry that rewards decisiveness. Crews, studio production experts, and completion bond companies all demand it: It's as if no one cares if it's a good decision or a bad one—only if a decision is made. "My indecision is final," is Christine Vachon's joke about the director who knew what mattered most to her crew. Tamara auditioned sixty-eight people for one role with a single speaking line; I don't even think the character ended up in the movie. But producers must trust their director's process. And if the result is a powerful film like *The Savages*, then perhaps all those auditions were worth it.

Indecisiveness, however, is not conducive to short shooting schedules. We had twenty-five days to shoot *The Savages*. We didn't have time for anything other than definitive choices. The financing we had—which was the only financing we could get—did not provide for any more shooting time. I was confident that we could get it done in the time allotted, but in discussions with my partners, I heard that the contracted schedule was our enemy. And apparently, the tight schedule was my fault, and Tamara and Jim seemed to hint that in my committing to it, I had undermined Tamara. While I don't believe this was the case, I do think the producer is responsible for everything. And yet, to make the movie for the money we had available necessitated such a limited schedule. And that meant it was going to be a real challenge to get a Tamara Jenkins movie. I could not demand decisiveness from her without also taking away what she was all about. And I knew her well enough that working this way wasn't going to be true to who she was. I was trying to do both: fit Tamara into a preconceived box and appease an angry financier.

But the crew didn't agree that allowing Tamara the time she needed to get things right was what was best for the film. And Fox Searchlight and the bond company certainly didn't, either. Bond companies—which insure that a film is delivered in accordance with agreed-on terms—aren't all that bad, by the way. They help productions from spinning out of control. Generally, distributors or financiers are happy to pay a small percentage of the overall cost of the budget—from 1.5 to 3 percent—to have an outside party review and track a film's finances and schedule. It keeps everyone honest.

Soon enough, we were shooting sixteen-, seventeen-, eighteen-hour days. On the last day of shooting at Silver Cup Studios, we had been shooting for seventeen hours when the union finally came in and pulled the plug. It was brutal. People were really upset about the grueling length of our workdays—and rightfully so. I was told I had to fire the assistant director, because someone had to take the fall, but I knew that this was blaming an innocent party and I wasn't going to support it. Everyone wanted a true Tamara Jenkins film, and working at her deliberate pace was what it took.

This wasn't the first time that our working hours had brought about such tensions. Previously, around the third or fourth day of shooting, the crew members had called for a meeting, where they made it clear they wanted to see Tamara reined in. They wanted to see the working hours shrink and a commitment to honoring certain breaks. We reached a resolution on those issues, and then I said to Tamara, "You have to lock yourself down and make a decision before lunch." I didn't suggest the possibility that the crew would revolt or that the bond company would shut us down, but this was, in fact, the case. The challenge of reconciling Tamara's methods with the crew's, the studio's, and the bond company's had sparked a slew of simmering tensions—between Jim and me, between Tamara and me, and between Erika and me. Something was going to blow.

As the film went forward, we were getting great footage. But that was not enough to keep the financiers at bay; we were also going into over-time on a daily basis. Fred Westheimer came to New York and insisted on meeting me at 11:15 PM at the Pierre Hotel. I am used to meeting my financiers during filming, but usually they recognize that I'm getting up at 5 AM every morning. Set visits are common, but this seemed different.

I hadn't met Fred face-to-face during the entire production, and when I saw him, he cut a distinguished figure. In his late sixties, he clearly enjoyed working out, and he wore a very expensive, embroidered T-shirt, the kind favored by much younger men. He didn't make much small talk and jumped to the point: He may not have been to the set or had much general producing experience, but he felt he knew what was what. And he told me that the crew had no respect for Tamara or me, because I was allowing the long hours. I could argue that many of the crew had signed up because we had worked together before and this was the type of movie they wanted to be associated with. Some of the crew I had known for over twenty years. But Fred felt he knew better. Tamara's excesses were all my fault, and she would have to go sooner rather than later. He said they were doing the movie only because of Alexander Payne, and they were going to install Alexander to edit the movie: Either I needed to bring in a twelve-hour day and respect my crew, or Payne was going to take over the film.

I don't believe Fred ever had a conversation with Alexander about editing the film. I don't believe Alexander would ever go behind a director's back; he was always incredibly supportive of Tamara. But my financier was calling into question how I was managing the set, and this made me furious. I said to him what I really believed: Knowing most of the crew people, who were not there because of the pay but for a love for the project, they weren't going to leave. They wanted to work specifically on this movie, as opposed to some New York cop show. And despite the trouble, I wasn't accepting otherwise. And knowing Tamara, and having been in the edit room with her, I knew that to make the movie right, she had to finish the film and do it in the style that was true to her. I admitted that it was a difficult process, one that I was not enjoying, but it was the only way to get the movie to its highest level.

This was not a reasoned discussion, and it very quickly deteriorated to a point where I said, "I'm not having this conversation." And he said something like, "Don't you dare walk away, or I'll hit you in the fucking face." I've been in testy situations before, and I've been in a few fights—a long time ago—but I've never been challenged by someone thirty years my senior and someone who is my partner on a film, whose child's film career I helped elevate, and for whom I was going to deliver an Oscar-nominated movie.

I got up from the table and left the hotel, thinking, what kind of fucked-up world is this? I can't go and tell Jim or Tamara that our financier said he's going to fire Tamara from the edit room; I need them to believe that Fred supports them. I can't call Erika and tell her that her father just threatened me; I have to deal with her for the rest of the show. How the hell did I get into this situation? I'm working more than fifteen hours a day, I'm getting yelled at, I don't have trust, and I'm trying to defend a filmmaker whom I truly believe in and feel some emotional debt to, and the net result is I am getting attacked from all sides.

Is a good movie worth all the battles we have to go through to get there? I find myself asking this question so much. I take great satisfaction that *The Savages* found its audience, received great critical acclaim, and even received two Oscar nominations. That's what most people will see when they watch the film, but for me, I see the scars that we all received along the way.

The lesson from *The Savages* seemed clear: Only work on movies you believe in. You go through all of this hassle, where you're questioning how to make the best movie and how to be a good person, and at the end of the day, after all that suffering and sacrifice, if you're not mostly mesmerized by the results, you're going to have a hard time gearing up to make another film. (It might also be wise not to make a film with your ex.)

At its core, *The Savages* is a story about children coming to terms with the fact that their parents did not love them. You can't love all the movies you make, but if the process is going to be hell and you want to make another movie, you'd better be proud of the results, or your retirement will loom large before you.

Producing films is a bit like childbirth: A beautiful baby makes all the pain go away. *The Savages* found its audience and became part of Fox Searchlight's 2007 banner year, which also saw the releases of the company's breakout smash *Juno*, as well as other indie sleeper hits *Waitress* and *Once*. At the 2008 Academy Awards, Laura was nominated for Best Actress, and Tamara received her first Oscar nomination, for Best Original Screenplay. I sat at home watching the spectacle, completely satisfied that I had helped bring a funny and truly touching film that would help families discuss their parents and their future in hopefully more honest terms. Maybe all those battles were worth it. Maybe, after all, I was winning the war and would continue the good fight.

Chapter 5

Ambition

I first met Todd Solondz in the early 1990s, when he was trying to make his film *Welcome to the Dollhouse*. He gave me a copy of his short film *Schatt's Last Shot* and a script called *Middle Child*. I had read some of his other scripts previously and considered him a lovely and truly unique guy with the ability to capture horrible moments that are both heartbreaking and hilarious. Eventually, *Middle Child* would become *Dawn Wiener* and then *Wiener Dog* on the way to becoming *Welcome to the Dollhouse*. James Schamus and I had talked about doing the project, but felt we'd be lucky to raise half a million dollars, and the fact that the film was all kids (requiring shorter work hours, and tutors) would make producing it even more difficult.

Welcome to the Dollhouse went on to win the Sundance Grand Jury Prize. Sony Pictures Classics acquired the film for distribution, and it became a modest box-office hit, launching Todd's career—one of the most distinctive in independent film. After the success of *Dollhouse*, Todd confided in me that he had a new script and asked me to produce it. He had also sent the script to Christine Vachon, figuring there would be no way that two producers would actually like it.

I knew Christine, of course. She had produced *Office Killer* and Todd Haynes's *Safe* with Good Machine, and even though I had executive producer credit on those films, we worked together strictly on a distanced, business level. It turned out that my close collaboration with Christine on the new film would be crucial.

It's rare that a director and single producer are so simpatico that they can go through the whole shoot without help. Directors often need more support than what one producer can give. And one reason I've found it so useful to have business partners and producing partners is that the job of producer can be a lonely and alienating gig. I don't know many individuals who are strong enough to do it on their own. Making Todd Solondz's film, which would become *Happiness*, was extremely tough, and I don't think I could have gotten through it without a partner, and one as strong as Christine.

Happiness tells the story of three sisters—a self-hating author; a suburban housewife; and the youngest, a hapless, hopeful loser—and the dysfunctional relationships that surround them. The plot turns on the revelation that all is not well in suburbia: The middle sister's husband, a psychiatrist, is sexually molesting his young son's friend.

Early on, we were thinking about making the movie for a bigger budget, and we had a long list of actors we were thinking about for the leading roles. But then we started sending the script out, and the response went like this: "I can't believe you're asking my client to do this role." People were afraid that the role of the psychiatrist would forever brand them as a pedophile. One of the agencies, Gersh, even told us that it wouldn't even show the script to its clients. I had good friends who said to me, "I can't do this movie, Ted; I have children."

It wasn't as if we were sanctioning the character's behavior, but the problem for most was that we weren't judging it, either. To me, it was clear from the script that no matter what horrible psychological disorders the characters had and no matter what horrible humiliations they endured, Todd had immense sympathy for them. Some might call the film misanthropic, but I have always found the story a profoundly humanist work. I have always been attracted to material that helps me better understand people with whom have I absolutely nothing in common. But the majority of the people who read the script were completely shocked. I don't think we ever got close to casting a single well-known actor in the controversial role.

In addition to the agencies, the unions also distanced themselves from the project. We heard that the Screen Actors Guild was concerned about the content. And when we asked the technical unions for their support, we had to assure them we weren't making pornography. After reading the script, Matt Loeb, who was the head of the crafts union, called up and said, "You don't have to worry about signing a contract with us. Go ahead on your own. We don't need this film." Which was fine with us: If the unions thought it was too risqué, we could more easily afford a nonunion crew with a tight shooting schedule.

With some good fortune, we were able to get financing through foreign sales and a commitment from a new distributor called October Films, which had launched in 1991. I was very nervous giving the script to our new partner, David Linde, at our foreign-sales division, Good Machine International. David had come from Miramax. I feared he was going to leave the company when he read it. We weren't even sure it could qualify for an R rating. But he read it and became very excited. He saw in it a bold piece of filmmaking that could define who we were as a company. David and James started working with Christine and me to figure out how we could put it all together. David picked two overseas distributors, Kinovelt in Germany and BIM in Italy, sent them the script, and asked them to come aboard for traditional fee percentages of the budget—somewhere between 10 and 12 percent. With that in place, David took the film and these contracts to Bingham Ray at October Films. It looked like a new model: Based on the presales, foreign sales alone could finance the cost of the shoot. October agreed to finance the rest of the film and David and our company would license it internationally on their behalf. That contract would many years later lead to the sale of Good Machine to Universal, merging it with what then was October.

Meanwhile, Todd and his casting director, Ann Goulder, were holding auditions, though the auditions might as well have been rehearsals. Todd met lots of actors, and when he liked an actor, he would bring the person back for a second and third time. These weren't minor casting sessions; Todd would do the other roles and give the actors real direction for hours and hours. Phillip Seymour Hoffman's agent asked us, "Are you casting my client in your movie? Because he's been to three sessions already, and the third one lasted an hour and a half!" Evidently that was the last role Phil ever had to audition for; his career took off after that. He was an unknown then, but he knew enough to know that Todd's audition process was not the usual way of doing things.

Todd figured out something that most young directors never learn. Before making a movie, you need to have a couple versions in your head, because of how the pieces fit together—or don't. Especially if you're making something that's controversial and you're not paying anybody and you're not proven, the possibility that one of the pieces will fall through and collapse the entire production is very strong, so you have to explore every option. You need to have an answer in place for all the what-ifs. If Todd often shoots a lot more material than he uses, it's because he's aware of the problems that might occur. He does what is necessary to make sure that, no matter what, he'll have a movie he's proud to have made.

Happiness was one of the tenser sets I've ever been on. The sense that we're all in this together was absent, because some crew members felt, "This guy won Sundance, so they must have gotten a lot of money to make this film, so why aren't we getting paid better?" Because of the union's decision to distance itself from the film, we were working with nonunion crew who did not enjoy the same protections that union people did. Specific protocols were not in place for how certain issues should be handled. We were in constant battles just to sort out our shooting schedule. Many producers try to work nonunion to get around certain rules, but I wished we had a union contract so that we could focus on the work and not the negotiation. After the first day of shooting, people wanted to fire the caterer. But I was just happy to have a hot-meal truck, which I don't think we'd ever had before on a shoot. It felt like the crew members just wanted to use their power, and they wanted to have someone canned. We held out; we knew a warm breakfast would later be appreciated. But we ended up firing the caterer in the last five days and bringing in a new one: When the crew is out for blood, it's hard to say no.

Todd always knew what he wanted, and he was extremely precise. He wanted the dialogue delivered exactly as written. Certain actors would try to take liberties with the script and make it their own, but Todd wouldn't have any of their improvisations. During one emotional scene, Jane Adams's character is going into work after a particularly bad night. There are strikers outside, and she feels vulnerable and scared. It was cold outside, the wind was blowing, and in one line of dialogue, she was supposed to say "cannot." But it frequently came out "can't." Todd kept yelling, "Cut!" and the crew was starting to lose it. But this is precisely the point where you need to trust your director. The crew may not have known it then, but it's incredibly clear to me now: There will never be another director like Todd Solondz, and as his producer, I needed to give him the room to be himself. One of the key aspects of good producing is finding ways for the directors to trust themselves and the crew to trust the directors in return.

One of the most difficult moments in making *Happiness* was the scene on the couch with the psychiatrist, played by Dylan Baker, and his son, Billy, played by Rufus Read. In the scene, the father confesses to his son that he is a pedophile. By that point in the shoot, the work-days were getting longer and we realized we couldn't complete all of the scheduled shots. It was Friday night, and we had to be out of the main location by Monday.

Generally, we shoot the kids first and then the adults, because the kids often get tired. And that's exactly what we did. We shot a single of the kid, and then Dylan's single. But in the midst of doing Dylan's single, we suddenly saw this incredible performance from Rufus. So Todd said, "Let's do it again. Pull the camera back. Now let's do it in a two-shot." And then he said, "Let's go back and do the single again on the kid." And there were people on the crew saying, "I can't believe you're going back to get the single on the kid. You just did that. You had it. Move on." But they weren't seeing that something truly incredible was going on: Rufus and Dylan were connecting emotionally to their characters and each other. In a child's perfor-mance, you often see the strength of the adult they are playing off. Dylan was giving Rufus what he needed to go deep into the reality of the scene. Today, when you watch the film, you can see it: a son asking for his father's love, without recognizing the profound prob-lems of his dad's behavior.

As a producer, you're watching this incredible thing happen, and you want to be in the center of it, while on the other hand, you have this fire blazing out of control amid the crew behind you. But undeterred, Todd knew what he was getting and he knew what he needed to get.

But even after capturing the incredible serendipity that elevated the scene into the realm of art, we still had to face the pressures of reality. We were falling behind schedule and decided we had to come back on set for a sixth day. The problem was, we hadn't booked crew people for a six-day week. And everyone was exhausted, and we didn't have much good-will at that point, because of the long hours we had been shooting. On Saturday, we had to hire two-thirds of a new crew. I certainly understood that people needed a break after a week of fifteen-hour days, but those of us who stayed felt abandoned by the department heads that left us.

As a producer, you have to constantly put yourself in other people's shoes and see things from their perspective, but at the same time, you have to produce the necessary results to make the best possible movie. When the bulk of the crew didn't come to work on Saturday and then returned on Monday looking chipper, it was tense: I didn't want to see our "deserters"—even if it had been their right to not participate.

Early in the film, there was another tough scene where the character played by Jon Lovitz (a popular *Saturday Night Live* actor at the time) commits suicide, asphyxiating himself with a plastic bag. We knew we had the shot, or at least, we thought we had it, but Todd wanted more. This was the first time I questioned why we were doing additional takes. Christine and I didn't know Todd that well yet. But Todd knew that sometimes, a director has to be tough to get that ineffable thing out of the actors. It was always just one more take. One more take. I'd look at Jon with that plastic bag around his head, and I'd think, Is he okay? And then after Todd promised me that this was the last take, he insisted on an additional take. I was going crazy.

I remember I had the call sheet in front of me that day, and I read,

"Good Machine," and suddenly this vision came to me: I saw in "Good Machine" an anagram for "Him once a dog." In my youth, I had a reoccurring dream that I was the Pharaoh's dog in ancient Europe. The Pharaoh would sit on a throne, and I was a jackal, with big ears and an arched back, and he would sit with his hand on my head.

When I thought of the anagram for "Good Machine" on the call sheet during that last take of Jon Lovitz trying to kill himself, I let out a big snort and ruined the shot. I don't know exactly what the anagram meant, but maybe in that moment, I felt again like the dog, and Todd was the Pharaoh, whose bidding I was there to follow. Like a good pet, I sat still on the next shot, and we were finally able to move on.

Most talented artists have some idiosyncrasies. When people describe Todd, they often emphasize certain "nerdish" qualities—a nasally voice, a keen intellect, a dry sense of humor. But I think of how brave Todd Solondz is. During the editing of *Happiness*, he insisted that we should conduct test screenings to see how audiences would react. Many directors fear such screenings, and with *Happiness*, despite the controversial subject matter, Todd was the one suggesting it. During one of those early screenings, a brawl nearly broke out, because someone in the audience said we'd gone too far and violated codes of decency and morality; then there were some folks who felt we didn't go far enough and wanted more. And these two sides were steadfast and wanted to keep debating even after the building management was insisting we leave. And that's when Christine and I realized that we'd created something special, because what is an art film if not a movie that provokes discussion?

Todd went back and forth with many versions. A lot of it was about how much an audience could take. Could we find that place where people wouldn't just react, but would truly feel? Todd loves his characters despite their afflictions, but for some people, empathy is like change:

They won't embrace it until they have no other choice. Some people laugh precisely at actions that make others tear up. Todd's work is very much a litmus test for his audiences, even if they're not always in on the experiment.

By the time Todd found the version of *Happiness* that he wanted, we were up against the Cannes deadline. We had great partners at October. Both of the founders, Bingham Ray and Jeff Lipsky, were film lovers and real filmmakers, but that didn't mean we would always agree. The battle of art versus business rages in every film, and the people involved rarely find it easy to reach consensus. There was no denying that our version of *Happiness* was long and a challenge for audiences. And October Films had a lot riding on it. We were the company's first production. It needed our film to work with audiences, critics, and the industry at large. No one wants to produce a movie, only to hear everyone in the business say it's too long.

We went back and forth over the length of the film for several days, but fortunately, Bingham and Jeff decided to table the argument. To their credit, they didn't insist on their own way. Todd would have liked more time to consider the edit, but commitment is something you have to live with, and the Cannes deadline was short-circuiting our decision-making process.

It turned out that Todd was right all along. Cannes Film Festival audiences embraced the movie in all of its demanding two hours and twenty minutes; it even won the FIPRESCI Prize from the International Federation of Film Critics. Although many people didn't know it at the time, Todd proved, among all the duress, that the director is always right—at least most of the time.

While we were in Cannes, rumors started to swirl that Geri Halliwell—a.k.a. Ginger Spice—was going to leave the Spice Girls.

The stock at EMI, the Spice Girls' record label, dropped significantly. Incredibly, one person's actions could deeply affect all of those share-holders' fortune—and as I suspected, what happened next to Solondz's *Happiness*.

October Films had recently acquired two other controversial films, Trey Parker and Matt Stone's *Orgazmo* and Lars von Triers's *The Idiots*. I seem to remember that the *Hollywood Reporter* had run a blurb on this upstart distributor and its three X-rated films. And I think that both the publicity around *Orgazmo* and *The Idiots* and Ginger Spice's departure, affected the film's fate.

I don't know what goes on in corporate headquarters, but Edgar Bronfman, the CEO of Seagram's, which owned both EMI and Universal (the latter of which owned October Films), might well have thought, "A subsidiary of my company has a film with a sympathetic portrait of a pedophile. And we're going to watch our stock price tumble further because of this little movie? No way." Bronfman's other company had been burned by one pop star pursuing her interests; he wasn't about to have Universal suffer a similar fate from a gang of indie filmmakers. Whatever happened in the boardrooms of power, October Films aban-doned the movie. Despite all the prizes and critical acclaim, we were an orphan, with no one to look after us.

As horrible it was, it was worse for October's Bingham Ray and Jeff Lipsky. Years later, Chris McGurk, who was head of business strategies at Universal, told me that Bingham and Jeff's mistake was that when they were told they had autonomy from the parent company, they actu-ally believed it.

Even though October dropped the film, Universal helped facilitate a two-million-dollar loan—utilizing Good Machine's assets, including the film itself, as collateral—for us to release the film ourselves. People always say Hollywood doesn't care about independent film. But this wasn't the first disaster I survived because people in Hollywood behaved honorably. Universal gave us the proper support to protect the film. Sure, it meant a tremendous amount of additional work on our part, but the company recognized we were up for it. And yes, Universal wasn't going to risk damaging its brand or stock price, but the situation could have been far worse: The company could have completely buried the movie. In the corporate world, this was the chivalrous thing to do. Turnaround agreements are similar; they give producers the chance to move on. But these days, studios often hold on to projects, fearing that if they let a project go, another company might make a hit out of it and then they'd have egg on their face. So ultimately, we were treated well.

When Good Machine set up the operations to put the movie into theaters, we faced further hurdles from the Motion Picture Association of America's (MPAA's) Ratings Board, which had branded the movie with an NC-17 rating. James requested a hearing, claiming that the film may have been inappropriate for children, but it was a very humanistic tale and parents should be the sole arbiter of whether people under the age of seventeen could see it. After all, we had no nudity and very little violence in the film. But the ratings board said there was no way we could ever get an R rating. Todd could cut out the scene where the dog licks the boy's cum, or Philip Seymour Hoffman's masturbation scenes, but we'd still get tarnished with an NC-17. The MPAA felt that the overall impact of the film was such that young minds needed to be protected from it.

We knew all along that we weren't going to change any of the content to get a better rating. We also knew that this was by far the best cut, with the richest storylines. As a result, we ended up releasing the film as it was, unrated, without the MPAA's seal of approval. The film earned a modest $2.8 million in the United States, but ended the year on many critic's top-ten lists. It also received a special ensemble acting honor from the National Board of Review and a Golden Globe nomination for Todd's screenplay.

I remember using the term "cinema of audacity" to describe *Happiness*. At the time, a lot of films had crass content—*There's Something About Mary*, with its infamous "hair gel" scene, was released that very same year. But Todd manages to take audacious content and deliver it with style and grace. It's never just to shock; it's profoundly revealing about human nature. That's what makes his work ambitious. And Todd has continued to employ that technique in film after film. To this day, it surprises me how few filmmakers try to be ambitious. It's *cinema*, after all; it should be cinematic. Make each frame pop; make each character distinct; leave the audience awed and surprised.

When I helped produce Solondz's 2001 film *Storytelling* together with New Line's indie division Fine Line, we made sure that within the financing agreement, Todd could obscure any scenes deemed offensive to the MPAA with a big red box. It might have seemed like a strange choice—who would want a big red box covering up part of their film? But we were contractually obliged to deliver a film with an R rating, and the MPAA is careful to avoid charges of censorship, even self-censorship, so if an artist wants to block something that might otherwise get it a more severe rating, it has to be a creative act and not something done after the fact. For example, a filmmaker can't insert a "censored" band over a particular image. So this big red box was our preemptive move to ensure that Todd would not have to cut any scenes from the film.

Now, when you watch one of the most provocative scenes in *Storytelling*, where an African American college professor has sex with one of his female students from behind, all the while telling her, "Say,

'Nigger, fuck me hard,'" the big red box appears in the American rated version, obscuring the action. The technique works both artistically and commercially. Todd's films always play with questions of what is socially appropriate or permissible behavior, and the big red box became a prominent signifier of these very issues. Todd was able to ingrain his pet themes into the very material of the film. And we got an R rating.

This kind of audacious storytelling has defined Todd's career, but it's also at odds with the industry's changing bottom line. I think Todd enters every film thinking that it will be his last. Maybe it's his shtick, but it's also somewhat real. For his film *Dark Horse*, I had thirteen distribution offers after the film premiered at Toronto in 2011. But the top offer was for less than 10 percent of the budget, a fee level that demonstrated an unfortunate trend in sales. Companies were willing to release the movie, but they weren't going to risk spending any money beyond what it would cost to market it. I hoped distributors could do better. The film has a great cast, and Todd is a major director. But lots of companies didn't even try to see the film when it premiered in Venice or screened later in Toronto. After the festivals, I had to chase down executives, set up screenings, and send them Blu-rays.

Ultimately, we decided to release *Dark Horse* in theaters ourselves, as we had done with *Happiness* before. The money offers did not equal what we saw the value of the film to be. If someone had said, "We'll take this film on for such a low price, but we'll only buy the rights for three years," I would have considered it. But the offers were a third of where they had been previously (and they expected the licensing period to remain just as long as before). At the time, I had also been writing and speaking a lot about self-distribution, and I felt I should not just talk the talk, but also walk the walk. So I thought, "I should be a part of the foundation for this do-it-yourself approach and have some faith in different releasing strategies."

Distribution takes a village: It is such an undertaking and it's by no means as exciting as development, production, and selling the film after your festival premiere. Those are high-adrenaline sprints, but distribution is a marathon. It requires a whole new body type. It requires careful pacing and keeping your stamina up.

Dark Horse didn't do much business theatrically, but the film proved yet again Todd's unceasing commitment to pushing his craft further. It is the ambitious film that does more than just give the audience what it wants. To simply provide is to pander. And Todd's films have never done that. They take us to new ground, where we question ourselves and where we are; they unlock the peculiarities, expose the wonder in the everyday, and forbid us to take our lives and our perceptions for granted. And in that body of bold and uncompromising work, I still believe there is immense value.

Even if the box-office numbers don't always show it, the audience for ambitious, idiosyncratic cinema is expanding. Somewhere out there is a model to bring Todd's films to a global audience. It's just so hard to get penetration beyond the small, self-selecting audience that's already receptive to his work. I do think the methods to identify and connect with audiences improve on an hourly basis. And if I can have an ongoing direct communication with any niche group, and I can reward people for their participation, that group will grow into an audience and, eventually, a community.

But like a lot of other directors, Todd has to make some big decisions. When Whit Stillman, writer-director of the 1990 indie breakthrough *Metropolitan*, made a film in 2011, he did it for around a million dollars. Hal Hartley has made that decision, too. He works regularly on lower and lower budgets. Though Todd did work with a significantly lower budget on his 2004 film *Palindromes,* he hasn't yet made the decision to commit to that level overall. He still has grand ambitions. But unfortunately, the question nowadays often comes down to how low can a filmmaking team go in terms of driving a budget down. And is there a way to do that and still earn the fees to have a feasible and sustainable career? I sincerely believe virtually any film can be made for any budget. But lower budgets require compromises in terms of content and aesthetics (you can't have expansive scenes with huge crowds, for instance). But do we want artists like Todd Solondz, who are trying to push their craft further, to be limited? Or do we want them to keep making films and keep making them bigger and better? Can we build an industry that rewards such groundbreaking filmmaking? It's my ambition to keep trying.

Chapter 6

Collaboration

Hal Hartley's experimental film *Flirt* came together on a napkin at Cannes 1995. Although I had already produced well over ten features, it was the first movie for which I put the financing together totally by myself. We had already shot a third of the film in Manhattan and had plans to complete the filming of the other two parts in Berlin and in Japan. In February, we had taken the project to the international Cinemart in Rotterdam, where we conducted some preliminary meetings to get the ball rolling. Cannes was the perfect place to close it up. All we needed to do was figure out exactly how we'd split the financing and recouping of the investor's money. At the Carlton Hotel, I sat with Reinhard Brundig, one of the founders of the German company Pandora (which backed films by Emir Kusturica and Jim Jarmusch), and Japan's Satoru Iseki (who financed films by Chen Kaige and Wayne Wang), and we sorted out a tidy, equitable three-way agreement while looking out over the French Riviera. It was an ambitious project for a one-million-dollar budget, but I was confident that I could pull it off. And now I had the signed napkin to prove it.

Japan's production methods, however, are very different from those of independent film in America. Iseki-san wanted to take care of us. When we arrived in Tokyo to prep, he set us up with the Kurosawa Group—founded by the great Japanese director Akira Kurosawa—to manage the production. Iseki initially insisted that we stay at a prestigious luxury hotel, the Rihga Royal, the perfect place in his mind to convey our status for impending meetings. Watching the film's funds dwindle rapidly under the Rihga's roof, I wanted to find a more affordable place to live. I was also frustrated about how long it was taking to schedule and arrange meetings with the owners of locations and to close deals. Evidently it was Japanese custom that I, as the producer of the film, meet the owners of every location we wanted to book. And only the owners would do; I couldn't meet with managers or representatives. It was about proper respect, and nothing else would do, in our financier's opinion.

Meanwhile, I had gotten hold of *Tokyo Decadence*—a controversial film that was one part Antonioni and one part S&M porno—and had shown it to Hal, who immediately wanted to meet the actress Miho Nikaido from the film. But because of that movie's graphic content, the Kurosawa Group didn't look favorably upon her and we couldn't get a meeting. The group had been encouraging us to meet with another actress who was achieving a level of mainstream success. Hal met her, and the actress had seemingly been led to believe that she was already cast, despite Hal's not saying anything of the sort. But Hal kept insisting that we find Miho Nikaido, as he thought she'd be perfect for the role.

Time and money continued to slip away. And it became clear that our method of producing movies was quite different from the Kurosawa Group's. It felt like I was left with no choice: I had to fire Kurosawa, which for me—a film aficionado—as well as to all of Japan, was akin to firing God. For the good of the movie, I had to find a team more accustomed to an American indie way of working.

I moved us out of the Rihga Royal and into a "businessman's" hotel. The difference between that and an "economy" room, which was the next step down, was that in the "businessman's" room you couldn't reach everything from the bed. It wasn't living in a pod, but it was close. And it was certainly not the kind of place where you could conduct meetings, let alone try to impress anyone. But it was what we could afford.

Around the same time, we got word that the Kurosawa Group's actress wanted to meet again with Hal. Respect demanded that Hal take the meeting. He arrived in his then-customary white shirt, tweed jacket, and Timberland boots. I waited outside the coffee shop, looking in from the outside. Their conversation seemed curiously formal. She ordered a coffee, but it just sat there untouched and ominous. The conversation got heated as the coffee grew cold. Animated and passionate discussions were something you did not see much in Japan. And then, boom: Splash! Hal's white shirt was brown. The actress was so horrified about not being cast, she had set up the whole tête-à-tête just so she could throw a cup of coffee at my director.

Unbeknownst to me, the one-two punch of the actress debacle and firing of the Kurosawa Group looked as if it might destroy Iseki-san's standing in the community—it cost him face. He called me and told me he was going to withdraw from the production. The contract was structured in a way that this meant he would forfeit the money already spent. For him to quit and lose the money he had spent indicated how serious he had taken this offense. But I still needed more money to shoot and to get us back to the States. Good Machine was relatively young at the time. I didn't have much money to do the film, I was using some of our corporate funds to float the production, and even that had run out. I had all my

American crew stranded in Japan and didn't know what to do. I felt if I spoke to anyone—Hal, my business partner, even my wife—they would panic and make the situation worse. My first attempt at producing soup to nuts, complete with securing all the financing, was collapsing before my eyes. I was on my own without a penny to my name, in a foreign land, having fired God and lost the one ally who could get me out of there intact. To top it all off, at my side were friends who expected me not just to produce a movie, but also to pay them along the way.

One trait that helps producers is an imagination that can take you to the worst-case scenario, so that you can guard against it. I am prone to many dark thoughts, but I hadn't anticipated this. What the hell could I do? I took a deep breath and decided to stay calm and just see where things would go. I have long felt that a bias toward action is a great plan, but sometimes situations demand just the opposite.

Thirty-six hours later, Iseki-san called me and said, "We're going to go to the mountains; I'm picking you up at seven AM." Before I could ask anything, he hung up. He was waiting the next morning at sunrise in front of my pathetic hotel. I opened the door of his BMW, but he didn't say a word. He just kept staring ahead as we drove up higher and higher into the mountains. I had seen movies like this, and they always seemed to end with an execution in the snow.

It felt like an eternity had passed. We had listened to about half the Miles Davis catalog, when Iseki-san stopped in front of a mountain inn. It turned out to be a traditional bathhouse with large, communal, natural hot spring pools. The two of us spent the next few hours still not talking, but stewing away in the bath together with about twenty other guys (who I don't think had the same problems to work out that we did). It was clear that this was no minor matter: I had put Iseki-san in a very difficult situation, and he was going to be sure that I understood the situation. He wished the movie did not have to take precedence over human respect; in short, and without any words, he told me I had let him down as a friend, even if he understood it was on behalf of the film. With nothing but a few careful looks into my eyes and a tremendous amount of patience, Iseki-san told me that ultimately, he felt that he could survive this situation professionally and he trusted Hal and my judgment. As we drove back down the mountain on the dark, unlit roads, it became clear he would continue to fund and produce the film with us. If the art of the samurai is *not* having to draw one's sword, I had just witnessed the technique in a Japanese bathhouse.

This wasn't just an instance of wanting to see me sweat; Iseki-san was sincere. I came to understand his situation. And I was deeply respectful of it. It was a critical moment for me because I learned how important it was to understand the psychology and motivations of the financier, and that many factors weigh in when financiers choose to get involved. The Kurosawa Group had helped Iseki-san in his career, so when we fired the group, it was like the son rebelling against his father.

When we returned from the mountains, the crew and I went out for sushi with Iseki and drank very, very heavily. It was the first time I had both beer and sake over the course of a single night, but it is now my custom whenever I eat sushi—it is my salute to Iseki. I don't think any of the crew knew what the alcohol was purging that night, but I was toasting my survival and the trust of a good friend and business partner and hoping it might spare me similar situations in the future.

✳

In the fall of 2000, during one of the craziest times in my life, with the production of three features—Michel Gondry's *Human Nature*, Todd

Field's *In the Bedroom*, and Todd Solondz's *Storytelling*—and the birth of my son, I was trying to hold it all together. While trafficking between the three films in Los Angeles, Maine, and New York, I felt like I was continually dripping in sweat and covered with dust. I might have been a film producer, but I was always the most haggard man around, counting my blessings that indie film had no dress code or much concern with hygiene.

After much *Sturm und Drang*, *In the Bedroom* was finally in the can, but the writer and director Todd Field said he wanted to quit the project altogether. Todd doesn't kid around a lot, and he certainly wasn't joking now. Suffering from a bleeding ulcer, peeved at numerous crew people along the way, and frustrated with creative differences he had with the financial backers over the film's final cut, he sent me an email asking to terminate his involvement. "I do not wish to stand in the way of what is inevitable," he wrote. "It is a game I'm too tired and have no interest in playing. I will no longer be working on the film."

In the Bedroom would go on to receive Oscar nominations for Best Picture; Best Actor (for Tom Wilkinson, as a grieving father who seeks revenge for his son's death); Best Actress (for Sissy Spacek, as his cold and anguished wife); Best Supporting Actress (for Marisa Tomei, as a working-class young wife and mother who has ripped the family apart); and Best Adapted Screenplay (for Todd and another writer, Robert Festinger). But at the time, few of the film's backers seemed to have faith in Todd's unrelenting vision. My role as a producer was to protect the film and, in doing so, manage the needs of both my director and my financiers.

I first met Todd as an actor on the set of Nicole Holofcener's *Walking and Talking*. We had cast him from seeing him in Victor Nuñez's *Ruby in Paradise*; in that movie, he has a loose yet serious feel as a laid-back, left-wing greenhouse worker. My assistant at the time had a movie-star crush on him and had convinced Nicole and me to cast him, no audition required. She campaigned every day, inserting photos of him into the stack of papers on my desk. One day I started to think that it had been my idea to cast Todd; apparently, her brainwashing had worked.

Todd is a serious man. He told me on the set of *Walking and Talking* that what he really wanted to do was direct. We talked about his time at the American Film Institute and his love for the writing of Andre Dubus. (*In the Bedroom* was based on a Dubus short story called "Killings.") He didn't know that my own dad was drinking buddies with Andre, and I had grown up alongside the author's kids in Massachusetts. I told Todd that if he ever needed help, he should just reach out to me. I frequently tell people this sort of thing, and I mean it with all sincerity, but Todd is one of the rare ones to take me up on it.

Six years later, Todd came into the Good Machine offices with a well-thought-out "look book," a scrapbook filled with images, refer-ences, influences, color palettes, wardrobes, props—you name it—for the movie he wanted to make. He was the first director I knew to do that; such books are standard operating procedure now, but back then, it felt both revolutionary and completely commonsensical. You could visualize the movie by looking at Todd's book. If you think about film as a busi-ness of images and ideas, Todd had it down. And he had a script that communicated the emotional content of the story with specificity. He not only commanded the material, but also had to be the one to direct it. What could better serve a first-time director than such preparation and clarity of vision?

When we shot *In the Bedroom* in Maine in the summer of 2000, my pri   *Nature*, which was wrapping, and
So   prepping. I based these priorities on

the depth of my relationship with the people involved and the budget level, and thus the fees it would earn our company. By this point, Good Machine had a staff of over forty people whose salaries we consistently had to raise, and the potential return on investment was higher for those two films. I had structured it so that my associate at Good Machine, Ross Katz, was to be the on-set producer during the filming of *In the Bedroom*.

Ross had come off his first producing gig, the gay romantic comedy *Trick*, and he loved Todd's material; in the months leading up to the production, Ross had deservedly won the trust of Todd and GreeneStreet Films, our financing producing partners on the film. *In the Bedroom* was a small-scale story, in a manageable location where Todd knew every detail. We did not see the signs of what it was to become: a production fraught with bitterness, conflicting agendas, angry outbursts, and the firing of various crew people.

My third trip to the *In the Bedroom* location on Maine's mid-coast was on the first day of shooting. Todd had terrible stomach pains. He wasn't eating. He had already lost twenty or thirty pounds; clearly the movie was getting to him. We were shooting in a harbor off the coast of Camden. The shoot suffered from tidal issues—at low tide, the gangway was incredibly steep, making the setup time difficult and strenuous; during high tide, the gangway was nearly flush with the docks, creating an excruciating noise that made recording sound impossible.

We were already falling behind schedule, and Todd would shoot his scenes in more concise, innovative ways, but he wasn't finding the rhythm that allowed the production to gain momentum. He was also asking a lot from his team. Todd had come off working as an actor on Stanley Kubrick's *Eyes Wide Shut*, and he wanted to display the same sort of intensity that Kubrick had. He thought that concentrated behavior like Kubrick's would produce the results he wanted. People took our job because they wanted to make this movie, but Todd didn't want anyone to have a newspaper or book to read between takes; he wanted everyone to be focused on the film. He didn't even want anyone sitting down. The key crew people were behind him—the director of photography, the soundman, the costumer person; they recognized his vision—but Todd wasn't winning over the rest of the crew. Far from it. Tensions were high.

Adding insult to the crew's injuries, our financial partners at GreeneStreet decided that we had to have trailers with the casting of Sissy Spacek, Tom Wilkinson, and Marisa Tomei. It was the right decision, because the actors delivered phenomenally, but this fifty-thousand-dollar budget line also sent out a strange message to the crew: How much money does the production *really* have? And why are we trying to fit the production into this number of days when it clearly can't be done? Nerves were exposed, and each difference of opinion was fresh salt in everyone's wounds.

Todd was very clear about what he wanted: total devotion from the cast and crew, just like what Kubrick had had. But it was also clear to me that I needed to be Todd's conduit, helping produce a constructive environment around the actors, not just while in front of the camera, but also behind them. Todd needed support. We would not continue to capture the promise that was in his script and early footage if we allowed dissent to flourish. Yet I had not committed to being on set regularly, and Camden, Maine, was hardly a short trip from my Manhattan apartment.

The next time I got off the plane in Maine, Todd had just fired the production designer as we were moving into the film's main house location. He decided he didn't need a production designer, so he, his wife, and Sissy Spacek went out shopping and dressed the house. When Sissy brought things back for her character, the process actually gave her, as an actor, a much deeper connection to the world she was living. It was her house, and she was designing the house as if her character were designing it. Sometimes situations that look like true problems turn out to be real blessings.

Then, a few days later, Todd fired the assistant director. Todd wanted to get rid of the line producer, too, but we were able to hold him back. I didn't know how many relatives Todd had, but I doubted it would be enough to fill the entire crew. We didn't have anyone nearby who could be assistant director, and even though I had two other movies that I needed to tend to, I wasn't going to leave and hope that it would be solved, so I took on the job of assistant director for a day and a half. Acting as assistant director is not like riding a bike; the walkie-talkie may fit in your hand, but no amount of experience in other areas is a substitute for the consistency that comes from those who make it their profession. Consequently, despite my years as an assistant director before I became a producer, I felt I was on wobbly legs stepping into the assistant director role again.

The schedule was still overly ambitious: Cuts needed to be made; costs were spiraling out of control; everything was operating outside the team's experience level; and the other producer, Graham Leader, kept asking the accountant at GreeneStreet for cost reports and budgets. These were normal things to request, but impossible to turn around in the time available and with the staff at hand. It's easy to ask for things, but you also have to make do with the tools you have. It would be great if everyone on a shoot shared the same priorities, but that's rarely the case. Hell, it's seldom the case that the producers on a film even share the same priorities.

And that's where real trouble starts. We look to producers to solve problems, but Graham seemed to bring more problems with him each day. The rights to the short story had been controlled and optioned by

Graham, who had previously hired Rob Festinger to write a draft called *Killings*. Long before he brought the project to us, Todd had reached out to Graham on his own, and since nothing was happening with the earlier version, Graham agreed that Todd could do another draft, provided Todd wrote it for free, and Graham and Rob had to be credited. (Because of this early deal and the nature of "chain of title" law, the film's eventual Oscar nomination for best adapted screenplay was shared by Todd and Rob.) When the contracts later came through, it became clear that Graham's rights had lapsed, and Todd actually never needed Graham's permission to adapt it.

When the script was brought to us, it turned out that the underlying story rights were actually still held by Andre Dubus and his family. I let Andre know that I was interested in making this movie and that, because of his relationship with my father, the story was personal to me. The Dubus family had lived just a mile away from my parents' house. My dad had passed away when I was six years old, and in his final days, he had told Andre he always regretted never having written a screenplay with him.

Andre had a Hemmingway-like fortitude, but in 1986, he was hit by a car while trying to help some people in a motorcycle accident and lost his legs. He was very frustrated with the hand he was dealt, which in this case included the loss of control of his own material; Hollywood had not been kind to Andre Dubus. He displayed no love for Graham and his lawyers, either. Andre wanted us to take them out of the equation. We started to strategize.

Two months later, Andre died. But he wanted *In the Bedroom* made in the right way. It was one of his dying wishes. And in some ways, it was my father's wish, too. And there I was, thinking that I wasn't ever going to get to honor those wishes because of some legal issues.

Because Todd had "based" his script on the one that Graham had commissioned and because Graham had the rights to the original version that Todd had based his draft on (even if he did not have the rights to the original story), we needed Graham's involvement. If Todd had written it six months later, it would not have mattered. Todd's script was clearly his and not an adaptation. But in order to keep the legal chain of title complete, we also had to take Graham on as a partner. In the film business, it doesn't matter what the truth of the situation is. It's all about what the perception could be. I recognized that there was a potential lawsuit if we disregarded Graham. And thus, we really had no choice but to partner. *Partnership* has as many different meanings in the film business as *producing* does.

Throughout the production and postproduction, Graham kept coming to us with different debtors, who apparently were owed money from his development of the project. We had no idea what the money they gave Graham was for, but he had evidently promised them reimbursement, even credits on the film. There was no original deal regarding any of this. It felt like a scam and seemed totally absurd, but there was no escape. We couldn't risk anyone's suing Graham for some promise he had made concerning the project. We were in bed with him now, and if he had dug a grave for himself, we would have to share it. We were "partners."

Through it all, Graham kept feeling out of the loop. Rightly so, because people on the team just did not want to talk to him. You have to make people want to communicate with you, and if all you deliver is bad news, they stop reaching out. I did my best to make Graham's wishes heard and accommodated—even though no one else was listening to him. I didn't respect his process, but he had more potential to make trouble if we distanced ourselves.

The industry always encourages a cover-your-ass, control-everything mentality. But again and again, I've also sought to protect the people who are contributing to a project and let them have some control—and as a result, they have been very generous to me, in return. You need to earn the right to collaborate with others, and often that means you have to lead by giving up something first. Production is about establishing trust and confidence. Finding a way to do that is any leader's job, particularly that of producers.

At one point, I wrote to Leader, in one of many efforts to placate him:

I think everyone would have liked to involve you more on the creative side, but time did not allow for much discussion. The film was full steam ahead from day one. There is the adage that "all mistakes are made in preparation" and I think it never was truer than it was here. I am sorry that you feel a bit alienated, but you will be quite proud of the final product, I am sure.

Despite the staffing issues and the problems with our partners, what I saw on set—the work Todd was doing, and what the cast and crew were delivering—impressed me, and when I returned home, it seemed like there was finally some consistency on the project. While I continued to receive reports of crankiness, tirades, and internal warfare on the set, I was also receiving good news about the actors. Scenes were working. Wilkinson's lead performance was coming across as complex, scary, sad, and surprising. Ross and GreeneStreet producer Tim Williams would bring the film home.

But shooting it was only the beginning.

Everybody felt that *In the Bedroom* was a long viewing experience. The script was a deep, dense 120-plus pages. There are some films that are long and slow, and this doesn't have to be a negative. But bringing home the final cut of *In the Bedroom* wasn't going to be easy. In September, I wrote to Todd, outlining a series of edit suggestions that I thought would make the film stronger:

You know I love the film, or at least you should . . . However watching it this time, and I watched it two times through, I convinced myself we have some serious work ahead of us.

If you put yourself in the head of a virgin viewer, one who knows nothing about the film, throughout the first act, you would be swimming, looking for a clue as to what the film is about, where it is headed. As deliberate as the pacing is (not because of it—but in spite of that deliberation), we are held back from surrendering our trust because we do not receive enough information on a regular basis. We are denied the right of developing expectations, which in turn shuts us out of participating in the narrative, because the initial clues we receive are small and gentle and misleading. All of this is a long-winded way of saying I feel we have real first act problems.

My note continued at some length. I suggested he try out a "bold" drastic recut that we could screen for some "virgin viewers." I told him that he wasn't trusting his own material and that "shortened elements" would have a "greater impact." I warned him that "pretension, repetition, or any unwarranted delay in bringing us into the story" would jeopardize our chances of distribution. And it went on.

Todd was not happy. Together with more notes from GreeneStreet and a small but disastrous test screening, which included directors Boaz Yakin and Ang Lee, who had their own thoughts, Todd decided he wanted to quit the film. Ang had been very gentle, focusing on small notes regarding the actors' performances, but Boaz was coming off of a number one box-office smash with *Remember the Titans*, and to him, the film was indulgent and misguided. Todd couldn't take it and said he'd had enough. But I urged him not to give up on his vision. And in a lengthy follow-up email, I wrote:

> You owe it to everyone to help them realize what it is that you made. It is not a game; it is a process. The film will triumph in the end. You are confident what works and what doesn't—so let people see what doesn't work and maybe you will see something that does that you did not originally see yourself.

I asked Todd to take my notes without malice, "because I honestly think they may improve the film, not because I think they may help sell the film." I continued to press on him that the slowness of the current version was not a commercial problem, but an aesthetic one, and that the narrative was "not progressing" with the expectations that the film had set up for itself. I even told him that to quit over some notes was "not just stupid, but childish, selfish and overly dramatic."

Then my email ended with a final plea:

> Take a deep breath. Look at everyone's intent. No one wants anything other than your film; everyone just wants to make sure that every effort has been made to make a film that speaks to the audience for that film. You have to allow for some participation from those that got your film made. As alone as you have felt you have not been, just as you are not now, people are ready to support you if you give them the tools.

Such situations are difficult for everyone and very emotional. Not surprisingly, it was hard to get Todd to listen, but we finally sat down together. Directors, as a breed, are prone to flights of exaggeration. When it comes to protecting your vision, how can it not be all or nothing? But because I said what I had to say, and I said it with empathy for Todd's position, he heard it. Todd then decided that he would sit with me and go over every cut. But he wouldn't sit with anyone else. That was his demand. It was a two-day process that yielded a lot, and it got us to the 138-minute Sundance cut.

At the film's Sundance premiere, all the distributors were there, including Harvey Weinstein. The trade reviews were strong, but measured. *Variety*'s lead critic, Todd McCarthy, called the movie "an almost startlingly accomplished directorial debut" and "beautifully acted by a diverse ensemble," but noted that its "deliberate pacing" would win "accolades from critics and serious-minded viewers but will limit its commercial potential."

Both Fox Searchlight and Miramax made one-million-dollar offers, but then Miramax came up another hundred thousand. Though Harvey had already garnered the nickname "Scissorhands," I had final cut, contractually, which satisfied both Todd and Miramax. We would go with Harvey.

After the festival, Todd was confident that the movie he had was the best version. It wasn't out of arrogance. He knew the footage, and he knew why it mattered. So when Miramax asked to edit the movie down another twenty minutes to fall under two hours, Todd knew the editing wouldn't yield a better movie. We had only about three cuts we wanted to make, which amounted to just two minutes of screen time.

From January to March, Todd agreed to work with an editor that Miramax assigned, and they made a shorter version. Todd recognized that this was all part of Miramax's corporate culture. We had to play along if we wanted the company to push the film in release. Todd strove to find a shorter version. He did, but that's all it was: shorter. It wasn't better. Miramax "tested" it again, but it didn't work. The test screening numbers went down. The Miramax team claimed that Todd deliberately made it worse. Then the team wanted to do its own edit. Months passed and we heard nothing.

Finally, one day in August, we got a mysterious phone call from one of our supporters inside the company. He said Harvey would be eating dinner with several friends that night at the Mercer Hotel in Soho and Todd should confront Harvey publicly there. The only problem was that Todd was in Los Angeles. But nothing was going to stop Todd from protecting his film, so he hopped on the first plane to New York City. He raced from the airport to the restaurant, and sure enough, Todd just "happened" to run into Harvey at the Mercer.

Ultimately, they made a bargain that they would screen it for Martin Scorsese, who Harvey had a relationship with, and see what he thought. We never got a clear answer on Marty's verdict, but Thelma Schoonmaker, Marty's editor, called me and said Marty liked it but had some notes. She said she would call me the next day, but it never happened. I called and called, but never heard back.

Then we got another surprise phone call: Harvey wanted to meet with us, in person. When we went up to his office, we found him sitting inside with two VCRs and a different version of the film in each one. We went through each film, cut by cut, and made a decision on each one. Though the meeting was intense and heated, Harvey eventually agreed that Todd's was the best cut of the movie.

The title, *In the Bedroom*, by the way, was not some Miramax marketing ploy, even though it may sound this way. Todd had relocated the story from the Massachusetts–New Hampshire border, where I grew up, to mid-coast Maine, which is famous, of course, for its lobsters. And the "bedroom" is the part of the lobster trap that holds the crustacean; it's often said that two lobsters together in the same cage will attack each other.

But to his credit, Harvey never tried to strong-arm us or make the movie his way. He wanted what was best for the film; it was just that he was not confident that our cut was precisely that. In the end, being the great lover of film that he is, Harvey saw that our version was the one that the audiences would appreciate most. And Todd realized that at the end of the day, you have to end up with a distributor that's going to market your film. When we sold the movie to Harvey, I told Todd that we had to recognize Miramax's corporate culture, but we would endure. It's not about winning or losing. It's about making sure that the distributor will still want to sell and promote the movie. That's the end goal. And that's why Todd sat with the Miramax folks and went through the whole process with them. For someone who on the set appeared to be a combative, short-fused sort, Todd managed the Harvey Weinstein relationship surprisingly well.

But there was one final piece to *In the Bedroom*'s success.

After the strenuous time of getting to a final cut, we had to figure out a score. We were using some music from the Kronos Quartet. But then Todd told us that he knew someone who would score the film for free. At that point, we were already over budget. It seemed too good to be true. And it was. Having Oscar-nominated composer Thomas Newman (*American Beauty*) score your movie because he loved it was still an incredibly significant expense, because we needed to record it with live musicians, and record it and mix it wherever he wanted. But everybody loved the idea. A major award-winning composer could help position the film in foreign buyers' eyes and make it an Oscar contender.

But how were we supposed to find the money to do it? GreeneStreet ultimately decided it was the right decision and authorized another three hundred thousand dollars to make it happen. You could argue that this was just one other factor that led the film to reach the level it did. But the problem was that after the Miramax Sundance sale, we projected a net shortfall of three hundred thousand. Had we shot ourselves in the foot by spending that additional money?

David Linde, our third partner at Good Machine and the one who had built our foreign-sales business, advocated waiting until the U.S. release of the film before selling the rights to remaining foreign territories, and GreeneStreet went with it. We held back on bringing it out to the international marketplace, because we thought if we waited for the Miramax campaign in the fall, international sales would pop. Film is often thought of as a perishable good. You don't want to hold on for too long, or it'll begin to rot. GreeneStreet's commitment looked to many like a foolish gamble.

It was also incredibly rare. Usually, a film is worth the most when it first hits the marketplace. Consider all of those festival premiere bidding wars that we used to enjoy. But here we decided to wait. And sure enough, Harvey Weinstein spent twenty million on his one-million investment, promoting the film to a thirty-two-million gross, and the foreign value went up and up and up. When the film received five Oscar nominations, its value ascended even higher. What first looked like a bunch of risky bets ultimately seemed like genius.

There were six masters on *In the Bedroom*—Todd Field, Graham Leader, Ross Katz, GreeneStreet, and Miramax—and they all empowered me to keep going, working in pursuit of Todd's vision. They didn't always give me the support that I wanted, because it was all too brutal while we were in the thick of it. Everyone was battling everyone else. I believe that I was necessary to keep all those personalities in check. If there hadn't been a producer like me to soften all the blows, fists would have flown and the movie might not have ended up as it did.

To be sure, Todd was not an easy person to work with. Frankly, directors don't need to be, if they have something to say. And it's easy to overlook someone's shortcomings when you meet a person who has vision and a movie that you want to make. I still continue to make the same apparent mistake. And I have had tough experiences with difficult directors over the years. I am not sure it can be avoided if you want every film you make to strive for greatness.

I can now look at *In the Bedroom* and see the tremendous effort and consideration that Todd put into every aspect of it. I think it is that commitment that bolsters his work. I see it in his subsequent film *Little Children* and I suspect it has been a barrier to getting subsequent work off the ground for him. You'd think that other filmmakers would make such effort, but the fragility of the process probably discourages most. It takes incredible strength to put so much heart and thought into so many decisions. Todd could do it, but many filmmakers will never even try.

It's so hard to make a good movie. I'm not ever sure if it's worth the pain, particularly if you're only getting paid thirty-five thousand dollars (which is what my fee was on *In the Bedroom*). But *In the Bedroom* was personally important for me as a way to contribute to Andre Dubus's legacy. And my father's too. Dubus's short story "Killings," on which the movie is based, opens in a cemetery, one in which both my father and my stepfather are now buried. Andre is there, too. And the movie is a monument to him. But the movie is also a monument to them. It is a monument to the loss that we all too often suffer.

I started making movies because I believed movies could change the world. And I think *In the Bedroom* did, in a way. With its penetrating inquiry into questions of vengeance, responsibility, guilt, and grief, it helped contribute to the cultural conversation at the time it was released, in the immediate months after September 11, 2001.

Chapter 7

Creativity

Michel Gondry wanted live flies.

A prolific French music-video director, Michel had already earned a reputation for his remarkably imaginative visual sense, thanks to his videos, most famously of Icelandic singer Bjork (*Army of Me, Bachelorette*). Working with Michel on his first feature, *Human Nature*, was to witness a truly original artist. Michel had a mind like no other—the way he put together filmic space and saw visual possibilities was completely different from anyone I've ever encountered. Thinking differently often goes hand in hand with behaving differently though, so Michel had requests and processes far from what I had experienced before.

For one particular scene, he wanted real flies swarming around actor Rhys Ifans, who plays a man who has been raised by apes and believes he is one. Michel didn't want to do it digitally. He wanted live flies. But flies are living creatures, of course, and under the rules of our times, if you order flies, you have to work with the American Society for the Prevention of Cruelty to Animals—and they would require that the flies go unharmed and returned to their prior habitat, a luxury we could not afford or even conceive of managing. So that wasn't going to be a possibility.

Shortly after the fly problem was discovered, Michel's long-time line producer, Julie Fong, showed up at the set one day totally exhausted. "Julie, what's the matter?" I asked. It turned out, she was up all night catching flies. Julie was so tremendously loyal and devoted to her director that she had laid out different pieces of rotting meat throughout the night and had gathered a total of twenty-seven flies. But when it came to shooting, it didn't work. You couldn't contain the flies. You'd just put them in the shot, and they'd fly away. It was an impossible task, and ultimately, we had to move on without the flies, but Michel inspired that kind of commitment and creativity in the people around him. He was consistently reinventing the methods and the language of filmmaking, and it lifted the work of the entire team. I defy anyone to find that much production ingenuity on an eight-million-dollar movie.

James and I were introduced to Michel through fellow music-video maven Spike Jonze, who had shared an agent with Ang Lee. Spike was working with the Beastie Boys trying to make a mockumentary about the greatest film auteur that you've never heard of (the project never came together), but he also had some scripts by Charlie Kaufman that he wanted to produce. Spike famously went on to direct *Being John Malkovich*, his debut feature, but at the time, Kaufman's screenplays were notorious for being un-producible. They were great, but according to the industry wisdom of the time, not makeable.

One day, Spike called me and said he and Charlie wanted me to meet Michel. Although neither Spike nor Charlie had yet to make a feature, they were teaming up to produce Michel's directorial debut, *Human Nature*, and wanted my help. I watched some of Michel's music videos, which were so smart and audacious that I thought, "I absolutely have to make this guy's movie."

Michel Gondry clearly had a talent for visuals and music and putting them together. But U.S. financiers were reluctant to back a feature film by a director known for using digital effects to split up dramatic images into test patterns. (Michel's 1999 video for the Chemical Brothers' "Let Forever Be" remains a timeless classic.) His ability to "make strange" is unmatched by most; we see the world afresh when we observe it through Michel's eyes. So Good Machine International's David Linde rightly figured the only way we were going to make the movie was with the financial support of European companies. Ironically, one of the best ways to persuade European companies to back a project was to make them think they were scooping their American rivals, so they felt they needed to jump aboard quickly.

We attached actress Patricia Arquette and planned to unveil it at the Cannes Film Festival's market. A few weeks prior, we brought the package to Canal Plus, a big French company, and convinced company representatives that if they didn't back it then and there, they might lose it later during the heated competition of the festival's market. The Canal people committed eight million, and when we hammered out the deal in their luxurious hotel suite at the Carlton, pacing back and forth from room to room, they even offered Michel final cut, which their American rivals would never even contemplate for a first-time feature director. We signed the deal. Two months later, after healthy foreign presales, a good-sized budget, and everything we could have ever hoped for, Michel called and said he couldn't make the film for at least a year. His girlfriend had leukemia and he needed to tend to her. As producers who privilege people over business, we had to put a halt on the production.

As a producer, you're frequently worried that if you don't spend money when you have it, it won't last. But Canal Plus agreed to wait. And Michel then had the time to think through and plan out the entire movie meticulously. By the time we were finally ready to shoot the film, he had drawn detailed storyboards, some of them the size of postage stamps, on the back of the script's pages. But although he committed his vision to paper, we often didn't know how to interpret it.

During production one day, I looked over at him and saw that he was fuming.

"Where's the hat?" he said, in an angry French accent.

"What are you talking about?" I answered.

"Why did I prepare? Why did I do all of that work if no one is paying attention? There, look at the storyboard." He pointed to the scrawl on his screenplay.

I saw a sketch that was a bit larger than a pinhead.

"There," he said. "It's a hat."

Michel often became obsessive over things that might seem like they didn't matter, but they mattered a lot for Michel, and thus for the movie.

Once we finally got rolling, it became apparent how unique Michel's mind was. He fully understood that cinema was plastic, that it could be bent and folded in many ways. For instance, a lens wasn't just a lens with Michel. We might have a zoom lens that could go from 10 mm to 100 mm, which stretches out the image from a close shot to a long shot, but Michel wanted to go from 10 mm to 250 mm, to create the illusion of extraordinary depth. So he put two lenses side by side and morphed the two shots together in postproduction. In this way, he created the effect of a zoom out from very close up to extremely far away, in one continuous shot.

For all of Michel's visual trickery—he also carried mirrors around to put inside his shots to expand the space—he also believes in the reality of things. He doesn't look for CGI (computer-generated imagery) for solutions; he likes handmade effects, which sometimes even call attention to their artifice. For instance, in one shot, the forest is actually a miniature shot of broccoli. In several scenes, Patricia Arquette appears covered in body hair, head to toe, and we had to apply real hair to her entire body on a regular basis. It wasn't a special effect; it was just a hardworking makeup artist. Similarly, the mice that Tim Robbins's character tries to train to use forks and knives were real, though there was some CGI, obviously, to show them picking up the utensils. Michel's sense of imagination made for a kind of giddiness on set. We felt that the magic of cinema was alive again. To see the rules being reinvented is energizing for everyone and leads you to do more than you normally would. For example, Julie's all-night fly-hunting expedition: That was her own mission, but I think every person on the cast and crew was inspired to make some similar contribution. It served as a model for all of us.

As a producer, it is my job to enable that boundless creativity—and while it might have seemed mystical at the time, there were several down-to-earth ways that I and others at Good Machine helped it to happen. Most important was constructing a deal with Canal Plus to make the movie that Michel needed to make, when he needed to make it, and to have sufficient funds to do it.

We also allowed Michel to work with people that he was comfortable with, despite their relative inexperience. Julie Fong and the editor Russell Icke had only worked on Michel's music videos. Production designer K. K. Barrett, who has since been highly lauded for his work on Sofia Coppola's and Spike Jonze's movies, had only worked on one film, *Being John Malkovich* (which no one had seen yet). Same with the art director Peter Andrus. But one of the things you can do for first-time filmmakers that can have a profoundly positive effect is to produce an atmosphere of trust and confidence, and this often comes with hiring people they know.

Still, it was a challenging project, because what we were trying to do was so unique. Despite the adequate money, everything was pushed to the limit. Eight million dollars allowed us to shoot on a soundstage, but it was a dusty former airplane hangar. We were able to imagine and realize some wild scenarios, but time was short and we weren't rich. I was rooming with Anthony Bregman and his wife in Marina Del Rey far from the hip areas of the city; everything was just enough to get by, but never enough for an upgrade. It was not a sushi budget; it was a Baja Fresh budget, so named for the L.A. fast-food Mexican place across the street from our apartment and where we dined far too frequently.

And not only did Michel have the pressure of making his first feature and learning the limits of the shooting schedule, in contrast with a more compressed commercial or music-video shoot, he also had the added burden of creating scenes for a *sizzle reel*—footage that sells the movie to buyers—in the first week of shooting. We had no American distributor onboard, and getting one early would significantly enhance the value of the film internationally, so the pressure was on. On top of all that, he was also just getting his movie legs, straddling the delicate line between having enough funds to dream and not having enough to avoid compromise.

On the first day of the shoot, Michel got upset because he wasn't happy with what he was getting, but Anthony and I told him we needed to move on. Michel was embarrassed and felt like we were violating his authority. But letting him know of our time constraints helped clarify things going forward.

Making movies is never just about capturing that one shot or one line of dialogue that's right there in front of you; it's about making sure you get everything in a manner that will tell the whole story. The film has to work in total, not as individual parts. Along with that, you need to make sure you create moments of magnificence. There's always a careful balance of getting what you need and reaching for something that stands out. All of the directors that I've worked with who have gone on to great success have achieved this tricky balance between practicality and grandeur. And it's the producer-director relationship that helps preserve this balance. As a producer, you're often characterized as the person who says no (because of budgetary restraints), but you also have to be the person who says not just yes, but "abso-fucking-lutely we can do this" (rallying the troops and encouraging the director and his or her team to reach for excellence).

When you're still finding your footing, it's good to schedule shots that aren't absolutely critical to your story. On the other hand, and particularly if you are trying to sell your movie early before you finish it, you also want to shoot something phenomenal for that sizzle reel. It's one of the unfortunate paradoxes of making movies.

A U.S. distributor greatly improves the value of your film in international territories, and as *Human Nature* was financed by a foreign-sales company, part of our job was to bring on a U.S. distributor as early as possible. And to do that, we needed to put some pressure on Michel.

I'm a big believer in a Wednesday start date for film productions, which gives you three days to find out where the problems are. Everyone needs to settle in and find his or her rhythm. Inevitably, though, you need to fire somebody over the weekend, and you need time to replace the person.

Fortunately, on *Human Nature*, while Michel knew how to make every shot and scene dynamic, the music-video-trained editor was a fantastic clip cutter. So by the end of the first three days, we did have a kick-ass sizzle reel, and as a result of that sizzle reel, we sold the domestic distribution rights to Fine Line Features—a sale that in turn helped boost the international sales. Win-win. Even though the film didn't do well at the U.S. box office when it was released in 2002, it was a moneymaker for Good Machine, Canal Plus, and all the key creative participants (who shared in the upside) because the foreign territory sales on the film were so strong.

What often happens with a lot of directors who come from music videos or commercials is that they don't see the big-picture ninety-minute version; the whole isn't as good as the individual parts. There were some great scenes in *Human Nature*—Rhys falling from the tree, training to be civilized; Tim and Patricia's date; the mice learning table manners—and we were all so mesmerized by the individual scenes that Michel was creating that it was hard to see the forest for the trees. But I think Michel recognized this flaw, learned from it, and more than rectified the shortcoming in his superb next film, *Eternal Sunshine of the Spotless Mind*, which my colleague at Good Machine, Anthony Bregman, went on to produce with Steve Golin. And even if *Human Nature* isn't remembered today as much as *Eternal Sunshine*, I felt good about making a film that was creatively rejuvenating. I was also being true to myself.

Even though the rest of the industry may not necessarily embrace it, I always believe that uniqueness is better. It distinguishes you in the marketplace, gives you a signature that people remember, and can encourage discussion. But practically speaking, one of the downsides of earning your living by making movies is you have to be prolific—I figured I had to make at least two movies per year to raise a kid and pay a mortgage. And one of the downsides of being prolific is that it's difficult to be distinctive when you're working your ass off all the time. The more movies I made, the more I had that sinking feeling of, "Holy shit! Am I going to make another movie like everybody else's?" That fear and desire drove me to find stories that were truly unique. Creativity is about seeing patterns and then finding a way to differentiate from the standard conventions. The fact is that most indie film successes are idiosyncratic or weird or different in some way (see *Pulp Fiction*, *The Blair Witch Project*, *Memento*). If Hollywood wins with familiar formulas, indie films often triumph as a result of their originality.

Probably for that reason, when HBO Films came to us after *Human Nature* with a challenging new proposition, we wholeheartedly embraced it. The cable TV company had the film rights to *The Laramie Project*, Moisés Kaufman's 3½-hour play about the hate-crime killing of Matthew Shepard, a young gay man in Laramie, and the community's reaction to it. Constructed from interviews with the local townsfolk, the play had multiple characters and was about both the townspeople's views and the theater troupe's efforts to go in and record them. It was a very multilayered and complex piece and required some serious development. At that time, producer Ross Katz, who had produced both *Trick* and *In the Bedroom* for us before, and Anne Carey, who worked at Good Machine in development, had been wanting to grow. We thought the two of them would be perfect for whittling down the play to ninety minutes and for figuring out how to handle the dozens of speaking roles, and getting it made well.

We were a bit snobbish about TV in the early 2000s. We made feature films—not television. And yet we couldn't have gotten *Laramie* made as a movie. There were no big-name stars, and it was self-reflexive, documenting the theater troupe's activities as much as the story itself. It's really the prequel to the play. If you had gone around Hollywood or indie-film-land and pitched, "I want to make a movie about a theater troupe interviewing people in Laramie," no one would have listened. On top of that, Moisés, who had never directed a movie before, was going to shoot it on location with all those actors at a cost of just four million dollars. The budget was tight with little flexibility.

But everyone was willing to do it because it was an important story and because we were trying to do something creative with the medium and find a way to take the film's message further. It's how we got all the actors that we did (Laura Linney, Steve Buscemi, Christina Ricci, Janeane Garofalo, just to name a few) and for the cost that we got them (everyone worked for scale). HBO also made a donation equivalent to the actors' wages to one of three charities (the Matthew Shepard Foundation, the Southern Poverty Law Center, and Amnesty International). Not many entities would give money that they didn't have to spend. But it set the tone for why we were making the movie.

When we started planning the shoot, we figured we were going to have to do forty shots a day. A saner production might have twenty to twenty-five. Hollywood films often do half of that amount. It wasn't impossible, but it was hard. In the beginning, Moisés was feeling overwhelmed. He felt we were asking him to go too fast. He wasn't sure if he was getting what he needed. It was his first feature film, after all, and we were only able to get two or three takes before moving on to the next setup. Theater directors are often trained in performance, but here there wasn't room for much variation between takes.

In the edit-room, which was also new to Moisés, the task was weaving together these incredible performances to create a rich tapestry of experience. At one point, we started to get more radical, and we put these self-reflexive video "glitches"—which evoked someone changing channels—into the movie, and we became more playful with the material.

When Moisés realized that the film we were making wasn't a movie version of the play, but something completely different, it was liberating. The whole project came alive in a new way.

The Laramie Project opened the Sundance Film Festival in 2002. HBO didn't need to present it in theaters, but they made forty prints of the movie and screened it all over the country. Then, on HBO, more people watched it than they ever would have if a film company had distributed it. The movie also spurred the play, which surpassed *Our Town* as the most-staged theatrical production on high schools and college campuses around the country. It took this combination of social commentary, cultural reportage, and creative provocation to enable teachers and students to explore this difficult terrain and see all sides of a complex issue.

While Ross and Anne were moving mountains in Laramie, I was back in New York trying to realize an impossible project that I had dreamed about making for years. When I moved to the city in the 1980s, I had fallen in love with underground comics and would often frequent the comic book stores and head shops downtown, which is where I first discovered Harvey Pekar's comic book series *American Splendor.*

I marveled at how Harvey's story was about battling depression through creative output and finding meaning with his life by sharing it with others. It was such an oddball idea: Here's an average guy who works at a VA hospital, documenting his life in a comic book. And you'd think the person who wrote it would draw it, but Harvey had asked other comic book artists to illustrate his stories, which opened them up to further interpretation. I had envisioned that it would make a great omnibus film, with different filmmakers taking on different stories. I figured since Jim Jarmusch was from Cleveland, just like Harvey, maybe he could direct one part.

Late one freezing winter night in New York, I was changing my newborn son's diaper and noticed two men in ski masks kissing outside my window. It was getting hot and heavy, and the juxtaposition of the heated passion and the freezing weather was distracting me from the job at hand when the phone rang. It was Joyce Brabner, Pekar's wife. She had gotten my number from a comic book artist named Dean Hapspiel, who was our office secretary on *The Ice Storm*. Indie film is a very small world.

She told me the rights to Harvey's life and work had lapsed, they needed some money, they weren't asking for much, and they had heard that I was interested in optioning the material. Always on the lookout for random good fortune, I worked out a deal with Joyce immediately—even though I had no idea yet what a film version would look like. But I knew it had to be different from what was already in the marketplace. I felt we didn't have to settle for something traditional, and the film should mirror Pekar's own playfulness with form and content. I thought it could be a blend of documentary and fiction, like Haskell Wexler's *Medium Cool* or Jan Oxenberg's *Thank You and Good Night* (which my partner James Schamus helped produce). This sort of hybrid form always inspired me, and I was eager to try it myself.

So Harvey wrote a draft—all handwritten and faxed to us page by page, moments after he wrote each one—but it was a straightforward narrative, which just didn't feel right. I went out to Cleveland to visit Harvey and his family with director Chris Smith, whose movies *American Job* and *American Movie* had the sense of docu-fiction hybridity that I was seeking. Anthony Bregman, my former assistant and now a producer, joined us. Chris, Anthony, and I shot some video of Harvey and his family; we were hoping to find inspiration for the film. What we found instead was that Harvey and Chris didn't click.

I left Cleveland with some crucial information: Our story was about the whole family. Harvey's narrative was always about how he found comics. But here was a guy who never thought he'd have a family, who thought of himself as a reject, who couldn't maintain a relationship, and who, early on, even had undergone a vasectomy. But through his comics, he also forged a family. For me, that was the big beautiful thing we had to capture. That was the story. It wasn't just about creating one's art, but was about creating and sustaining human relationships in unexpected ways.

The other thing I discovered was that nobody could ever play Harvey as well as he plays himself. Besides, his comics were ultimately about interpretation and how different people perceive Harvey differently. How would audiences recognize this if they did not have something to measure it against? Harvey had to be in the movie, even if it were only going to be for a small amount of time. He was so idiosyncratic that the style of the entire film had to be similarly idiosyncratic to do him justice.

Everyone in our office had a Harvey story, about how obnoxious Harvey was and how much they loved him. During preproduction, Harvey had somehow gotten all our cell-phone numbers, and one time, he called Glen Basner, who is now a big deal sales agent, but then was just trying to decide what he was going to be. Harvey phoned him to berate him about the sad performance of the New York Giants—or some other New York sports team—and Glen thought it was just somebody from the office impersonating Harvey as a joke. That's what the film had to capture—Harvey's aggressive, yet affectionate personality. And this gave me the confidence that an unusual approach to storytelling would work, because it was true to Harvey's life.

I determined that the film definitely had to incorporate archival documentary footage as well as animation. It needed an innovative approach to the biopic, and ideally the director needed to be someone who truly understood the nature of relationships and how challenging they could be. Initially, the requirements seemed daunting; maybe I was aiming too high. But when Shari Springer Berman and Bob Pulcini—a married documentary filmmaking team—came into my office one day, alarm bells went off; they were the perfect fit. They were a couple that would get the story's family dynamics, and they had a unique understanding of nonfiction, which would provide a distinctive perspective for the biopic.

As unusual as our pitch was, we didn't need to work hard to convince HBO Films to finance the project. Brooklyn filmmaker Jim McKay had introduced me to HBO executive Maud Nadler. We all shared an affinity for telling stories that captured the lives of "everyday people" (which later became the title of one of Jim's movies for HBO). We clearly bonded over the need to communicate the struggles of working-class folks. Bob and Shari were getting ready to head to L.A. for a series of meetings on another project, and I urged Maud to meet them. Maud called me immediately after the meeting to tell me HBO wanted to make the movie. I could still hear the filmmakers saying good-bye in the background when Maud called me. There wasn't even a script yet, and Bob and Shari had never even read the comics until we met. Nonetheless, I had mapped out which stories I thought should be in the movie, and Bob and Shari added their touch and turned a script around in record time.

Maud loved the script as much as we did. *American Splendor* was green-lit on the first draft and put into production on the second draft— the very same draft that would earn an Oscar nomination. Everyone has stories about development hell, but sometimes a script is there from the beginning, and the trick is simply to stay true to it without mucking it up. You have to know when to leave well enough alone. It can be a producer's strongest gift.

Maud Nadler and HBO Films president, Colin Callender, approved the film with a budget of under $2.5 million. But upon seeing an early cut, they approved an even higher budget, which allowed us to do the animation we wanted. Unlike the production of most movies, where everything has to be decided in advance, we had the luxury of allowing the process to determine the outcome. This freedom was crucial, not only to the success of the movie—we could figure out what animation we needed, in light of the footage we had already shot of Harvey and our cast—but also vital to the way that I believe we should create all movies. Filmmaking is not, or shouldn't be, a strictly goal-oriented exercise. I've always preferred the process to the proof. This belief goes all the way back to grade school, when I realized that every time I took a test, I was no longer learning. It wasn't about education but was about proving your stature. When artists experiment, when they work without a net, the work becomes more alive. Such a method can also allow the audience to engage with the art on another level, because there is the additional question of whether the author can ultimately pull it all off.

The HBO team granted us even more funds to use the source music that Harvey had originally selected. These weren't cheap songs to license—with tracks from Marvin Gaye, Dizzy Gillespie, and John Coltrane—but HBO recognized the added authenticity that this music gave to the project and kicked in another couple hundred thousand dollars. It's not often that you have backers who believe in spending the money to get something right. Generally, producers are always asked to cut corners. As films budgets go, we didn't spend much money, but HBO allowed us to spend far more than initially anticipated.

How did this generosity happen? It all started with Harvey, of course. First, he inspired me with his creativity, and then I spread that enthusiasm to Bob and Shari, who got incredible work out of the crew—like our cinematographer Terry Stacey (who later worked with me on *Adventureland*), our production designer Therese DePrez (whose estimable credits now include *Mr. Magorium's Wonder Emporium* and *Black Swan*), and costume designer Michael Wilkinson (who went Hollywood, working on *300*, *Watchmen*, and *American Hustle*). Yet, as gifted as they are, I think *American Splendor* inspired all of us. In turn, all of us inspired Colin and Maud, and they gave us the freedom and resources needed to deliver the film. And when you look at the movie, for all of its challenges and wrinkles, you see complexity and confidence, warmth and love, and that's what is in Harvey and his comics.

I think such inspiration also came about as a reaction against the tiredness and jadedness that was beginning to surround independent film. There was a feeling that indie films were becoming clichéd and parodies of themselves—whether Tarantino rip-offs or quirky romantic comedies—all variations on stories that had been told before, the equivalent of Hollywood reboots. Most of us enter the film business with the goal of doing something great, of lifting the art and maybe even changing the world. But the process of getting your movies made, the people we often have to deal with, and the challenges of earning a sustainable living frequently lead us to make compromises we later regret. We need a constant dose of truly creative inspiration to keep us going.

There was something else, too.

Just a few weeks before we started prepping *American Splendor*, we were hoping to close a lucrative five-million-dollar distribution deal for Nicole Holofcener's *Lovely and Amazing*, which had just premiered at the Telluride Film Festival. For me, it was like striking it rich. Finally, the big payday I had long sought had arrived. The film had been made for only a million dollars, so this was a substantial victory for us. We were getting ready to celebrate. We had gotten an offer in writing from an executive at Fox Searchlight, but it was conditional on his higher-ups signing off on it. We suspected we were being played, but we were reassured repeatedly that this was just how it had to be done. The night turned to the morning, and the days turned into a week. The head honchos never came through. Suddenly, I feared I was never going to strike it rich; that wasn't why I made movies, but when the opportunity comes, it's hard not to dream about what it would be like to struggle less.

After Telluride, we needed our screening at the Toronto International Film Festival to breathe new life into *Lovely and Amazing* and bring it up for sale again. The morning of our big premiere, I decided to clear my head and go to a screening of Mira Nair's *Monsoon Wedding*. While I was sitting inside the theater, my cell-phone started to vibrate. And then it vibrated again and again. I finally left the theater to see what was going on, and that's when I saw the news of 9/11.

As a teenager, I had always had rock-and-roll dreams of apocalypse—of buildings crashing to the ground and cities burning up in flames. But I had never considered how infantile those fantasies were until I walked into a hotel in Toronto where a bunch of my friends were gathered around and I saw on the TV those images that I had once dreamed of—and realized their horrible repercussions in the real world.

In Toronto, we didn't know exactly what to make of the horrors that had taken place back home in New York, but the sense of community we felt toward each other was never greater. We spent a lot of time huddling together in hotel lobbies and restaurants and bars trying to process what had happened. I had been so frustrated and angry that we had lost our deal for *Lovely and Amazing* and that we had lost our Toronto screening (it was canceled). But very quickly, all of these emotions felt so unimportant. Like my adolescent dreams, my emphasis on the business and money felt infantile in the larger scheme of things. My priorities started to shift.

Some friends and I rented a minivan and drove over Canada's Rainbow Bridge back into New York State and down toward the city. My family and I lived in the West Village at the time. My son was less than a year old, and he and his mom had escaped across the Hudson River because the smoke was so bad. When the sun rose the morning after the tragedy, I took my son out for a walk. We looked out at the smoldering remains of Lower Manhattan, and I was completely unsure of what to do with my life.

The Good Machine offices were downtown on Canal Street, and you could see the Towers from our windows. Many of the staffers who were in the office on 9/11 were pretty shaken up. Some decided they would leave the film business and do something more meaningful with their lives. I wasn't sure what to do. Having been apart from my son when the attack happened, I did not feel like traveling again—to make another movie or to attend another film festival—anytime soon.

But *American Splendor* was that seemingly impossible dream project that I could not let go. Two months after 9/11, we were shooting in Cleveland. And making that film brought those of us working on the movie together as a team and helped reaffirm the importance of creative output—of making something distinct, and the universality of uniqueness. We weren't saving the world, but *American Splendor* resonated with audiences. People felt close to those characters. They were brought to understand people different from themselves. And that felt significant, too.

After making *American Splendor*, I continued to have that same feeling of wanting to create movies that were different from everything else. I had loved a 2000 Mexican film called *Amores Perros* and thought this kind of innovation was where independent film needed to go. It was adventurous, kinetic, with no individual protagonist, really pushing the envelope. I remember lamenting to one of my Good Machine colleagues, Mary Jane Skalski, that there wasn't a single filmmaker I wanted to work with, other than the *Perros* director, Alejandro González Iñárritu. But how would I ever meet, let alone work with, a Mexican director? Literally, the next day, I got a call from Alejandro. I have never believed in heaven's intervention or that the universe provides much beyond chaos, but this was weird. Just like Bob and Shari's walking into my office and providing the exact fit that I needed for *American Splendor*, Alejandro came to me exactly when I wished he would. But it wasn't God working in splendorous ways. It was Alfonso Cuarón, the Mexican director who had made *Y Tu Mama Tambien* with Good Machine International (and would later make the best of the Harry Potter films and the 3-D masterpiece *Gravity*); knowing that Alejandro was looking for an English-language producer for his next project, Alfonso recommended me.

After a number of failed attempts, I finally met Alejandro in Los Angeles at the Coffee Bean & Tea Leaf, a gathering hole for people in the indie film industry. He first approached the producer Albert Berger (*Little Miss Sunshine*), who was also sitting in the café and who Alejandro thought was me—I considered it a compliment. Alejandro finally found me, and we bonded over the possibility of taking film form to new places. We discussed how cinema was a hundred years old but we were doing it the same way we always had. After 9/11, I felt that if I was going to continue to make movies, they had to be movies that mattered. And if the cinema purports to be the art that most captures what it means to be in our world, the challenge was how to create something that feels new and of the moment. I hadn't yet read the script for *21 Grams*, but I knew Alejandro wanted to capture the subject of free will, which sounded enticing.

Alejandro and his scriptwriter Guillermo Arriaga had developed a nonlinear approach to their story, which skillfully captured some complex ideas. But it was funny because the two of them were coming at the concept from opposite philosophical positions. A lot of times, we believe we need collaborators who think like we do. But Alejandro and Guillermo demonstrated that it's sometimes beneficial to find collaborators who make you think harder and force you to take chances. Alejandro is a believer—his religion is very important to him—and Guillermo is an atheist. And yet, both men wanted to tackle this question of fate through a unique storytelling strategy. The complicated structure of *21 Grams*, with its intricate shifts back and forth in time, may seem chaotic—which reflected Guillermo's position—but the precision of that nonlinear form shows the hand of the director even more. To capture that feeling of free will, inadvertently perhaps, the film ultimately reflects the presence of a divine order. Or to think about it more in creative terms, perhaps the more elaborately constructed a story, the more you see the hand of the writer-director. There were a lot of heady conversations about the script. Alejandro and Guillermo did a few additional drafts of the script with me, which delayed us by about six months and probably only pushed the script another 5 percent further, but they wanted it to be as strong as possible so there was no room for financiers or film company executives to give us development notes.

For the casting, Alejandro had already been working with an experienced casting director, Francine Maisler (who had cast *Spider-Man, Out of Sight*, and dozens of other big films). But he wanted to make sure that what we saw on screen were his characters, not celebrities. With a $23 million budget, it was not a cheap film, and Alejandro didn't want to make it cheaper. So we needed actors who had value. The actor Benecio Del Toro didn't work very much, being very choosey with his roles, and because of that, his personae wouldn't get in the way of the character that Alejandro wanted him to be. But the director was concerned about Sean Penn—a major star—and decided the actor needed to wear a prosthetic nose to make him less recognizable.

At the time, Naomi Watts wasn't yet a name. She had done David Lynch's *Mulholland Drive*, but her first big break was on the horizon. She had just been cast in a 20th Century Fox's adaptation of John Grisham's *Runaway Jury*. But Alejandro felt very strongly that she shouldn't do the Fox project, so that she could stay fresh for the audience. So we asked Naomi's agent and manager if she would step down from that movie. It was a bold move on our parts, but an even riskier proposition for Naomi. Put yourself in her shoes: She had been slugging it out in the trenches in L.A. for a long time, and when her number finally came up, we were asking her to walk away—which she eventually did. That takes guts and a lot of integrity. Ultimately, I think it was the best thing for her career—she received an Oscar nomination for Best Leading Actress for *21 Grams*—but of course, none of us knew this at the time.

One evening, during preproduction, I was having dinner at the Chateau Marmont—not my usual stomping grounds in L.A.—with Alejandro, Sean Penn, and Benecio Del Toro. At one point, Robert Downey Jr. and Tobey Maguire dropped by. As the cool night air made the candles on the patio shiver, I felt a strange sensation. I was surrounded by some of my favorite actors and what may well be the smartest director I had ever met, and yet, I felt a bit like I was in that Groucho Marx joke of not wanting to belong to any club that would have me as a member. These were precisely the type of talents at the top of their game—people I always wanted to work with. Yet simultaneously, I feared I could be corrupted and I might lose sight of the revolution that we were seeking.

But ultimately, that wasn't the case. Though I didn't know the *21 Grams* team that well, we had come together because we all felt we were reaching for something extraordinary. Whether it was the courageous act of Guillermo's script or Naomi's sacrifice, there was the collective sense that here were creative people who wanted the opportunity to step outside the box and try something different, which they are rarely allowed to do. And this sensibility has meaning and value and is one of the ways that *21 Grams* got made. I should emphasize that it's not just the director who wants to take creative risks; the actors do too, whether they are established stars or those getting their first break.

21 Grams also got made because my partners and I were extremely meticulous in putting the deal together. Because this was such challenging material, we had to visualize it as much as possible for the eventual financiers. Film is usually a business of known unknowns, so we kept busy eradicating those known unknowns. When someone reads a script, he or she don't usually picture a specific house, let alone a street or a town. We wanted to shoot in Memphis, so we scouted locations, had photos of Memphis, and kept them available for discussions with the possible financiers. We also came up with a concrete list of the cast, crew, budget, and business plan. We wanted to make the film feel inevitable. We wanted to make sure any possible partner saw the same movie we wanted to make and, in trusting us, would leave us alone to make that movie. Every component was planned out, along with the timing of bringing the film to the marketplace.

We decided to take the gamble of holding it until after Cannes, because the marketplace was looking subdued that year and we bet that companies would still have money left over in their acquisition budgets. Then John Lesher, Alejandro's Hollywood agent, devised a strategy to play two people at the same company against each other. We had just sold Good Machine to Universal, and my partners James Schamus and David Linde were now busy running Universal's new specialized division Focus Features. They knew the project well; with its international roots and reach, it was a perfect film to help launch Focus, and they wanted it badly. But meanwhile, Lesher suggested to Universal's top executive, Stacey Snyder, that she meet with Alejandro and pursue him. Ultimately, both groups wanted the project and the credit for it, but James and David had more limits on what they could spend. With Stacey involved, she could step in and come in for a more complex financial arrangement. Finally, Universal and Focus agreed to this very unique deal structure, where we retained distribution rights to the film in Mexico and Spain and would receive any revenue from those territories, while they got the rights to the rest of the world. Because we had been so specific, we were able to reach an agreement that would allow Alejandro what he wanted and that would actually make some money, too.

These days, everyone has to compromise when big money is involved, and compromise is often the antithesis of ambitious, creative work. As much as corporate executives secretly believe in their collaborators, the infrastructure itself encourages too much interference. Unless you build a deal to protect the integrity of the film, you won't get the final outcome you desire. So whether it was the deals we crafted for Alejandro on *21 Grams* and Michel on *Human Nature* or with HBO and the filmmakers on *The Laramie Project* and *American Splendor*, we obtained greater freedom on those projects than the system normally allows. The nature of financing usually forces you to compromise, but we were able to preserve these filmmakers' creative vision. As the noted film attorney John Sloss likes to say, quoting Robert Frost, "Good fences make good neighbors."

Chapter 8

Time

Time was running out.

The film business was changing. We could try to keep going the way we had for years, but I suspected that soon, we'd hit a wall.

Ang Lee's *Crouching Tiger, Hidden Dragon* had a huge impact on me, my partners James Schamus and David Linde, and Good Machine, to such an extent that we considered selling the business to Barry Diller's company, USA Films, in 2000 on the understanding that he was then going to flip it to Universal Studios. One of our final steps was a sit-down with Diller. It was an intimidating meeting. Here was this infamous media mogul, and we walked into this big boardroom, and he was the only one sitting at this colossal table. On the way up in the elevator, James, knowing that the whole meeting was a formality, told David and me that he wanted to ask Diller one question.

In the middle of the meeting, James finally looked Diller in the eye and said, "We want to ask just one question." And Diller agreed, but being the consummate dealmaker, he insisted that he get to ask one too—but we had to go first. So James asked, "Why do you want to go into the art film business?" And Diller answered something like, "Film is more than just a business. I love the art of it, and there is a real potential to create great culture and good business." (You can tell how much he was committed to that statement by what he subsequently did in the specialty film business. Nothing at all.)

But then it was Diller's turn to ask us a question: "How the fuck did you guys make so little money on *Crouching Tiger*?"

The answer was, essentially, the independent model.

Over the years, some nine different companies had made offers to buy Good Machine. The eighth company was British mogul Nigel Sinclair's Intermedia. We were close to a deal with them, but the negotiations eventually broke down. Intermedia was then a public company on the new German Media Stock Exchange and wanted to have everything structured to drive a profit, which meant that if our projects weren't generating lots of profit, we would lose control of them. This new stock exchange also looked to be weakening at the time. What we thought we were going to get paid wasn't necessarily what we would get paid; as the price was based on stock, there was little opportunity to fix it in place (or incentive to do so). We ended up killing the deal in the final hour after both sides had gone through a grueling due-diligence process.

But one of the key things that allowed the Universal deal to eventually go through, particularly as fast as it did, was that we had all of our financial and legal books in shape, thanks to Intermedia and all those other offers. By the time Diller and Universal came knocking, we were ready. Our bookkeeping was in order, James and David were eager to go on to the big leagues, and the model as it was working for ambitious independent films no longer seemed so functional without a guarantee of U.S. distribution in place. And most importantly for me, I was ready to focus on a new method that would put the movies first. Although they would be lifted by the business, they'd be driven by our individual passion. I thought I had a way that would support a more sustainable and creative indie film industry. (It proved not to be that easy.)

Fortunately, it turned out that as fast as things were changing, the old models for making, financing, and distributing movies would exist for some time—longer than I suspected, actually. And in the interim, there were some wonderful movies to make. But the traditional ways of indie film, as we all knew it, were coming to an end.

When it became clear that Good Machine was finally going to be sold, a number of my colleagues told me they wanted to keep working together. There was Diana Victor, our business affairs person; Anne Carey, our development executive; and Anthony Bregman, one of our producers.

I'll never forget the day Anthony first walked into the Good Machine offices with a photograph of the Angelika Film Center marquee. When he realized that Good Machine had something to do with most of the films playing there, he wanted to become a part of our enterprise. He offered to be my assistant and said he would work for free for five months. At that very moment, my current assistant had accidentally blown up the office cappuccino machine, sending froth splattering all over the place. "Okay, you're hired," I told Anthony.

Anthony's first major assignment at Good Machine was to retrieve a Nagra reel-to-reel sound recorder that a Coney Island hoodlum had liberated from our equipment truck. We had gotten a call demanding a ransom. Not only was Anthony brave enough to make the journey, but he somehow managed to return with the equipment and all the money we gave him to retrieve it. We knew from then on that Anthony would make a great producer.

When Anthony, Anne, Diana, and I talked about what we hoped to build together, it quickly became apparent that we all wanted the same thing: We didn't want to have huge overhead, so we wouldn't be forced to take jobs simply for the money. We wanted to work only with people we liked, and we wanted to work only on movies that we loved.

In the early 1990s, I remember having lunch with legendary film scion Samuel Goldwyn Jr., the son of one of the founders of Metro-Goldwyn-Mayer (MGM). We had just sold *The Wedding Banquet* to his film distribution company.

Right off the bat, he asked James and me, "Let me understand something. Are you guys artists, or are you businessmen?" That was his conversation starter.

And I responded, "Can't we be both?"

He paused and said no.

Through much of my professional career, I've tried to reconcile both sides of that line, and This is that—my new film production company—was our attempt to resolve the contradiction. It may be a more financially sound business model to build a slate of films, raise financing for the entire set and make a bunch of movies than it is to go from movie to movie. But you need a lot of money to finance a slate, and that takes a hell of a long time. Plus, movies are perishable goods. I would never say to a filmmaker, "We're going to wait on your movie until I get another five million for more of the slate." If I've raised money for a movie, I'm not going to want to wait around—even if waiting might turn out to be better business. Not waiting is a decision for that particular movie and that particular filmmaker. It's a good decision for the art. But it's not necessarily good business.

Likewise, when you meet a one-of-a-kind filmmaker, it's good business to stay in business with that one filmmaker. Sometime early in my career, around the time of Ang Lee's *Eat Drink Man Woman*, James had said we should only produce Ang's films. We could see his budding mastery, and James was asking, "Why would we want to work with anybody else?" Ang is a great guy and an adventurous spirit. What more did a producer need? That might have been fine if I had felt like I knew everything and I was comfortable with the world as it was—but that wasn't me. I knew that I was learning a lot by working with a mixture of directors and at a range of different budget levels, and I didn't want to give the variety up. That's how I've learned my craft, by mixing it up and taking on movies where I know I'm needed—where I know I'm not just another producer. It can't just be about getting the job or getting the movie made; I want to keep learning every step of the way.

So our new production company was formed on many of these principles: keeping our expenses lean and working only with the people and the movies we were passionate about.

But we needed to find a name.

In considering a purchase of Good Machine, everyone, from USA Films' Barry Diller to Universal's Ron Meyer, confessed how much they liked the name. They all wanted to keep it, but I was a tad sentimental about it. I didn't want it to be like a rock band touring the country and only having the lead singer from the third incarnation of the band. James and David felt the same way. Good Machine was all of us. The name represented the work that we all had done together. It couldn't stand without us.

Anne, Anthony, Diana, and I were all tired of grandiose brand names like Paramount, Summit, and Zenith. Come on, folks, it's entertainment! At the time, we happened to be working with British director Terry Gilliam (*Brazil*), and he had the best corporate name: Poo Poo Pictures. The name inspired us to come up with something equally irreverent, so we settled on the Rococo Cocoa Co. We thought it was genius, and we quickly came up with the logo of a cup of cocoa with a rococo-esque puff of steam coming out the top. But when I tried out the name, it was a disaster. I called up one of those über-powerful Hollywood-type attorneys and said, "This is Ted Hope, from Rococo Cocoa Co." And after the receptionist said, "What?" and after I repeated the name for the third time, I had had enough. And just said, "It's Ted Hope from Good Machine." So the Rococo Cocoa Co. was dead before it even launched.

But we still wanted a name that was fun and took the piss out of the seriousness of the trade. Back then, my son was just learning how to talk, and like all parents, I thought everything he said was brilliant. When he said, "Red car," I thought it was a perfect name. But it turned out there was already another film company with that name. Then another time, he said, 'This is that," and I thought it was perfect. We thought it was clever, because people would be saying, "This is that script," and "This is that deal memo." And we liked the inappropriateness of the acronym, TIT. Unfortunately, people still kept getting the name wrong, "This is that" became "This and that," which made us sound like a knickknack shop. What can you do? We had already named our company; we'd made our bed, and now we needed to sleep in it.

Eventually, This is that became official: three of us producers, pooling our fees, figuring out how to bankroll the movies we loved, and focusing on films budgeted from seven to twenty-five million dollars. Keeping our budgets in this range gave us both the most production value and creative freedom that the industry allows. At under twenty-five million, we wouldn't be as tightly scrutinized by the studios and could still be daring in subject matter. And seven million was the minimum to manage a six-week shooting schedule, dress the sets, elevate the costumes, and enhance the shots and lighting—the stuff that makes up production value. We could aim more for a niche audience than a mass market. And we could make movies that both meant something *and* made money.

But the sale of Good Machine to USA Films/Universal signaled, at least to me, that independent producers' days were numbered. It would become harder and harder to finance a film solely around international sales and the *prospect* of U.S. distribution. Everything had to be secured in advance, and all the distributors recognized this fact. Furthermore, the notion of independence was over, because the studios now owned the majority of the specialized distributors. Even though my former partners were in charge of one of them, it still felt like everyone was driven primarily by profit.

Despite these ominous signs, we were in a privileged position at This is that. At Good Machine, we had established a reputation of delivering high-quality yet artistically ambitious work and discovering directors of the highest order. And we had fear on our side, in that distributors would be afraid that our next film might be even better than the one before it. With fear on your side, you could enter into long-standing "output deals" with international distributors, where they agree up front to take every movie you make for a fixed percentage of the budget. And that's exactly what we did with companies like Village Roadshow in Australia and New Zealand, and Svensk in Scandinavia, all of which committed to buying the rights to our projects. We also had a first-look deal for all other territories with my former partners at Good Machine under their new corporate home, Focus Features. The first-look deal meant that Focus's own international division had first dibs to any of our projects, excluding Australia, New Zealand, and Scandinavia. This deal helped with the perception that our films would always have a home. As long as these factors stayed the same, we felt our model would work.

The deal I helped to structure with Focus Features would definitely keep This is that going. But unfortunately not by much. When we got our first overhead deal at Good Machine with Universal around the time of *Ride with the Devil*, it was incredibly lucrative, with $1 million to cover overhead costs, salary advances for James and me, as well as a discretionary fund to buy the rights to material and develop projects. By the time we formed This is that, we received around $350,000 to cover our annual expenses, which was the industry norm at the time. No development funds; no advances. With $350,000, you could run your company and staff your office, but on that kind of budget, it was difficult to take any creative risks. We couldn't afford to take on projects that wouldn't get made. But if your slate becomes full of films that you feel are definitely going to be produced—often, anything that can be positioned as a thriller, a horror film, a comedy, or anything with a rising popular actor attached to it—they are not necessarily the movies that you have the greatest ambitions for. These other projects need nurturing; only time can make them whole. And as much as you want to make the most amazing films possible, you are often not getting paid to work on those. You need to have some movies that you trust will go into production quickly and are likely to pay the bills.

Still, from about 2004 until the financial crisis of 2008, my colleagues and I, armed with our solid track record, felt that if we could conceive of a film that was unique and ambitious and had solid talent, we'd get the necessary funds to make it. And if everything lined up right, it might just change the world—or at least change some people's minds. It was always a long road to get from there to make such a game-changing film, but if you reached that goal, it was an incredibly inspiring feeling, and I wished it would never go away.

Fortunately for us, my colleagues and I could still rely on foreign sales for our films, and there was a model that developed around movies of medium-sized budgets, from approximately eight to fifteen million. Moreover, a huge influx of capital, mostly hedge-fund money, came into the industry during this period. But with that coin came changes—some good and some bad.

When we started making movies, video revenue from our films was accounted on a royalty basis—usually twenty cents for every dollar earned—which meant only a small portion of the revenue ended up in the hands of the filmmakers and their funders. Now every video dollar goes into one big accounting pot. Distributors still take a percentage fee of your earnings—usually between 5 and 30 percent—but at least they're taking a percentage of your *total* revenue, and not shortchanging you on every cent netted. The new businesspeople, thankfully, recognized that the old model was unfair and discouraged success or long-term involvement.

But not all the ensuing changes were so helpful.

One of our first goals at This is that was to raise a large investment fund to make our movies. We were not alone in this desire. Many other producers were trying to do the same thing at the time, raising huge financing deals to fund an entire slate of movies, but the deals were frequently on terms that I thought were bad for us, and the industry, at large. And three important changes in financing significantly mucked things up. First, the money folks kept asking us to put skin in the game, which meant deferring a significant portion of our fees—sometimes as much as 50 percent—across all of our films. Investors believed that producers had no incentive to make sure their movies succeeded, because producers received their fees during the making of the film. Thus, investors thought, producers had little incentive to keep pushing the film all the way through to distribution. But *all* independent producers have skin in the game, because they usually end up deferring some of their money; it's just usually done later. If you give up chunks of your salary or profit participation early in the process, you'll have less to bargain with when it really counts, like when you need to get approval for something that is critical to you, such as more shooting days, a certain actor, or creative control. I might be willing to lose, say, a quarter of my established fee to make a movie that I really want to get made, but when the concession comes at the start of the financing process and not the end of the negotiation, that starting 25 percent will inevitably grow larger. They start by cutting off your feet, and little by little, you keep on giving up more, compromising for the good of the film, until there's nothing left of you but a patch of hair being blown about by the wind. Our unwillingness to comply with these new terms became one of This is that's biggest roadblocks to raising funds.

Second, Wall Street investors also recognized that U.S. distributors had high distribution fees. Standard practice for distributors was to charge 30 percent of the total "film rentals," which is the amount that the distributors net after the exhibitors take their cut. No matter what their contracts say, producers rarely share in any of that money. It's as if the system were rigged against them. Marketing expenses must be paid back; then there is a time gap between when such costs are logged and when they are paid, and interest payments on that differential come out of film rentals. It's not a simple formula. Hedge-fund managers had studied the independent-film business closely and decided that this had to change. If movies often recouped their costs by just 10 to 15 percent, it was not surprising that financiers began to ask that distributors reduce their share by 15 percent to make sure the investment was worthwhile. But when the fees were lowered so dramatically, it also reduced the distributors' appetite for risk, and fewer movies were acquired.

And finally, when hedge funds or financial institutions provided money for a production, they expected to benefit, regardless of the film's success. In the hunger to raise funds for a production slate, we heard through the grapevine that another producer had agreed to have the interest on his fundraising kick in from day one. This meant the producer needed to pay back such a big chunk of money that his production company found itself overpaying for projects just so it could get movies into production and start to pay back their debt. The financial arrangement also forced the company to make its movies quickly, to reduce the amount of accumulating interest it would need to pay. The result: It was harder for this company to make a good movie and even harder for the producers to make a profit. You just can't rush good films. That producer's company eventually went bankrupt, which only further reinforced the notion that movies don't make money. (They can if done right.)

These changes—monetizing producer's fees, lowering distribution fees, quicker interest payments—might have benefited investors, but the shift hurt everyone else. Some significant production companies went down, but it could have been much worse if these alterations had been more widely adopted. There needs to be a more holistic approach to making movies. The best thing we can do is to make sure that both the artists and their supporters are direct financial beneficiaries of the work, not just one or the other. Historically, we built a system that bolsters the middlemen—the distributors and the agents—more than it does the others. But it should support the overall ecosystem.

During this time, This is that collaborated with a slew of high-networth individuals new to the independent-film business and eager to apply the lessons they had learned from other fields. Billionaire businessmen Steven Rales, who founded a company called Indian Paintbrush, financed our movie *Towelhead*, his first, after running a variety of successful companies. The owner of EMC, a data-storage company, put up the funds for *Door in the Floor*. Sidney Kimmel Entertainment, founded by clothing magnate Sidney Kimmel, financed our film *Adventureland*.

From a creative perspective, when it was working well, the wonderful thing about the foreign-sales model—in which financing is secured through advanced sales to international distributors—was that you had enough of a budget to pay people a living. It wasn't huge, but directors and producers still received a six-figure fee, which allowed you to think about a long-term career and dream about owning a house or having a family—ah, those simple luxuries. For films designed for the art house and not the multiplex, actors in those days could still earn somewhere between scale—a shifting figure, from as low as a hundred dollars per day, depending on budget levels, determined by the Screen Actors Guild— and five hundred thousand for the entire shoot.

When budgets for independent films still tipped beyond seven million dollars, we also had the time and resources to shoot a movie. Nowadays, it seems you're expected to shoot for twenty-five days, no matter what kind of movie it is, including period films with major stars. Time makes everything better. The more time you have, the better coverage and performances you get. It's a saner way of working. With lower budgets, the serendipitous possibility of delivering something more than what you set out to create goes out the window. You're expected to meticulously plan everything so that you can meet the impossible schedule. The lower budget leaves no room for spontaneous creativity. You're not learning from the process. You can't afford to think on your feet. When the budgets were at higher levels, you could still pursue ambitious cinema. You could elevate the material. Now you don't ever have the time to change your mind.

In 2003, during our second year at This is that, Anthony brought in Michel Gondry's second film, *Eternal Sunshine of the Spotless Mind,*

which I think ranks up there among the best films of that decade. I'm not gloating, because I did not produce the movie. It was producer Steve Golin's film to begin with, and Anthony, working at This is that, teamed up with him at Focus's urging. Anthony had the motivation to drive it and knew he had a great partner in Golin, so I could simply observe from a comfortable distance.

I find that it's important to only take on projects where I can contribute something unique to them. Often, I feel that I'm asked to do a film simply because of my track record—and not because of what I do well and what I can bring to the project. Despite everything I learned from working with Michel on *Human Nature*, and as inspiring as it was, I remained more excited about serving a new group of directors and looking for other experiences. And it wasn't clear to me how or why Michel and his group would need me to make *Eternal Sunshine* better. Over the years, I would have loved to work with Scorsese, Coppola, or Altman, but for the same reason, I might have passed on the opportunity because I'm not sure how I could have enhanced any of their movies— not that they ever called me!

Eternal Sunshine's script was developed with USA Films under Scott Greenstein. But the problem was that USA viewed it as a forty-million-dollar film. In contrast, my former partners James and David, who were starting up at Focus Features, didn't want to spend over ten million on this inherited project, as brilliant as they knew it was. Anthony was brought in to figure out how it could be done on the smaller budget. In some ways, that middle-sized budget gave Michel more freedom in terms of the aesthetic approach to the film. There was a playful spirit, where he was still permitted to do things on the fly. If the film had been green-lit at the higher budget, the production would have required everyone to stick to a more rigid plan. Instead, Michel was allowed to improvise, and Anthony and Steve could accommodate Michel's creativity. For instance, when Michel heard that the Ringling Bros. and Barnum & Bailey Circus was going to be walking its elephants through the midtown tunnel to Madison Garden, he wanted to film the spectacle for the movie, and Anthony, much like with the flies in *Human Nature*, had twenty-four hours to come up with a plan. Elephants are bigger than flies, but just as difficult to capture.

Anthony and Ray Angelic, the line producer, called everyone associated with the circus, the NYPD, and the mayor's office looking for a way to photograph the elephants. Fortunately, the New York Mayor's Office of Film and Television prides itself on getting things done and making things happen, and the next day, when the elephants marched through the tunnel, Jim Carrey, Michel Gondry, and the *Eternal Sunshine* team were there to capture the magical moment.

During postproduction, we had a rough-cut screening of *Eternal Sunshine* for friends and family at Technicolor. In watching the cut, we could clearly see how widely inventive the script was, but there was still something critical missing. Everyone else in the audience marveled at everything that Michel had gotten. It was going to be a marvelous movie—that was evident—but it wasn't yet perfect. Could he get there? How would he get there? Nobody in the audience was taking a hard line, but for me, it was obvious that *Sunshine* wasn't yet fully shining. I felt that it still wasn't clear how or why the two leads loved each other. Everyone else had accepted it as a given (they were movie stars and it was a love story, after all), but the attraction hadn't been demonstrated. When I spoke up during the screening to make the point, the tone of the conversation changed. My observation was a hard criticism to hear. Michel was furious with me. He said I had doomed his movie as the crowd then realized the film was not yet finished. And he stopped talking to me for a while.

But ultimately, Michel and his team were given the room to make the movie sing. He was editing at Good Edit, which occupied the space below the old Good Machine offices (I had created Good Edit to do postproduction in-house). Michel kept working at it and his team fully supported him. Trust and confidence. Time and money. It's possible to make a good movie without the latter two attributes, but I'm not so sure it can be done without the former two.

In the end, Michel did some additional photography (even though Jim Carrey's schedule wasn't exactly open), and he made the love story between the characters real. If you're trying to make original, authentic art—particularly if it seeks to reveal something of the human predicament—the closer you strive to get to it, sometimes the further the goal is away from you. And there's really no solution to that conundrum, except time. By taking the extra time to figure out what made those characters tick, Michel eventually found a way to connect them in a deep and emotional way.

On another early This is that production, *Thumbsucker*, directed by another music-video-director-turned-filmmaker, Mike Mills, we also spent a lot of time in the editing room. Mike knew that it was a good movie, but he hadn't completely captured it yet, so he just kept at the task, in the editing room. In this case, we were fortunate to be one of the first in a slate of films from a new financier called Bull's Eye Entertainment, and our executive producer, Cathy Shulman (who would go on to win the Oscar for *Crash*), helped make sure the project got the time and space it needed before we submitted it to Sundance. When you have the extra pressure of a set delivery date or festival deadline, it's often hard to find the nuance of the movie, but fortunately, Mike did finally find it. One reason many films end up mediocre is that filmmakers are dashing to finish them. We need to build into our process the time for creativity to spark. And often, the structure of the business doesn't allow for that.

Soon after we started up, This is that signed with the United Talent Agency, a big Hollywood-based firm, to have a bigger presence in Los Angeles. We wanted to see how we could expand and diversify. We also wanted more respect and more money, and UTA wanted us to be part of the Hollywood game and be the kind of producers who got gross profit participation—the Hollywood dream. We were pitched a variety of studio projects, but they were so inappropriate for us. There was *Must Love Dogs*, a romantic comedy with John Cusack and Diane Lane, and then there was another one about a mermaid. I thought to myself, "Come on, really?" We were about character development, strong plotting, and emotional truth. But the studios said, "No, no, no, we just want you to make sure the director does what we want." Needless to say, it didn't work out.

So in our quest (or maybe it was our agents' quest) to become the American version of Working Title (which produced all those successful upscale British comedies and dramas like *Four Weddings and a Funeral*, *Notting Hill*, and *Pride & Prejudice*), the question remained: How do we do it?

Word came out that Alan Ball, the Oscar-winning writer of *American Beauty* and the creator of HBO's acclaimed *Six Feet Under*, wanted to make his directorial debut. He had optioned the book *Towelhead*, Alicia Erian's novel about a thirteen-year-old Lebanese American girl coming of age in the cruelest of ways. We read it and we loved it. It was about something important, and it was sure to offend people, which is always something I enjoy. (Any movie worth making should have at least someone somewhere wanting to kill you for making it.) I got very excited. We told Alan's agents we wanted to do it.

Because of Alan's successful work in TV, he could afford to take the time to get the script right. While most artists struggle to earn a living to sustain their art, Alan could move slowly. He was one of the fortunate ones.

Now we just needed to find a great cast and secure the financing. Months earlier, Hal Sadoff, a financial consultant in the business, had gone over to the Hollywood agency ICM and become an agent. Hal called me and said there was this industrialist who was coming through New York and was interested in getting involved in the film business, and would I like to meet him? You bet.

Part of the producer's job is to meet with people who have money—or at least appear to have money. In reality, you rarely get to meet the actual person who has the money. But Steven Rales was different. He met with lots of people in Los Angeles and had wanted to work his way into the film business for quite some time, but he hadn't committed to anything yet. People started to wonder if he was for real.

Through a series of lunches, Anne, Anthony and I shared our philosophy of the business with Steven. We described how you could, with the right material, director, and cast, launch a film at a market like Cannes and make 70 to 120 percent of your budget from foreign sales and then sell it at a big domestic festival at 30 to 50 percent of your costs and eventually make money.

Steven was a good listener. Many folks new to the business do all the talking about how they are going to turn the industry on its head, but Steven was not like that. He was smart, confident, and easy to talk to and possessed a dry wit. If he was for real, I knew I wanted to be in business with him.

I have always thought Hollywood doesn't care about creating sustainable and long-standing financiers; it refers to new money as "dumb money" and often treats new financiers as such. Hollywood needs a constant supply of ignorant money-people to keep the entire system working. It is a system that Bernie Madoff would have been proud of.

I'm paranoid every time I feel I am competing for investors; I'm always afraid the film industry might exploit them and not help them stick around for the long haul. I wanted to keep Steven as a partner for This is that. My plan was to show Steven that he would do well with us and could stay with us. But if we were going to make more than one film with him, I needed to keep him away from Hollywood.

At one point after we had signed on to do *Towelhead*, our UTA agent Rich Klubeck said he was representing someone who would be a perfect financier to be involved: Steven Rales. I didn't realize how deeply Steven had already established himself out there. Hollywood may have few secrets, but there is definitely no such thing as a financier that nobody knows. We may have had to share him, but we were still very happy to have him on our film as his first feature. He agreed to put up eight million dollars, and we were already set to presell the foreign rights through Celluloid Dreams, a top international sales company.

Our agents explained that Steven had been an art buyer and he understood the value of blue-chip properties. He was trying to apply what he had learned in the art world to the cinema business. Alan Ball was going to be one of those blue-chip properties.

At the same time that we were courting Rales, New York–based Hollywood producer Scott Rudin also expressed interest in working with Alan. Rudin is deservedly a legend in the business. He was named president of Fox Studios before he turned thirty. He is the only producer to have won an Emmy, a Grammy, an Oscar, and a Tony. Hollywood agents call him when their top directors want a producer to protect them from the studio. Immediately, I thought, "Oh shit, how can we compete with Scott Rudin?" He had yet to go on his quality movie spree and was closer to his Lemony Snicket period than his Coen brothers period. But we recognized that he was a big threat.

I wasn't the type to immediately call Scott and sort things out. I prefer to take a breath and see how something unfolds. Thankfully, he phoned me and suggested, "Let's work together." It was a huge relief and an incredible opportunity. I must admit I *was* worried that everyone would credit the legendary Scott Rudin as the producer and forget about my contributions. But I tried not to let my pride get in the way—after all, I had done plenty of movies already and established a reputation. So I thought, "Let's move forward and see what happens."

We met with Alan. He is not someone you can take lightly. For one, he's tall, over six feet. He may have laughed a lot, but his brow was often furrowed. His intense eyes also shot through everything, his mind moving faster than everything else around him, always looking for a solution. I often felt that everything I did on the production was a test that I did not want to fail.

As passionate a writer and filmmaker as he was, Alan also knew how to navigate crises. Here was a guy who had been through some of TV's toughest times. He had worked on shows from *Roseanne* to *The Golden Girls* and had seen it all. If I identify one phrase with Alan, it was "This, too, shall pass." When something went wrong, you could see it on his face: a deep take-it-slow sign that fully embodied that phrase.

I moved out to Los Angeles to work on the film. I have never felt that I belonged in L.A. Rather than drive, I prefer to walk wherever I can. New York is like a respite from the film business, because most people you meet don't care anything about it. But when you're making movies in L.A., not only is everyone around you in the business, but you also begin to believe you're doing the most important thing under the sun—which it isn't. I often take perverse pride in the fact that other than *Human Nature* and *Towelhead*, I have not worked on movies made in Hollywood.

But the L.A. film community often teases you when you're an outsider. And if you don't spend time in Hollywood people's faces, they quickly forget about you. I needed them to take me seriously, and I felt that I needed to do my time in L.A. It helped to have a film I wanted to make and a filmmaker I wanted to work with.

However, I knew if we were going to stay out there for the shoot, I needed to find a place that would be more than a house, but a place that might make me comfortable. On independent films, that's never easy. But I got lucky, very lucky. In Michael Mann's famous L.A. cop movie *Heat*, there is this absurd element where Amy Brenneman's character—a school teacher—lives in a beautiful glass house in the Hollywood Hills. It is the kind of place that a producer of indie films could never afford in real life, either. It turned out that the owner dug my films and cut the rent in half so we could stay there, high above it all, where the hawks circle out your window and the city lights sparkle at night. There are some perks that come from making the films you love.

In the beginning, agents told me that *Towelhead* would be a perfect project for their big-name clients like Matt Damon, Naomi Watts, and so on. Every role had big names being bandied about. It was a hot subject, a funny and heartbreaking book with unique characters. It was also an ambitious project, but most importantly, it was Alan Ball, the man who won had just won the Oscar for writing an uncompromising movie that had captured the zeitgeist.

But it was still a movie about a teen who gets raped by a man she trusts—and to whom the audience can relate.

The movie was also a challenge because the central character was a young girl—and that meant no star in the center. The adult roles for which the stars were auditioning were merely supporting roles. And even though Scott Rudin made calls to all the representatives of top actors, they ultimately saw it for what it was. And as bold and exciting as the film was, no big-name actors were saying they had to do this film to revive or redefine their career. It had *risk* written all over it.

We might not have gotten Matt Damon, but Aaron Eckhart was a great choice for the role and delivered a terrific performance. Same for Toni Collette, Maria Bello, and Peter MacDissi. And we did a nation-wide casting search for the young girl and couldn't have been more fortunate to find Summer Bishil, a method actress who came to the set for most of the shoot looking like an innocent teenager when, in fact, and much to our surprise, she revealed on the last day, clad in a red dress, that she was actually a sophisticated young woman.

When we started hiring the crew, we were working out of Alan's bungalow on the former RKO lot. We had top cinematographers, top production designers, and top costume designers lining up, all asking to work with Alan on this unique project. The director of photography, Newton Thomas Sigel, was way outside our price range, but he not only reduced his rate but also brought the top-of-the-line high-definition digital Genesis camera with him—essentially for free. He had developed it himself with the manufacturer and knew the equipment better than anyone else. James Chinlund, the production designer, had vision, understanding, and sympathy and was hired on the spot. He had worked with me before on Todd Solondz's *Storytelling*. Later, he would go on to design *The Avengers*. Our costume designer Danny Glicker got the job by having one of the most thoroughly researched presentations we had seen. Although he was pretty green at the time, the thoroughness and dedication he exhibited then paved the way for even more good work. I also brought on a top line producer, Peggy Rajski, who had won an Oscar for a short film she had directed. Indie films are known for launching actors, but so many of the crew people who annually get nominated for Oscars also come from the indie trenches. If the film business ever forgets how indies launch the most creative talents, it will be shooting itself in the foot.

Towelhead was an experience in good fortune. At every step, we were getting great people—cast, crew, and financiers. It's a stretch to make a full "stage" production on only eight million, but it's still a lot of money. We decided to shoot it on a soundstage, because Summer had just turned eighteen and didn't have much acting experience. Doing these sexually provocative scenes on location might have inhibited her work. We needed to protect her, and that became a priority in how we designed the entire production. If we had been working for a corporation, the company might have put cost savings first, sacrificing human respect as a result. By working independently, we could prioritize what we felt would make the film work best, knowing everything was riding on the performances.

Similarly, it would have been cheaper to shoot somewhere other than Los Angeles, but one reason we chose L.A. was because it would keep the actress close to her family and keep the entire production on a more professional level (as opposed to shooting away on location, when things sometimes devolve into summer-camp antics or hotel sleepover parties). Had we been working for a company, rather than independently, these decisions about where and how to shoot would have come down to dollars.

The movie business is known for its colossal egos. Having won an Oscar and created an incredibly successful and popular television show, Alan might have been similarly affected. But he always maintained the excitement and energy that make first-time directors such a pleasure to work with. He didn't take it for granted that he was getting to make a movie. He worked as hard as, if not harder than, anyone else, recognizing that he was the leader. And yet, his experience was wide-reaching too. He was an adult. He knew what it took to make things happen and was appreciative of the extra effort people were giving. He also knew he had to listen to and take advice from others. Rarely do you find these two different aspects in one director: the pleasure and innocence of the first-timer combined with the maturity and respect of the seasoned pro.

I'll admit that, like most directors, he occasionally snapped. A lot of directors lose their shit, and you don't want to work with them ever again. But then there are those who you understand why they snapped. Making movies is a stressful process. Directors are asked to make so many decisions, and there is always a lot at stake. I like working with collaborative filmmakers like Alan who solicit input. But comments, like questions, can overwhelm you. We would be at the monitor, watching the scenes, and Alan liked to get notes—except when he didn't like to get them, which wasn't always easy to suss out. When to speak up to a director and when to keep your mouth shut is a tricky art. Is it after Take 3 or Take 4, or do you wait further to see if the director can find the scene himself? I'd like to think I've mostly mastered this delicate balance, but more than a few times, I'd give Alan a note on something that he didn't want to hear, and it would upset him and break his concentration.

For instance, in one very subtle scene, Mario Bello's mother character brushes the hair of her daughter, played by Summer. We were running out of time, and somewhere around Take 6, I decided to speak up. But I should have held back. It turned out that I wasn't as tuned into what was already going on between Alan and the actors; he had been finessing the scene already, and when he came over to me and Peggy and heard my comment, he blew up. But then he quickly regained his composure and got back to the scene. It turned out to be a beautiful moment on screen, both visually and in the performances, but in the heat of the production, the fear of not getting a moment completely perfect can stress everyone out.

But with Alan, we'd both apologize and move on. Alan knew how to put his own frustrations in a context that people could understand, and his loyalty to those he worked with allowed for a more open and productive dialogue.

When we realized we could use a couple hundred thousand dollars more to shoot an additional three days and build both of our key locations on the stage, Steven came through with the money. Sure, we had to justify it and consider alternatives, but he listened to us when we explained to him why it would make the film better and why it didn't mean we wouldn't still keep a tight rein on the budget. I didn't realize this kind of supportive funder was lightning in a bottle. And it might not come again. But looking back on it, I realize that Steven's level of support was a freak of nature. We faced a tight shooting schedule of about seven weeks, but we had it great in comparison with standard operating procedure today.

In postproduction, we did some test screenings in Pasadena to see how the film was playing. People were eager to see it, and during the screening, you could hear people laughing and then getting upset. But on the questionnaires we handed out, men forty and over hated the film. It was strange because in the beginning, they were always the ones laughing the loudest. Then you could tell that they were really becoming angry with the movie, perhaps because they found themselves identifying with a character who would become a rapist, or were frustrated that the sex was not titillating. Some of those early audiences loved the film, but others thought it was too long or repetitive. But whatever the public criticism, we were confident that we were putting subtlety and richness and complexity onto the screen, and we didn't need to listen to the test results. If we had a studio, we would have *had* to listen to the audience.

We got the film ready to premiere at the 2007 Toronto International Film Festival. Because of the controversial nature of the book's title, we didn't want to scare off buyers, so from the start, we figured we needed to change the title. We settled on *Nothing Is Private*, which I always liked because it represented the way that people feel ownership over each other. I also liked its declarative form; plus, it is a line one of the characters says. Yet when you are adapting a novel, if you remain true to the work, it feels disingenuous to abandon the title. On the other hand, you don't put book titles on a marquee. *Towelhead* is a hate-filled term, and we feared that the irony of using it could easily be lost on audiences. But then again, we knew that some people would chastise us for not using it and perhaps accuse us of wimping out. We went back and forth, and I don't think anyone ever truly committed one way over the other. How do you know what is right in such a situation?

In Toronto, the film played really well; it was a hot-button subject, and people wanted to talk about it. But there weren't a ton of buyers. I was starting to get nervous. If you don't have an offer within twenty-four hours of your premiere, the perceived value of your movie goes down. That night in Toronto, I counted every hour that passed. I started to sweat.

Finally, Warner Independent, the independent-film division of Warner Bros., surfaced with a deal. Hallelujah! And the company offered about 30 to 35 percent of the budget, which was an acceptable price. We closed that night with Warner.

But when it came time to release the movie, all of the initial excitement had worn off. Unfortunately, this old independent-film festival sale system doesn't capitalize on the premiere buzz. You're able to use it to sell the film, but not to release it. Though the film sparked online discussions among attendees and critics during the Toronto festival, this was a very small group. The wider American audience, which wouldn't see the movie for another six months, wasn't allowed to join in on that conversation. In hindsight, I can say that the release's delay wasn't a good strategy for this type of hot-button movie, and we should have launched the film in theaters right after the heated festival premiere. Ironically, the industry has allowed a system of sales to develop, via the festival system, that helps a few films maximize recoupment earlier, but ultimately diminishes revenues for most films. It's one of those things that if we put some thought into it, we could build it better.

To bring back some of the controversy, we chose to go back to the book's original name for *Towelhead*'s film title. It was polarizing, perhaps too much so. I don't think anyone really wants to see a movie that uses a racial slur for a title, no matter what the film is about. It makes an audience complicit in endorsing the slur. But my opinion was the minority. I may have produced the movie, but it was not just my film—particularly after we sold it to Warner.

The title didn't help our distributor, either. Warner Independent was going through a lot of changes; the entire specialized-film distribution business was undergoing seismic change. Here was a company that had been the talk of the industry when it released *March of the Penguins*; the documentary about the little Arctic animals earned an amazing $77.4 million in U.S. theaters. But the priorities of the company's corporate parents were shifting, and Warner Indie was among several divisions sent to the scrap heap (including New Line, Fine Line, Picturehouse, and Paramount Classics). *Towelhead* turned out to be the last film that Warner Independent acquired. Our movie didn't destroy the company—Warner Independent was already on the outs. In fact, by the time *Towelhead* was in theaters, there was only one employee at Warner Independent, marketing executive Laura Kim. She had been a supporter of the film from the start, but as we limped to the starting gate, I kept imagining a big, open office, piled high with posters, DVD screeners, and film prints—and Laura all alone. In my nightmares, the phones never stopped ringing, because everyone wanted to book our film, but poor Laura, she was just one person and couldn't possibly field all the calls. In reality, though, it was probably a pretty quiet place.

Despite the shifting of the landscape, there were still opportunities to be found. And with Greg Motolla's *Adventureland*, we still had the time to get things right.

I had initially heard about Greg when I was working with Nicole Holofcener on her first movie, *Walking and Talking*, in the early 1990s. She was worried that the project would never happen and said, "Why are we doing this? It's not going to work. You should meet this guy named Greg Mottola."

Greg Mottola had made this great short film called *Swingin' in the Painter's Room*. It was essentially a one-shot movie set during a wild party, focusing on a couple that was breaking up. In 1995, Greg went on to make *The Daytrippers*, which was a perfect example of what low-budget filmmaking can be: well-conceived, wonderfully cast, smart and funny. I liked Greg, but he already had a producer at the time, and I have never believed in poaching other people's projects.

To this day, if a director brings me a project, I ask about his or her prior producing relationship, and I like to call that producer to clear my involvement. But I ran into Greg eight years after *The Daytrippers*, and things were different. He had spent a lot of time trying to make a film for Miramax, had worked in TV for a while, and was itching to get back into movies. Most importantly for me, he had also left his prior producing partnership.

He brought us *Adventureland*, and Anne and I agreed to produce it on the spot after reading the script. We thought it was incredibly fresh, but once we started speaking to agents and executives about it, we discovered something that our own agents had never told us. We learned that the script had previously been shopped everywhere, which made it harder to get the movie made. But what first looked like a script that was ready to go was actually something that needed to be reinvented. When we sat down with Greg and dug into the script, we immediately started recognizing ways to make it richer.

Adventureland was always a period piece, but the reality of the time did not initially resonate. It was set around 1980, the era of Ronald Reagan, Iran Contra, corporate downsizing, and the outbreak of AIDS and this feeling among young people that they could no longer trust the authorities. It was important stuff, and though the historical context only made up a few minutes of screen time, we thought it was necessary, and we worked on it for a long time to get it right. Greg strove for emotional truth, but it's not easy to make a film where the characters and their inner lives comes first and where the plot doesn't undermine the audience's faith in the reality of the film. But this was the kind of movie—one that achieves just the right balance of character and story—that I loved most.

We labored to get it exactly right. It took time, but we got there. We were poised to start to send it to agents to lock in some cast members, but then one day, Greg called me and said a guy he knew from TV was producing a feature film comedy with some unknown actors who needed a director. Since it was fully financed and ready to go, it made sense for Greg to do it. He thought it would go straight to video. We all thought it would be good training for the "real" movie we would do next. It was an immensely good thing that Greg went forward with it, too, because the producer guy was Judd Apatow, the unknown talents were Jonah Hill and Michael Cera, and the movie was *Superbad*, which ended up grossing over a hundred million dollars at the U.S. box office.

After *Superbad*, Greg's credibility skyrocketed. Not only did it help that Greg was hot, which enabled us to boost the projected budget by an additional three million, but the extra time before and after *Superbad* gave him some fresh perspective on the *Adventureland* script. He went back and worked another five or six months on a script that everyone else thought was already finished. (When you finish a film, you are often at your best. Your mistakes and successes are in sharper focus, and you know better how to avoid mistakes or create successes next time. Being prolific is a gift, because it starts to feel inevitable: Better work often begets even better work.)

By mid-July, our script was complete; now we just had to finance and cast it. We got Ryan Reynolds as our "star," even though our two "unknown" romantic leads, Jesse Eisenberg (before *The Social Network*) and Kristen Stewart (before *Twilight*), would turn out to be pretty big names themselves. With them in the package and some solid ideas for supporting actors, we could look for financing.

Before we had really shopped the package, we had heard that the post-Weinsteins Miramax had passed on the script, even though we formally hadn't reached out to Miramax with it yet. It's not that surprising, because a good executive will always hunt down a hot project. And you can't cast a film without sending out the screenplay. These early script offerings are a favor in the buzz economy, and sometimes you can use it to your advantage. But here it seemed like the early offering might stop us even before we had a chance to go forward.

I ran into the new chief of Miramax, a British executive named Daniel Battsek, at the premiere party for Angelina Jolie's Daniel Pearl movie, *A Mighty Heart*. The bash took place in an old-time Fifth Avenue social club, all marble and top-shelf alcohol, sushi, and lamb chops, waiters with gloves, and guests decked out in their finest. I was counting the celebrities gathered around Brad and Angelina when Daniel came up and said hello.

"You passed on my script before I had a chance to pitch it," I said. "You're way too efficient."

"Okay," he said, "talk to me about it."

It turned out that the Miramax people had read one of the earlier drafts—before our rewrites and before *Superbad*. Agencies and reps and companies frequently keep submitted drafts in their library. Sometimes, they can say yes when it's the wrong draft—remember Nicole's *Walking and Talking*. But more often than not, if they get hold of an initial draft, it can mess you up. Daniel promised to look at the correct one and invited me to come by his office afterward.

When I went into meet with Daniel, I knew it was going to be very challenging to reintroduce the project. Daniel said it was a great script, but tough to market. But I was prepared for that. A good producer will always think of fifteen different ways to market a film. Not only may some of the ideas actually inspire the marketing team, but real marketers also never want to be outdone by the film's producer. They'll work harder to prove they can do the job better.

The next day, Daniel's team had read the new draft and said they wanted to do the movie. But they were still nervous about committing eight million. It was too great of a risk for any one company, particularly with a cast centered around a couple of unknowns (like Jesse and Kristen). But as long as there were cofinanciers out there, there was room to play. Even as we were in discussion with Miramax, Anne and

I kept sending the script around, and it was gaining heat. Financing is also a lot like casting and setting up a crew: You need a team that has chemistry, and the producers' job is to find it. Although they hadn't yet worked together, we thought the new Miramax would fit well with Sidney Kimmel Entertainment. Both companies exhibited a true love of movies, from smart top executives down to the supporting staff.

You might expect that all film companies are staffed with folks who love film, but it's not always the case. Fortunately, Miramax had Battsek, Keri Putnam (who would go on to become the executive director of Sundance), and a great junior executive named Mike Falbo while Sidney Kimmel had William Horbert as chief of production as well as my old colleague Bingham Ray, whom they had brought on for marketing, and another strong junior executive, Jodi Hildebrand. All of these so-called businesspeople were always aiming for the best movie, not just the most marketable or commercially viable one.

It was already late summer, and we needed *Adventureland* to be a summer movie. It was set in an amusement park, after all. But no theme parks would let us shoot until after Labor Day, as they couldn't afford to cut into their prime business. Once Miramax and Sidney Kimmel Entertainment were committed, we only had seven or eight weeks to prep, which was relatively short, but we had scheduled a thirty-five-day shoot, which meant we had time on the set.

Each day on a movie set entails a thousand decisions, but the scale of the scenes on *Adventureland* made it even more challenging than the average indie film. The longer shooting schedule went a long way. We had the time to organize a hundred extras, with multiple lines of action in the foreground and background. We had the time to make sure the actors were connected; the chemistry between them was strong; and the solid comedic cast, all gifted improvisers, from Jesse Eisenberg to

Saturday Night Live alumni Kristen Wiig and Bill Hader, could riff and keep it real. Even Ryan Reynolds had come out of comedy and was a natural at being natural. And the time we had on set helped create the necessary room to play.

In many ways, time is the essence of directing: Greg had the time to find a specific spot on location, block out a scene, and make adjustments, and then the cinematographer Terry Stacey would light it, first roughing it in and then fine-tuning it. The movie became more than the script. The script was good, but a movie should always be more, and this time, we all knew that it was happening. When we were trying to figure out a pivotal scene when Jesse's character kisses his love interest during a huge fireworks show, it took time to find the rhythm and pace of it, but Greg and the team found it. In another scene, where Jesse and Margarita Levieva's characters get stoned on a broken teacup ride, it took time to find the right balance of sweetness and humanity, but we found it. In both of those instances, Greg was able to stay centered on the actors and the characters, despite everything else that might have been going on around him—whether the timing of the fire bursts in the sky or the sunset taking away our light. We had reached a point in the production where everyone on set, from cast to crew, had confidence in what we were doing and felt that it wasn't just a job, but was something special. We had found our groove.

We were also able to book all the actors for the run of the show, so they were there the whole time and could develop a level of camaraderie, like the kids who actually worked in the amusement park. The actors went to video-game arcades and partied together and became friends. And I think that's reflected on screen. And Greg knew that if he wanted to bring an actor in for a scene, even if it wasn't in the script, the person was generally available.

Producing is not just making sure everything scripted is there for the camera. You have to produce an environment and a sense of community. You need to inspire people to have the trust and confidence that they can make more of what they have. And when everyone is aiming for greatness, the atmosphere becomes kind of heady. It's not just a job anymore. Everyone wants to be there, and it's infectious and inspiring.

Talent, attitude, time, and money are the key ingredients to lots of great movies, and in *Adventureland*, we possessed all of them. The budget also allowed us to get what we needed in postproduction. Greg had specified a lot of music in his script. I think there were some forty-five different cues. A period soundtrack was necessary to capture the era. But even though Miramax also wanted it, there wasn't quite the budget for it.

Fortunately, in those days, we had a 10 percent contingency, which means an extra 10 percent of the budget is set aside for things that can go wrong. We took that contingency and allocated the funds to get Greg's wish list of songs by Lou Reed, the Replacements, and the Rolling Stones.

A few years later, production companies and financiers started chipping away at contingency allocations, dropping them from 8 to 5 percent, all the way down to 3.5 percent. That's a very small margin of error. As a consequence, savvy line producers will now inflate other costs or hide them in areas where they're hard to spot, so there is padding in the budget. Then funders started employing people to root those things out. So now the funders are, paradoxically, spending money to avoid spending money.

Because of all these tight financial controls, production is different today. With contingency funds and padding trimmed down to the bone, you have little room to deviate or otherwise play. But prior to 2008, that wasn't the case and the end product benefitted. Today, I don't think a movie made by someone who is not an established auteur would ever get green-lit without the project's having everything already preconceived, particularly if the film stars unknowns. But on *Adventureland*, we were able to figure things out as we went and to find those unforeseeable acts of magic that come out of the spontaneous moment.

After *Adventureland*, I foolishly thought that I had *earned* my place—that I had consistently done enough good work to keep producing in this fashion. I took it for granted that this is how we could make movies going forward: Hire the best crews and top-of-the-line actors, design how you want the production, and avoid piecing together financing from a dozen sources, but have a single financier who is aligned with your goals and doesn't need an immediate return on his investment.

I always believed that independent film was about trying to make the greatest movie. Period. But when the budgets became tighter, the goal became making a movie within the means available. Time (and money) makes for better movies. Every film requires thousands of decisions, and you're moving at such a pace that you can't consider all the repercussions of those choices. So you need a chance to breathe. If you don't have time on your side, you're just shooting what's on the page—the bare minimum—and when something goes wrong (and something always goes wrong), you may have to sacrifice something potentially wonderful. And this doesn't make for great movies.

I love all the films I did after the economic crash of 2008, but the job was no longer to make the best movie, because financiers are not going to give you enough money to do that. And when a distributor buys the film, they're not going to pay enough money for it. And finally, when the film is released, it's not going to make enough ripples in the culture. As the 2000s came to a close, it was clear to me that we were at the end of an era. And it was time for a change.

Chapter 9

Community

At a certain point, living an independent life, you start to recognize how fragile the whole enterprise is. You can't afford to ignore the big picture. And you can't do it alone.

Though technically the word *independent* evokes isolationism, in reality, it's about community. I got my first taste of this in a big way in the early 1990s, when I worked on a project with documentary filmmaker Jill Godmilow. She had always been a fan of the Wooster Group, an experimental theater troupe in New York that featured, most famously, Willem Dafoe and Spalding Gray, but there was another fine actor involved, Ron Vawter. He was dying of AIDS, and he had a one-man show called *Roy Cohn/Jack Smith*, which was basically two monologues of the two gay eponymous characters. Roy Cohn, the famous McCarthy-era lawyer, was known as gay, but spoke in a homophobic way, and Jack Smith was a flamboyant pioneer of performance art. Ron wanted to put this performance on film before he passed away, and he asked Jill to help him get a movie made. Having not been able to make Jill's earlier film *What We Talk About When We Talk About Love*, which was an adaptation of

Raymond Carver stories that initially brought James Schamus and me together as producers, I was not going to let this opportunity pass.

When Jill asked me to help get the money together, I figured we could do it for $100,000. We'd shoot it over three or four days on stage with Ron, with multiple cameras. We figured it wasn't such a big budget, and because Ron was well loved and people wanted to support him and an artistic project, we would be able to find two hundred people who would give us small amounts of money. I started calling people to help out. We got up to $10,000, then $20,000, then $25,000, but it was going to be tough to hit our goal. Then one day, Michael Stipe, the front man for the band R.E.M., called. Having heard about the project through his business partner and filmmaker Jim McKay, Stipe came through with a big chunk of money. The other band members gave, too. Then I cold-called Steven Soderbergh, who had cast Ron in *sex, lies and videotape*, and he too made a pledge. Soon, we were within reach of our goal. It wasn't two hundred people, but it had to be about a hundred. This venture was, of course, well before Kickstarter, but it was definitely a crowd-funded movie. The experience reminded me how important it is to have a partner or a team or community behind you, always encouraging you. Without them, it might well be impossible.

At first, all that a producer worries about is just getting the movies made. Then you start thinking, "Can I actually make a living doing this?" And then, after you've been making movies consistently, you start wondering how to get them seen and resonating with audiences. And then you begin to decide whether you're about making movies as good as they can be or you are just about making money. And finally, you begin to look around, outside yourself, and strive for ways to make the system work better for everyone around you. That is, unless you decide not to, but that's not how my story goes.

That's where I was in 2003, ready to look beyond myself. Eighteen months after I had left my marriage and was finally ready to look for a new relationship, a crisis hit the independent-film industry. Suddenly, I had to switch my focus away from personal concerns and more to the needs of the business. In September of that year, the Motion Picture Association of American (MPAA) forbade the Hollywood studios and their indie subsidiaries from sending out VHS and DVD promo copies to Academy members, critics groups, and guilds. The move was part of a wide-ranging antipiracy campaign—at least that is what the MPAA said it was all about.

Nonetheless, the prohibition was an affront to the indies, which depended on end-of-the-year award-season screeners to get the critical acclaim, attention, and accolades they deserved. In a roundabout way, screeners also helped indie producers obtain overhead deals—which helped pay our daily expenses and development costs—because sending out review copies got our movies out to the people who were influential. Most of my films didn't play in Peoria or break the box-office top ten, but when they arrived in the mailboxes of critics and Academy members, those tastemakers could see that the films were made with a level of quality and artistry. If it weren't for screeners, many of my films that were nominated for Oscars might never have been considered. Even more unfair than the ban itself, no one at the MPAA consulted the indie community about even the idea of a ban. Not only was that unthinking and insensitive, but it felt like a slap in the face. How could we not respond?

So I began to help organize a number of directors to make an appeal. Several prominent directors, including Robert Altman, began to speak out. The Independent Filmmaker Project, which was then a national organization, with main offices in Los Angeles and New York, organized a meeting between Bill Condon and Sean Penn, among others, and long-standing MPAA chief Jack Valenti, who promised to take action. But nothing happened afterward. I felt as if we were getting played.

I then wrote a talking-points memo, which listed all the reasons that the screener ban hurt independent filmmakers, and we distributed it far and wide. It was a solid case. But most people in the indie industry seemed reluctant to join in the struggle, because of MPAA affiliations. Most of our friends at the studio art-house divisions—like Michael Barker and Tom Bernard at Sony Pictures Classics and my former Good Machine partners James Schamus and David Linde, now at Universal's Focus Features—were sympathetic to our crusade against the screener ban, but they couldn't speak out, because of their corporate parents. And because everyone else depended on these companies for overhead and distribution deals, they were afraid to fight, out of fear of hurting their relationships and their careers. We may have been independent in name, but the reality was that we were all dependent on the studios. Later, the only indie mogul who was bold enough to join us was Harvey Weinstein, whose company, Miramax, was owned at the time by MPAA signatory Disney. Even then he did it on paper, not in person.

During the whole flap, I was working on John Waters's film *A Dirty Shame*, and my train rides back and forth between New York and Baltimore gave me more time to think and strategize. One problem we were trying to work through was the division between Independent Filmmaker Project (IFP) East and IFP West. Because of its proximity to Hollywood, the L.A.-based IFP was not willing to make a unified statement against the ban. That was a big difference between the two sides, and it was probably one of the reasons that the organization eventually split into two distinct entities, Film Independent in Los Angeles and IFP in New York.

I soon realized that if we were to make any progress, we would have to file a lawsuit against the MPAA. Nobody wanted to have to resort to legal action, but the interests of the indies were continually being ignored. Through producer Jeffrey Levy-Hinte, who was just as community minded and politically committed as I, but who had a lot more financial resources, we hired the kind of white-shoe, high-prestige law firm that Hollywood would take seriously. A friend of Jeff's, Greg Curtner, was a successful antitrust lawyer, who had worked in the automobile industry and now represents the National Collegiate Athletic Association (NCAA). Now we had game.

From a legal perspective, we were clearly in the right. It came down to the argument that a trade organization, in this case, the MPAA, couldn't dictate policy to its members. The relationship is supposed to work the other way around. And that key argument gave us confidence. But when I looked at how many people the legal case took, and how much energy, time, dialogue, and legal fees, I began to wonder whether organizations could really be the force for change that the industry needed.

The film business attracts a certain kind of maverick personality—I don't think we're a big group of joiners—so even though I was on the board of the IFP, I always doubted whether such support organizations were the most effective way to facilitate change and build the community. For our legal case, we simplified things by making Jeff and me the two key plaintiffs, freeing the lawsuit from the politics of a larger organization. In preparation for the trial, our attorney had drilled us repeatedly on antitrust law, as everything was going to hinge on our ability to tell the story in a manner that would prove the case.

At the court hearing, I was scanning the crowd of onlookers milling about the courtroom when I spotted an attractive, professional-looking woman. (For the New York indie-film scene, if you're not wearing a black T-shirt, you're dressed professionally.) When you're in the same film community for twenty-five years, you figure you know just about everyone. But as I had never seen this woman before, I thought she worked for the other side and I fantasized about having a torrid love affair with an MPAA attorney.

On the stand, I realized that our attorney's questions didn't allow me to address my salient points regarding antitrust law. So I did what I have learned from many great actors. I went off script, speaking freely about how the screener ban would affect me personally. Although it threw our lawyer off, the judge understood what I was doing. As he started laying out questions that signaled he was on our side, I recognized that we were winning the lawsuit. I felt more confident—I was glowing. Then I thought, "Not only are we going to triumph over the MPAA, but this beautiful woman is going to notice me and be impressed with how I won the case. I might have a chance with her . . ."

After I finished my testimony, I went over to Jeff, and surprisingly, the woman was standing next to him. I found out she worked with Jeff at his company Antidote Films. Turns out she had just come in to hear Jeff and had missed my testimony completely. Now I felt doomed; how was I going to impress her? I quickly suggested we all head to lunch afterward at Wo-Hop in Chinatown.

After several months of my pursuing her, we finally started dating. Then we fell in love, and a few years later, we got married. She is now Vanessa Hope, my partner in all things. (Thank you, MPAA. Thank you, indie film community.)

Around the time Vanessa and I got married, in March 2009, the social-media revolution was taking off. I had joined Facebook only a few months before. It felt like an alien planet to me. And I opened a Twitter account on the day before New Year's Eve 2008. Social media would soon change my life and my habits, and all for the better. Finally, I had a more effective way to facilitate change, a way that was more personal and didn't need any official organization or infrastructure to get things done.

As I've noted already, the entertainment business was experiencing a massive transformation, from both a creative and a business perspective. Good movies were not being seen. Good movies were not getting released—and those that did often got paid a fraction of what they previously received from distributors. When you consider the standard U.S. licensing fees for an independent film—which today may be as little as 10 percent of its negative costs, down from 30 percent ten years ago and 50 percent twenty years ago—only very few filmmakers can ever hope to sustain themselves financially.

Although no one had declared it yet, this period of transformation was becoming a war between two models: artistic-centric versus gatekeeper-controlled; capital-intensive versus low-cost; consumers' impulse-driven transactions versus considered choices; and the collaborative efforts of self-empowered creators versus the corporate monolith.

Like most political issues in this country, the battle is often seen along two party lines, like capitalism versus communism or, more appropriately in this case, fascism versus anarchy. We are told that the future of entertainment will either be a system brought about by further media consolidation and the closing of a free and open Internet, or the utter chaos of rampant piracy and intellectual-property theft. But again like most politics in this country, there is a third way, which takes the best of both sides and offers a far stronger alternative—a third way that never gets the consideration it deserves.

Initially, I was reluctant to put myself out on the web. It's hard not to be overwhelmed by all the negative possibilities. As mentioned earlier, part of a producer's job is to anticipate anything that can go wrong. A healthy level of paranoia is good. Unless you have the ability to run dark scenarios rapidly in your head at every juncture, you're not going to be able to prevent those disasters from happening. And when you start thinking about social media, most people over the age of thirty fear a loss of control. They worry that people might come after them, criticize them, and say, "What makes you an expert, anyway?"

In late September 2008, I was asked to deliver a keynote talk at a film-maker's forum for the nonprofit group Film Independent. Distribution executive Mark Gill had recently delivered his "sky-is-falling" speech, which painted the independent-film industry in a desperate way. ("If you decide to make a movie budgeted under ten million on your own tomorrow, you have a ninety-nine-point-nine percent chance of failure," he famously said.) I wanted to counteract that cynicism. Mark had been the chief witness on behalf of the MPAA during the "screener ban" antitrust suit, and it seemed fitting that I once again would counter him. Mark was only addressing the *business* members of the film community—the old, crumbling gatekeepers. But I started thinking about the community of independent creators and how we needed to create a unified front. And it was clear to me that social media could do part of that.

Social media could enable widespread connectivity, help us discover talent, build a network, and get the word out about quality art. This new form of human interaction could create an ongoing conversation with the audience, somewhat akin to what many musicians are doing, engaging regularly with fans, collaborating with them, and transforming them from distant associates to close members of their family. We could finally build a new infrastructure that could unlock new audiences, new models, and new revenue streams. These ideas became a major part of *my* speech, which I called "A Thousand Phoenixes Rising." So once I talked the talk, I had to learn how to walk as they do on social media platforms. I suspected I would get a few blisters along the way.

I had been pondering the need for something akin to Pitchfork Media for the indie-film business at a couple of investor summits. Pitchfork is a Chicago-based, daily Internet publication focusing on independent music offering criticism, commentary, artist interviews, and news. It was the number one influencer for the music-buying public then, even ahead of *Rolling Stone*. Started by a few University of Wisconsin students with a whole lot of attitude, the venture inspired me. Although it is mainstream now, when it launched, it was a bunch of upstarts—the outsider's voice. The film world needed something similar to help audiences discover the cream of the crop. If there are seven thousand independent films being made every year in the United States, and only thirty were being released in theaters, that leaves a whole lot of movies in limbo.

With the help of producer Mike Ryan (who first worked as a location scout for me on *The Ice Storm*), filmmaker Michael Tully, and Corbin Day, a friend with a background in venture capital and a love for indie film, we launched the website HammerToNail.com in a small way at Sundance 2008. The purpose of the site was simply to write about good, under-the-radar movies that often get lost in the festival shuffle and to provide a filter for the core audience, letting them know which under-million-dollar American films were out there. The site would be filmmakers writing about film for people who love film. Suddenly, I had this whole new way of finding out about talented filmmakers.

Up until then, I had always felt that each year, there were only about three or four new directors who would go on to make significant bodies of work. But that year, I discovered eighteen filmmakers whose movies impressed me. This was a seismic shift. Maybe they were always out there and I hadn't had the proper filtering mechanisms to find them, or maybe we were entering a great new moment in independent film. But because of our new website, it became clear to me that there was a tremendous number of talented filmmakers making films that deserved to be seen. This new knowledge was inspiring, but it was also frightening. It made me realize how much work there was to do, how little was getting done, and how the current system and support structure did not serve either the creative community or the indie-film audience.

The issue of net neutrality was also heating up around this time, and I felt that an open Internet seemed like the best opportunity filmmakers had for delivering a truly independent cinema. By maintaining the freedom to put up and pull down what we want, the artist becomes the entrepreneur who can speak directly to his or her audience, and people can vote with their dollars for the culture they want to support. Consequently, at that time I was sending out regular email blasts to people about net neutrality issues (along with blasts on parenting issues to my friends with kids). People kept telling me, "You should collect these things and do something with them." After a year of debating— "To blog or not to blog?"—I finally started my first blog, "Info Wants to Be Free." I meant *free* as in "liberty" (as opposed to a pricing structure).

Simultaneously, I was thinking about new models of self-sufficient indie-film careers and came up with a term to define them: *truly free*. Social media offered the chance to create without following the dictates of a large market, but the ability to reach many niche markets. Being a 100 percent market-based culture, American indie film is perhaps one of the most uncensored national film industries in the world, but consciously or not, we indie creators still self-censor. We write for the market, for what we think will sell, and as a result, up until recently, we limited ourselves in the subjects, forms, and techniques we explore. The Internet promises to free us from the dictates of mass-market creation, so we can create content around any subject matter and any form, and the enterprise could be financially sound, as long as the price point for that content was enough to make a profit, but not too high to scare away consumers. And thus, "Truly Free Film" was born as a second blog.

At the time, my son was around six and I was dismayed by the lack of online material that was cool and enticing to both of us. So he and I picked a name, "Bowl of Noses," based on a drawing that I had done for him that made him laugh, and together we started sourcing content to put on a blog. So all of a sudden I had three blogs—"Info Wants to Be Free," "Truly Free Film," and "Bowl of Noses." But I was not yet engaged with Facebook and Twitter or any other tools that could aid and amplify both discussion and participation.

Contact with strangers is a scary thought, often more so in the imagination than in practice. I struggled to get over it; I was intimidated by the idea of being accessible to mostly everyone I didn't know. I first reached out to my friend and fellow indie producer Christine Vachon to ask her about Facebook. I was already getting too many emails, and I was afraid of what might happen if I had another service that allowed people to talk to me. I had an assistant named Ellie Burrows, who had been at Northwestern University, one of the first schools where Facebook launched, and I remember I was shocked that she had three thousand friends already. The immediate thing that struck me about Facebook (and, later, Twitter) was that it wasn't a social group per se; it was a broadcast platform. Here was a way to immediately reach out to some three thousand people, or more. They may not be tuned in, but you essentially had a cable line directly into these people's homes, phones, and brains.

I asked another new media filmmaker, Lance Weiler, about Twitter and how it was being used, and he, like Christine Vachon before him, gave me the confidence to step in. Despite these communication platforms being completely new and daunting to me, I applied the same core beliefs I always had about film production: that everything you do should be about inspiring and earning both trust and confidence. There's no trick or game about revealing who you are and what you think. And that's not to say you're revealing personal details about what you ate for breakfast or who you were hanging out with, but rather, the simple, real passion you feel for certain things.

Online, like in life, I've always made it a point to go beyond my core conversation of "how to make better movies" and open up the discussion to other concerns along the way: politics, culture, and championing worthy causes. That additional information could help people in deciding whether they really wanted to follow my advice in the first place, along with, hopefully, tipping me off to other things they think I might like. As a result, I started another blog called "The Next Good Idea"; I already had a list titled "Over 100 Ways to Make a Lot of Money" and thought the list would make good fodder for "The Next Good Idea" blog.

After a few months, I was then working on six blogs: "Truly Free Film" (devoted to film practice); "Let's Make Better Films" (focusing on aesthetics and, later, folded into "Hammer to Nail"); "Information Wants to Be Free" (now called "Issues and Actions" and focusing on the general politics and other concerns of the film world); "These Are Those Things" (a curatorial space for things that I like); "The Next Good Idea" (about good ideas); and "Bowl of Noses" (for smart and demanding kids of all ages). My wife, Vanessa, finally pointed out to me that if Freud were writing today, he'd probably point out that having six blogs is obviously insane. His nephew, Edward Bernays, would have pointed out that having six blogs and none of them serving your brand is bad business. I took Vanessa's advice and combined them into one blog, "Hope for Film," whose brand I have appropriated for the title of this book. Both of the Freuds should be pleased.

What did I learn from this sudden burst of online activity? Obviously and most importantly, it broadened my contacts. When you engage with people over the Internet and then you have the opportunity to meet them, there's this crazy phenomenon where you actually recognize them before they introduce themselves. There's a feeling of kinship that's extremely refreshing. When you speak at an event, you're no longer in a room full of strangers. In 2010, during one conference in New York called DIY Days, I remember feeling like I was with a united community. Whether it was folks I hadn't seen face-to-face in thirty years or people I had never physically met, everyone was on the same page.

Then you start to recognize the group problem-solving techniques that the Internet facilitates—the way ideas are fleshed out and people can think out loud without embarrassment. When people get older, I think there's a tendency to be closed off to this sort of open discussion. Older folks want the proof—the endpoint, the final outcome—of whatever new venture you're embarking on. But I never felt this approach was effective. One reason I always wanted partners was to be able to bat ideas around with others. Much to my disappointment, I found that partners like to brainstorm less and less as the company matures, as if keeping it going saps all the energy. My leap into social media brought brainstorming back with a vengeance. Now, my collaborators—brainstorming comrades—didn't need to be my corporate business partners. Without the complications of a financial partnership, we could now make things better together, by proposing hypotheses, fleshing out thoughts, and putting more elements into the stew. It's refreshing and inspiring, and

I can get a hell of a lot more done now if I'm not doing it alone or demanding instantaneous results.

Because of the corporate hierarchy and the way we judge stature and success, most industry professionals operate on an elitist level, and as a result, the conversation can sometimes be very professorial and buttoned up. It doesn't invite dialogue; it's all monologue, ego, or self-justification. Such an attitude is a brick wall. Once I started letting go of that attitude and began putting things out into the world, asking for comments and discussion, phrasing ideas as thoughts rather than answers, it changed the whole discourse. There is too much naval-gazing and self-justification in the world. But if we want to protect and promote ourselves, we need to focus on the community. If creators don't want to help each other, in a few years, they will stop being able to talk about their *work* in their chosen field, and instead, they'll be discussing their *hobbies*. In lectures, I often beg people to do one thing—one simple thing—that I truly believe can change our world: Do at least one thing to help or promote another person and his or her work. That chain of support is the key to a sustainable diverse culture. We must shed the hierarchy that we have imposed upon ourselves. At public events, I am always surprised that audience members don't introduce themselves when asking questions: It would put us all on common ground.

Filmmakers often make the common mistake of thinking they are all in competition with each other. It is not a zero-sum game. When I was just starting out, it took me a long time to realize that when I was applying for a job (as an assistant director or a line producer), the challenge wasn't to beat someone else out for the job, but to find the best fit. Now I try to share what I have learned with others, and their responses, in turn, sharpen my focus. When a friend's business improves, so do my opportunities. I try to introduce the people I like to the people who I know can help them. Sometimes, their success eclipses mine, and that is fantastic. I have had the joy of mentoring many individuals, watching my assistants like Anthony Bregman, Glen Basner, and others rise up the ladder and contribute to the improvement of others' work. Community building is in all of our interests. Helping others rarely hurts anyone, particularly yourself.

Because of my embrace of a more open culture, I now have a highly collaborative atmosphere all around me. On my blogs, there are frequent comments; I'm not trying to be an authority, but I'm more of a facilitator. I can start a conversation, but others give it life. Frankly, I need other people to help me solve problems. Because I am doing a million things at once, the web provides a new way of finding solutions collectively.

My current method of problem solving relies fully on the community. I'll send out questions through Twitter, which spreads the information wide, then repost it on my Facebook pages and on Google+, which produces some additional and more in-depth feedback on Facebook as a result. I next extract that conversation, which becomes an initial blog post jointly written with the comments I've received. After I post the blog, I then tweet about that blog post; the tweet also goes to Facebook and reengages the conversation, and then, hopefully, this feedback loop brings a level of understanding for all of us. It's a group endeavor, and although I may be the instigator, we are all responsible for it. I wouldn't be surprised if friends and followers recognize many of the lines in this book; I've been constantly tweeting and posting them throughout the writing process, looking for sparks and feedback.

In March 2009, the Internet, social media, and my life as an independent producer came together in the most exciting and unexpected way, confirming everything I had been saying in speeches and to friends and collaborators for the previous six months. While surfing the Internet one night, I came across stories of real-life superheroes, ordinary people whose behavior was verging on vigilante activity or who sometimes simply brought groceries to a bedridden person or helped an elderly person get a cat out of a tree. But these heroes did it with a little flair and an awesome costume. I thought, "This is funny."

And I was particularly drawn to this notion that superheroes are these pop-culture representations of masculinity that distance men from their identity. People complain about the tyranny of supermodels on young girls' self-images, but what about a muscle-bound person with superpowers on top of it? How is a boy ever to feel adequate? I became convinced that there was a movie in these thoughts.

I found an article in *Rolling Stone* about these real-life superheroes and soon found a website that was a database of real-life superheroes. When I inquired about the film rights to the article, I discovered that it had been commissioned precisely to become a film property, so the rights were unavailable.

I had always wanted to make a film that could be aptly titled *Taxi Driver in Spandex*, and the *Rolling Stone* article about everyday superheroes was the perfect material to spur such a movie. I wondered, how do you tell a visceral, emotionally truthful tale about someone in tights? Our culture is now obsessed with comic books and heroes, and it felt like basing a movie on everyday superheroes was a way to simultaneously both revel in this obsession and comment on it. I couldn't get the rights to that article, but there were a couple of book proposals on the subject. I knew the clock was ticking; such ideas are not original. Very soon, someone would be attempting to make the type of movie I was dreaming about. If I wanted to be the one to get it done first, I had to move fast.

I was having these ideas around the time that *Watchmen*, a movie adaptation of a comic book, was being released, but I thought the film's budget was diametrically opposed to the aesthetic and themes of the comic book. In the film business, there seldom is a halfway point; once you've committed to a large budget, you have to bring in a broad audience. Consequently, the elements that had made the *Watchmen* comic book so surprising were totally removed from the film. You couldn't truly deliver what-the-fuck moments in a hundred-million-dollar movie; you had to deliver action for everyone. In contrast, real-life superheroes understood the absurdity of their situation. Even though they wanted to be super, they were also in on the joke.

I heard through the grapevine that filmmaker and writer James Gunn had written a script on the real-life superhero phenomenon five years earlier. The script was funny and pulled no punches (and, hence, would be too radical to be produced). James Gunn was renowned for his early work on Troma Entertainment exploitation pics like *Tromeo and Juliet* and went on to write the screenplay for *Scooby-Doo* and to write and direct *Slither*. Maybe his script could be the answer.

Three nights later, I glanced at actor Rainn Wilson's Twitter feed. He was one of the most-followed people, and heck, if everyone else was following him, why shouldn't I? He was funny and sometimes even profound in less than 140 characters. And that night, on March 21, 2009, he tweeted this: "Going out to indie producers w/ @James_ gunn s brilliant new/old script. Like a f'd up low rent watchmen! We'll see . . ."

And I said to myself, "Holy shit, this is that project," and I knew I wanted to make it. I called up Rainn's agent and told her that I wanted to see the script and asked if there was a producer attached. They sent it, and although they had no producer working with them, James and Rainn were not sure they needed one, either. It took me some time to gain their trust. It turned out that I knew one of James's brothers and another guy, who was the brother of the woman James was dating. I reached out to them to get James to call me back. Finally, James and I met and bonded over the belief that the film would only work if it was raw, and embraced a lo-fi aesthetic that the subject was begging for. The key to all of it was emotional truth, something that was defiantly indie and often disproportionate to the size of one's budget.

I didn't yet know what sort of phenomenon James was on the Internet. He had a webisode series on Spike TV, with over ten million hits, called *PG Porn*—"everything you love about porn except the sex." One of his blog posts, "Which superhero would you like to have sex with and why?" had a million hits. Clearly, he was onto something big. (He also has a fondness for weird animals and sushi—maybe that will be his next film.)

There's always been a fairly straightforward way of putting together low-budget indie movies like the one we had in mind. It's not rocket science: You package it with talent that appeals to domestic and international audiences, along with some cast members who bring a sense of discovery. Then you bring the package to international sales companies, which provide you their estimates of how much they think they can sell it to foreign countries. Finally, you bring private equity to it, using a discounted percentage of those estimates. On paper, at least, the method seems fail-safe.

But the foreign-sales model is also corrupted by design. Foreign-sales agents generally earn the same commission rate whether the agents meet their estimates or not. There's no penalty if those numbers aren't accurate. So say you're making a $5 million movie, and the foreign-sales agents estimate you will make $6 million in foreign sales. They take 20 percent of their sales, $1.2 million in this case, and the backers would net just shy of $5 million. But what if foreign sales only hit $5 million? The sales agent still gets $1 million, but then the investor only gets $4 million—not enough to pay for the film. Foreign-sales agents are then incentivized to push their estimates higher, thinking that they'll not only sell the film but also maybe even get more money in return. But, of course, it doesn't always work that way. The same goes for the producer's reps who handle the U.S. sale of a movie. They also work on a commission basis, and they too are incentivized to make the budget higher. Both sides will tell a financier they can do more sales with a higher budget, regardless if they believe they can hit their target. They have nothing to lose, and the higher the budget, the more likely they can sell it for more and thus get a higher amount from their commission. Both sides make money without putting up any risk capital—regardless of a film's success. Everyone but the equity investor is in on the game. The filmmaker gets the movie made, the sales agent gets the commission, the distributor gets their film, but the investor loses their shirt.

When foreign television started to reduce its acquisitions of American movies, foreign buyers could not protect what they had advanced, and they also started to offer less—and sales agents started to miss their estimates. When piracy took over specific territories, and films didn't sell, you couldn't sell movies to those countries, at all. By 2009, there was little blood left in the model, but we managed to make it work for our real-life super-hero film, which we had titled, simply enough, *Super*.

We packaged *Super*, and I brought it to the UK sales company HanWay, which was looking for a unique, comedic project that was aggressive, fresh, and provocative. When submitting projects to any company, you often have to find a way to convey urgency to it. If company reps believe that something new is happening and that the project will do well and will go out into the open marketplace very soon, they might read it fast and even make an offer. Luckily, HanWay's head of acquisitions, Matthew Baker, came to my office and told me what the company wanted. Fortunately, we had just secured Ellen Page (whom buyers saw as hot because of her role in *Juno*). The Toronto International

Film Festival—a good market to launch new projects—was right around the corner. Everything was lining up.

But it's never that easy. I am always reminded how applicable the Zen koan "It takes the entire world to spin for one leaf to fall" is to the art of making movies. So many things have to be in place and contextualized in the right way for a film to get made—even more so, for people to make it well.

The film industry in the United States is entirely market driven, and stars are our core currency. In 2009, the U.S. market for feature-film acquisitions seemed at an all-time low. The perceived value of *Super* was inevitably going to be dictated by its international value. When I mentioned the project to industry folks in passing, they felt we were doomed; neither Rainn nor Ellen were perceived as having any foreign box-office potential. We were fortunate, however, to have a very forward-thinking partner in HanWay. Even though Rainn might not have yet had international sales value, HanWay knew that he was one of the top fifty people followed on Twitter, and that meant something to the company. And it also meant something that James had millions of hits on his webisodes. Social media was making our film happen.

During preproduction and production on the film, we also convinced members of the cast and crew to join the Twitterverse. We had about 50 of our team join a *Super* Twitter list, which other people could follow. About 350 people were following that list as we were shooting. The number wasn't large, but it provided a base, and those people got to know other people, and folks throughout the film world seemed to be inspired by the list. We may have only had a few hundred people following us, but every one of the 50 people on our list had 350 or so more following them, and each of those had their own circle of friends, family, and followers. Transparency, sharing, collaboration—the hallmarks of social media—each give a substantial amount of penetration into the populace. Awareness can be created; it doesn't have to be bought. This is a considerable shift in the way films have been marketed. When you start to recognize that audience aggregation means something, you get a lot closer to the new business model that is starting to emerge in our industries.

Imagine a world where a filmmaker could go to a studio and say, "My team has five million followers. Through crowd-funding, we've done twenty-five thousand preorders for the video that we haven't begun to shoot, and I want to be your partner in the producing and marketing of this movie." How could that not be enticing? And we're almost at that point. This is the beginning of the third way. And you can already see it peeking out from under the horizon. Each day, it grows larger, better, and, perhaps for some, more threatening.

You're already seeing people thinking about how to motivate their followers and friends. The Hollywood studios find social media—and the greater transparency that comes along with it—incredibly terrifying, because it has the potential to create negative buzz for their heavily invested products. Yet I find openness healthy. We police ourselves better than any outside force ever could, provided we feel part of the community and not outside of it. Let people in, and they generally will reward you for it.

Yes, the Internet splinters people into niche partisan groups, but it also leads people to be more invested in the things they hold dear. People need to vote and speak out about the world that they want. I think we need to encourage this sort of behavior. We have been a quiet, dormant populace for far too long. And all of this online discussion helps change that.

Can social media translate into real audience build? Since making *Super*, I am often reminded that the movie didn't exactly set the box office on fire. Some people may be gloating that despite our social-media activities, we still had difficulty putting butts in seats. But our social media on that film remained focused on our first core circle—which was geared primarily to get our movie made and then to get our investors' money back by licensing it to distributors. And we will be able to do that, eventually. We sold the film to IFC Films for $1 million ($750,000 for U.S. rights and $250,000 for Canadian rights) for a period of ten years; we also preserved the right to sell DVDs and digital downloads off our websites.

But after making the distribution deal, we faltered. The marketing of the actual release neglected to focus on social engagement and remained centered on old methods of traditional advertising and press. There should have been wild-posting of our posters all over the cities where our film was playing, and flash mobs of people in superhero costumes on the streets. We needed to create an event around the release of the film, but people didn't feel that level of urgency. We neglected to create a sense of participation or collaboration that is rewarding for an audience.

. Is social-media activity just the domain of the superfan and politically obsessed, or is it something that's more widespread among the general populace? People trust the people they're closest to. That's the great crime in the firing of so many film critics in America over the last few years. Local audiences trusted those local critics; after years of engagement, the critics had developed a relationship with their audience, which came to know when to take something with a grain of salt and when to follow their advice like a close friend. Those critics may blog, but blogging does not have the same authority as when they were the voice of their local community. Today, we have to figure out the alternatives to those critics. Who are our filters? Who are our curators? What can we do to help sprout new ones? I personally find curating a necessary responsibility of producing and participating in film culture, but it's a flag waved by the few. It's a pressing problem that will continue to worsen if we don't act.

I know that if I have a screening for friends and family, I get a more positive reaction than I do from a screening in front of a bunch of strangers. So to extrapolate from that, the more numerous my friends, family, and followers, the more positive reaction to my work—unless I'm slacking on my art, and if I am, I deserve to be thrown out. I don't mind the hordes policing the elites. If that's the cost of the close-knit, bottom-up social-media universe, then I'm all for it.

For the first time, we have the potential to establish a broad middle class of creative individuals who support themselves through their art, aligning and collaborating with specifically defined audiences, and not having to conform to the limited dictates of the mass marketplace and its controllers. We now have the promise of a world that will deliver us better and more diverse work in a manner that is more accessible, collaborative, and participatory. With social media, we can now bring people together like never before. With a new focus on engagement, audience can also become community.

We—creators, entrepreneurs, and audiences—have to choose the type of culture we want and the type of art we want available to us. Do we decide for ourselves whether a work of art is worthwhile, or do we let the corporations decide? Who is our community, and how will we reach one another? We have to choose how we can all best contribute to this new system. And as we act on those choices, we have to get others to decide which content they want, too. Then we all become curators. We can all promote the culture we love, and we can reach out and mobilize others, not acting on impulses but motivated by our own shared knowledge and experience. And we must recognize that having as many others as possible share in that knowledge will make everything better: the culture, the business, and our pleasure in participating in it. We are walking into new territory, and we'd do best to map it out together.

We have to be sure to fortify ourselves for the long haul. And the best way to prepare for that journey is to recognize that it's going to take some time. I remember that on so many occasions, I have gotten excited over the changes I was sure were to come. Some did. Some didn't. Social media has not been the great leveler I first dreamed it to be, just as the foreign-sales model for indie films did not prove to be a long-lasting option for as many filmmakers as I initially had hoped. Most importantly, we need to learn how to keep our stamina. Then one day, the brick wall that we keep running up against will miraculously open and let us through. And it will happen a hell of a lot sooner if we can hit it with the force of many and not just by ourselves. Because of Twitter, Facebook, and my blog, I am attuned to others' struggles, particularly those just starting out, and their tribulations and solutions give me strength to know that if one option does not work, if one practice falls short of what I hoped, I will have the perseverance to keep going. As the famous activist cry goes, "The people, united, will never be defeated."

Chapter 10

Change

I thought I'd live in New York City producing independent films for the rest of my life. Ever since I moved there, I had always seen independent film as my profession and considered it a privilege to be working on movies in a city that I loved. But as the 2010s began, filmmaking essentially became my hobby. I was starting to fill my time with a host of other activities. Whether it was public speaking, writing blog entries, tweeting, communicating with people, or curating movie screenings at the Goldcrest Screening Room or Indie Nights at the Film Society of Lincoln Center, these *other* activities were immensely satisfying. But they weren't generally making me any money, and when they did, it wasn't nearly what producing films had generated at its height.

I didn't consciously pursue these changes, but I never felt that producing should be limited to the creation of films; I always believed that it should also be about helping the film communities sustain themselves. It also helped a lot that I dug doing those things. Even as I watched my income drop over a four- to five-year period, I didn't think I needed to do a complete 180-degree shift. I was still getting good movies made, although there was no denying they were being seen less, having less impact, and were less satisfying, as a result. I was also starting to feel that I wasn't being realistic about the changes that were coming to the industry. Or perhaps how these changes had already arrived.

One of the reasons I love the independent-film world and always enjoy discovering new directors is that I love change. I love having new experiences. Bouncing back and forth at different budget levels, different locations, different subject matter keeps me charged. But I realized that I personally hadn't changed in a long time. I was in a rut. And there is so much about indie film producing that annoys the hell out of me now. Many of the core business concepts that the whole industry is predicated on are antiquated, such as controlling content through centralized distribution, focusing on a mass-market audience, relying on transactional impulse buys, and hoping that audiences can focus their attention on one thing. And we are not taking advantage of all the innovations of the last few years, be it the great drop in cost to create or the ability to target audiences directly, derive hard data around audience engagement, or connect and collaborate with people all around the world.

I might be able to stomach all of that if it wasn't for my sense that so many filmmakers and film industry professionals seem so often to be just in it for themselves. Very few people seem able to think beyond their own individual film. I never get emails that say, "I'd like to help you, Ted." Or "Let's team up and try to tackle this problem." I'm no saint, but I try to offer such help regularly. I do introductions and recommendations. I advise and consult. I have written blog entries dedicated to the need for transparency. I do this, because I need it. We all need support groups. Besides, it's sound business practice. We're all in this together. My success is predicated on other people's success. My knowledge comes from the sharing of mistakes in addition to the successes that I myself and other people have made.

When we formed This is that, we were confident that we could get U.S. distribution slots for two films annually with budgets from $7 to $25 million. This was an ideal budget for many reasons, not the least of which was it afforded a salary you could run a company on. A typical producer's salary is somewhere between 3 and 5 percent of the budget (albeit often with a cap on that to limit how much in total you can make), but people often mistake that fee as an annual salary. The reality is, you are working three to five years on a project, sometimes far longer. The $7–$25 million film was still called low budget by the mainstream industry back when we formed the company. But these films actually had midsized budgets—low enough that you could take creative risks, but high enough that you could compete at the Academy Awards if you delivered the goods. Then, as some distributors folded, the cost of marketing continued to rise, fewer films were released, and the number of available distribution slots for those midsized outside productions shifted to one per year and then to one per two years. Now I'd say an independent producer couldn't make that $7–$25 million movie more than once every three to five years. If we weren't making the larger films, it also became difficult to justify the smaller films, because our fees couldn't cover our overhead.

So much of what we built This is that on was the idea of a cooperative effort. When we had overhead deals, we could front the rent for a larger office space and then sublease to other producers. It not only gave us a better location, but also gave us a collaborative atmosphere to work in. But after the economic collapse, tenants withdrew, and all of a sudden, we were paying full freight for an office space we couldn't afford.

We experimented for a while with a virtual office, doing meetings in coffee shops and bars and working out of our kitchens. But the month after we had both the number one film at the U.S. box office

(Anne Carey's production of *The American*) and the first film sale at the Toronto International Film Festival (James Gunn's film *Super*, which Miranda Bailey and I produced), we shut down This is that. Despite those triumphs, it became clear to us that the business no longer made sense. Even if *The American* was a box-office hit, Anne had worked on it for twelve years and cut the company's producing fee by two-thirds to make it happen.

So if I did not believe there was a business model to pursue these bigger films, I thought I'd focus on the smaller films while the world changed, and then see where we were. But the situation didn't improve. The downturn lasted more than three years. And the indie world wasn't changing for the better; it actually got harder to finance or sell those films. And yet, it was becoming easier, at least on a technical level, to make interesting movies on increasingly smaller budgets.

The optimist in me believed that both the indie-film culture and the indie business would bounce back, that this was just a blip caused by the economic crisis and that people (and the industry) would again hunger for quality tales told well. So I set myself a three-year goal of trying to make five films, regardless of budget, provided at least two had a budget of at least three million dollars so that I could earn enough to support myself and an assistant. I achieved this goal, with *Super* and *Dark Horse* hitting the "high" budget marks. And then there was *Collaborator* and the movies under a million—the critics' darlings *Martha Marcy May Marlene* and *Starlet*. We also financed a sixth film, *The Side Effect*, but it was never shot (an experience I never dreamed I would have and never want to go through again). But the challenge for those microbudget films was how to earn a living while doing them, because they generally lack any up-front fees for the producer. I realized I had set up my life as something that I could no longer afford. I had a family. I had a house and mortgage. I had to pay for health insurance. Sure, I was still making good movies happen, but was that enough?

Unfortunately, those low-budget films left me emotionally, creatively, professionally, and financially wanting. It wasn't like producing *The Ice Storm* or *21 Grams*, films that had the budget to deliver the fullest of visions. Or even *Adventureland* and *The Savages*. Although these movies didn't feel luxurious at the time, we still never had to compromise on them and they had significant promotional budgets behind them. Or *Happiness* and *In the Bedroom*, films that—thanks to the influence of critics at the time—had much greater penetration into the cultural landscape than their budgets would have predicted. Making some kind of impact is one of the reasons I love to make movies, after all. When good films don't get seen, something is wrong. So I looked back at the prior three years and thought, "Wait a second, this isn't making me happy. My investment of labor and emotion should give back more. I want more from all this."

I also had to come to terms with my dissatisfaction with just helping get good movies made. I wanted to make great movies—those that couldn't be ignored. And I started to wonder if maybe I could generate more movies, of a more interesting nature, if I didn't have to preserve my own hand in their day-to-day making.

Back in 2010, I posted on my blog a list of seventy-five things that I thought the film industry could do to make itself better (see Appendix, where this list has since been updated and expanded). But little happened as a result. I had hoped that my post might spark a fire among other filmmakers. I couldn't be the only person in the industry who realized how screwed up everything was and how, by working together, we could build it better.

But there were no concentrated efforts to figure out ways to allow filmmakers to retain the licensing rights, and the resulting financial upside (if ever), to their films (if filmmakers are not going to be paid up front, it should be common practice to at least give them a reasonable hope of future payment); to connect with audiences in a deeper, more sustainable way; or to ultimately move to a more prolific level of production. (And there still hasn't been any mobilization on these issues. We still don't share information or work together, though I hope that this will change someday.) I did work with another filmmaker, Jon Reiss, to design a new model to help integrate audience-building and engagement, as well entrepreneurial practices, into a filmmaker's toolkit. Unfortunately, we couldn't get much traction with it. The IFP in New York embraced a small part of the plan, and Jon has been running that minilab ever since, with positive results, but it wasn't the massive shift we were hoping to launch.

Without a business model fitted for the times we are living in— one that allows for filmmakers to have a more sustainable living and for investors to receive risk-appropriate returns—budgets will continue to shrink, which has a profound effect on the types of stories that are told, and how they're being realized. When microbudget movies become the majority of what indie film is, and they're less appealing to traditional distributors, then our cultural institutions must take a real hand in audience building and aggregation, film appreciation, the marketing and distribution of artist's work, and, ultimately, the protection of artist's rights. And that is ultimately why I came around to take on even more responsibilities as the executive director of the San Francisco Film Society, working in a city that I didn't really know, in a job I had never done before or had even imagined I wanted. If I wasn't going to try to fix the system, who would?

It started like this: One day in the early spring of 2012, when I was on my way to an IFP board meeting at HBO, I got a call from producer Jen

Chaiken from the San Francisco Film Society. I thought she wanted to talk about San Francisco's film programs and how I could help.

But she actually wanted to know if I wanted a job. It was the top post, which had recently been left empty after their former executive director Bingham Ray tragically died from a stroke at Sundance 2012. One of the many great things about Bingham was his tremendous enthusiasm for film. You'd think that everyone in the film business would have that sense of excitement, but it's actually rare. He was also a rabble-rouser. He loved to fuck things up—and in a positive way. Very few people have a true rock-and-roll spirit—that sense of "Let's cause some trouble," said with a wink. Bingham inspired me. And also being born with an inherent suspicion of authority and order, I definitely felt like I was a kindred spirit and relished the idea of carrying his torch.

I had never thought about shifting careers so dramatically. But when it happened, I could not resist the opportunity. A few weeks before I got that call, I had already planned a trip west. Spring break was coming up, and I had a lecture scheduled in Los Angeles. I decided to go with my son and drive up the Pacific Coast Highway. Twenty minutes out of San Francisco, finally through the fog and winding cliff-side roads of Big Sur, I heard my cell phone ring. The Film Society wanted to know if I would come in and talk about the future of film and what an organization like theirs could do to help. By this time, I was used to such "consultancy" calls and didn't think much of it. I was happy to share my thoughts, and much to the caller's surprise, I was just twenty minutes away.

When I arrived in the Presidio, I parked my car, hopped out, and saw a twenty-dollar bill lying in the mud. Thinking it was a good sign, I wiped off the mud, pocketed the money, and proceeded to the meeting. When I sat down with everyone, it quickly became apparent that this was no ordinary consultation. Sitting around me was the society's search committee (Melanie Blum, the interim executive director; Pat McBaine, board president; Howard Rothman, a LucasFilm executive; Marc Ruskin, a web entrepreneur; and Jen Chaiken, a producer). They asked me what they could do to make their organization more relevant. I hadn't fully thought it out, so my response came from my heart. I told them that to call yourself a film society and just screen movies at your festival was irresponsible; you also needed to try to improve the system. There was a huge need, and this was an opportunity to fill it.

Meeting those people also got me thinking about the culture of the Bay Area. It felt like a community to me, and a community that was very much concerned about the independent film business and finding innovative, even disruptive, ways to hasten change. Only one of the people at the table that day was actually a filmmaker, but I felt that they all cared deeply about film and wanted to do something about it. They suggested that they had the funds and labor to help make changes in the industry and culture of film. "Wow," I thought. "Wealth, labor, commitment, community, and mission—not to mention access to the tech world and a real entrepreneurial spirit." It's what I was always looking for; San Francisco seemed to have it all.

But I should have seen the signs that all the stars were not necessarily aligned. Perhaps I shouldn't have taken that twenty-dollar bill, after all. At the time, I took it as good fortune, but now I wonder if I should have paid more attention to the fact that it was muddy and wet and only twenty dollars.

After I realized they were offering me a job, I grew concerned that the organization wasn't attuned to the needs of the times, so I put together a list of forty things that I thought needed to be done. I told the group I wouldn't take the position unless the society committed to the recommendations as a plan. The members said they were on board. But it worried me that the organization had significant debt. I was told not to worry about it, that "this was how we've always operated; the board always comes through." And I was told that if I proved myself, they would find more money for my projects.

But I quickly learned that the debt was one barrier to receiving the necessary financial support and the ability to move forward. Without cash reserves, you're constantly wondering if you might have to let people go, because you don't have payroll. You have to plan for the worst, not dream of building the best. Nor do you have the resources to advance anything. Why hadn't they ever built a financial reserve for the organization? The Film Society was fifty-seven years old, many members had been on the board for a long time, and the maintenance of a financial reserve seemed to make common sense, but to them it was my problem and not theirs. When I started complaining to friends and seeking advice, everyone said, "Welcome to the nonprofit world."

I believe there are two types of producers and two types of directors: the producer who is the general and executes the director's orders and the producer who is a collaborator and strives to make the best movie possible along with the director. The directors, in turn, either want to give orders (dictators) or want to hear suggestions (collaborators). In corporate culture, you often hear about two types of CEOs: the builder armed with a vision for the future and the fixer who comes in and makes what is broken strong again. What soon became clear to me was that the organization needed a fixer to plug the leaks and buttress the foundation, not a builder looking to launch some solutions to what was ailing our industry.

The film society board members wanted me to come up with a way to generate some significant revenue: either a seven-figure revenue stream or several six-figure revenue streams. The organization needed over two million dollars to get itself out of the hole and build up reasonable reserves. Yet they also expected me to do it with no money to fund these initiatives. No one was even offering any substantial help, either. In fact, it was quite the opposite; they wanted me to continue concentrating on the same programs they had been doing for the previous fifty-seven years and then, in my spare time, find solutions to the cash-flow issues. But I had big goals that needed focus and commitment. I accepted the obvious responsibilities, but in addition to bringing in greater efficiencies and elevating the existing three programs (education, exhibition, and filmmaking services), I also wanted to instigate a forth program, entrepreneurial innovation. I felt that this approach was necessary to both preserve and advance film culture.

I needed more people to achieve my goal. The board members told me they wanted me to bring in a real "A team" and told me not to worry about how to pay the new hires' salaries. But each time I tried to make a hire, we didn't have the financials to support it. As a newbie to the nonprofit world, I was faced with the bracing reality. There was no money to grow, despite what I felt had been understood on accepting the job, and the priority was now going to be about getting the organization out of debt.

How do you sustain legacy programs that the organization has been identified with, while introducing innovation and embracing risk? At the San Francisco Film Society, it seemed we were fortunate in that I had secured a strategic planning grant from the Hewlett Foundation, and as I met with different consultants to help us with it, I kept hearing the same thing, "I've worked with organizations that have tried to do this before, and it usually ends in one of two ways: either your board quits or you get fired."

Under the leadership of the film society's Graham Leggat, who was executive director before Bingham, the San Francisco Film Society launched a period of extraordinary growth; when Graham died in 2011 and Bingham took over, he learned that this growth and love came with considerable debt, with no clear way out of it. Perhaps because they were so enamored with Graham, the board members did not realize that the organization had been spending money it didn't actually have. When they woke up to it, they were a million dollars in debt. One of the board members bailed the society out, and the board then recruited Bingham to guide the group forward. But when Bingham also died, the organization was left with all these great programs it had built up, significant debt, and the trauma of losing its two chiefs.

So my challenge wasn't just to create revenue without spending any money, but was also to work with people who were devastated by the past but who were also defined by, and devoted to, it—to one executive director they adored and another who hadn't really gotten started. No one helped the staff cope with these losses. In addition to these wounds, 40 percent of the team was fired by either Bingham or the interim director Melanie Blum, a decision that might have made sense financially, but shook everyone still further. Despite the staff cuts, programs weren't cut. As a result, there was still as much, if not more, to do, and with little to no increase in compensation. Sure, the staff members were still incredibly devoted to the mission of the film society, but they were also undergoing serious posttraumatic stress disorder.

Granted, I went out to San Francisco knowing that running an organization would not be just about building a new foundation for film culture. I would have to spend time doing the housekeeping too. But I quickly discovered that I needed to spend 85 percent of my time sweeping up dust and maintaining programs that I didn't think ultimately could be sustained without drastic change. The San Francisco Film Society's youth education and artists-in-resident programs, its filmmaker grants, and its spring festival—those are really good things. But if you want to have an organization that has a national impact, not just a local one, you have to put together an equal number of activities and services that are innovative and different from what other organizations do. Nearly every city has a film festival nowadays. The Bay Area itself has around eighty. If you're trying to build audiences and financial support, you have to do new things, but how could I without the staff and the funds?

It's funny, because when I was producing movies, I rarely had the funding in place when I took on a project. In film production, I always felt that hard work, strong leadership, an eye for innovation, commitment, and generosity all move projects forward. Couldn't it be the same in the world of nonprofit film societies? In movie producing, at least you have the advantage that every movie is a new project and the excitement that comes along with that. With an organization, however, you're bound to the programs that it has long been known for, which is never as thrilling as the shiny and new.

From the very beginning, everyone told me to focus on the film society's big event, the San Francisco International Film Festival, because it had always determined everything. "Just make it work. Don't reinvent it," they'd say. We did make some small changes to the festival, moving it into the new millennium: In order to bring more people to the website, we made online ticketing cheaper than buying in person; we gently raised the ticket prices and no one complained; we reduced the massive number of films a bit; and we axed a heavy and costly print catalog. Additionally, we had our most successful educational program ever at that year's festival. It all clearly added up to something. Our main focus, though, had to be on the festival gala, which is the organization's biggest fundraiser.

Putting the gala together is a lot like casting a movie, but without the benefit of knowing you'll have a movie at the end of the day to cheer for. The challenge is that the festival takes place in April-May, which is months away from award season. Usually, you can get stars for these types of events because the people are chasing awards, and the award season takes place in the fall and winter build-up to the Academy Awards. But the San Francisco Film Society gala is held at the wrong time to lure stars. As much as celebrities like to be honored, they also find honors that are unconnected to their films a little unseemly. So it's always a challenge to find celebrities who have the time to take part when it's not tied to award season.

Fortunately, soon after arriving I discovered that the fifty-year-old organization had never recognized a favorite filmmaker of mine, Philip Kaufman, an intellectual, highly regarded filmmaker who makes complex movies that are well received (*The Right Stuff*) and playful with form (*The Unbearable Lightness of Being*). On top of that, Philip was committed to living and working in the Bay Area. He had even shot his 2002 HBO film *Hemingway & Gellhorn* in the area, although it was set in Cuba. It was time to honor one of the city's favorites. With Kaufman locked, we were able to get Eric Roth (*The Insider*, *Munich*) for our screenwriter tribute and Harrison Ford as our actor honoree. As much as I was happy to honor these movie talents, the reaction I got from Hollywood agents and others in the industry was that we were putting on a show of fluff, something the local swells do just for themselves. Granted, the event kept the organization afloat, but the black tie and high-ticket prices made it feel elitist and superficial. It was lacking a community feel or a bigger message.

Still, all that money can lead to good. One of the wonderful things about the film society is that it gives away over one million dollars in grants and services to filmmakers, thanks to a donation from the

Kenneth Rainin Foundation. When filmmakers Ryan Coogler (*Fruitvale Station*) and Aurora Guerrero (*Mosquita y Mari*) spoke that night about how the funds enabled them to get their films made and seen, it was the highlight of the evening. We all love Indiana Jones, but getting quality films made always offers a unique thrill. Showing the impact the organization had on artists' lives was a new addition to the gala, and I believe it made the night a more fulfilling experience. And despite the value I put on such a spotlight, one of the board members responsible for organizing the event scoffed at the idea of having then unknown first-time filmmakers take center stage—the disconnect between our priorities was clear.

But the coup de grace of the entire festival was when Steven Soderbergh came to town. It meant a great deal to me, because even though I did not know him well, Steven had previously come through for me at different points in my career. And his speech wasn't just on the state of the industry, but it became his "retirement" speech. It was read and talked about all over the world. It became the bookend for film critic A. O. Scott's *New York Times* piece on the year in film. Steven's candor about how Hollywood no longer supports the art of cinema had shaken the industry to its core. For all the writing I had done and efforts I had taken to get people to wake up, Soderbergh's single speech about how it no longer made sense for him to make movies had considerably more impact.

That speech helped contextualize a program I had been passionately working on. The program, A2E (Artists to Entrepreneur), took place at the Kabuki Hotel during the festival. It was a unique workshop, where we had twelve filmmaking teams, twelve established film-distribution platforms, eight distribution consultants, and fifteen media tech start-up companies, all looking at new ways to distribute films and cultivate new audiences. It was the sort of thing I had wanted to launch for a long time, going back to the programs Jon Reiss and I had been pitching years earlier. Finally, now was my chance to build it.

A2E had grown out of my frustration with panels, which always devolved into self-promotion, and a general lack of transparency and openness in the industry. When I stepped into social media, I was motivated by the idea that if someone like me, a veteran of the business, started speaking openly and honestly, others would follow suit. I spoke up, on Twitter and in blogs and lectures, but few seemed to really join me. So I thought that if we could bring together a group of diverse stakeholders, involved at different parts of the process, and all were willing to share their experiences, hopes, and needs, we could develop new strategies and best practices for a way forward.

The focus of A2E was to take a business-minded approach to the art of storytelling and to teach entrepreneurial skills and offer other training to artists. If we could encourage filmmakers to act as owners-operators and not just as "crazy artists," perhaps we could encourage them to take responsibility for the life cycle of their work, from conception to theatrical release to its distribution on ancillary platforms (like video on demand [VOD] and DVD) to its eventual place in a company's film catalog. And then we could make these whole new paradigms less intimidating. My ultimate goal was to conduct several different programs under A2E, to make it an ongoing, multifaceted educational curriculum composed of multiple workshops. The first workshop was called A2E OnRamp: Direct Distribution. And it was exciting to see all these diverse constituencies meeting as equals and speaking openly. We had filmmakers about to shoot, in postproduction, or playing the festival circuit paired up with distribution and marketing strategists or meeting one-on-one with top digital distribution platforms, business-to-consumer platforms, and the hardware and software companies that were an integral part of the delivery process.

I knew a program like A2E wasn't something my board or my staff was interested in tackling. No one else seemed to shared my belief that the most important role of the film society was to be a leader of change. But the board wasn't going to give me money to launch A2E, even though I was confident that I'd find sponsors for it and this was precisely the sort of thing that, once launched, I could use to bring in more sponsors. No one wanted to look ahead. For the film society, other nonprofits, and even the film industry itself, change is often seen as too risky, the kind of thing people lose their jobs over.

I believed that our nonprofit could be a force for change; this was why I had traveled to San Francisco in the first place. Ironically, I had to turn to Australia to help make this vision happen. Screen Australia has a highly competitive intern program that sends experienced producers to apprentice with veteran filmmakers abroad. I had approached the organization about having a producer collaborate with me on building new models for the independent-film business. One applicant, Alicia Brown, was well versed in all aspects of the industry, and her enthusiasm for exploring new methods of film distribution matched my own, so Screen Australia and I awarded her the opportunity to come join us in San Francisco. It's a long way to travel, but we could not have launched A2E, let alone delivered it at such a high level without her and Screen Australia's participation.

In the end, A2E attracted over twenty new sponsors, mostly from the tech sector that the San Francisco Film Society had not yet cultivated. We forged alliances with all the other top film-support organizations, such as IFP, Film Independent, Sundance, and Cinereach, to put together an impressive group of filmmaker participants. A2E even returned a significant profit to the organization. And like many innovative endeavors, support for it came from outside the organization itself. When we look at all the changes that the industry needs, it's hard to believe that any of those changes will come from within. Look at all the companies that have hugely affected the film business: Kickstarter, Indiegogo, YouTube, Vimeo, and Netflix—all of them started as outsiders.

One filmmaker I asked to participate in the workshop, Adam Collis, had made a great short film in the 1990s, *'Mad Boy,' I'll Blow Your Blues Away. Be Mine.* After this initial success, he made a studio film called *Sunset Strip*, which was produced by the legendary Art Linson (*Fight Club*), but after the studio stepped in and took over the movie, he grew discouraged and left the industry. Adam then decided to get an MBA, and years later, we reconnected after he began teaching at Arizona University, where he brought me in to conduct master classes on film producing. I knew how committed he was to trying new things, and I wanted some films at A2E that were in the process of getting made, and he had been developing a project called *Car Dogs* about used-car salesmen. So I asked Adam to present his business-school dissertation, which was about why independent filmmakers should spend their own marketing dollars on their film. And at the end of the workshop, I asked him to pitch *Car Dogs* to the room, applying what he had learned from A2E. Adam is a very high-energy guy. He's a showman and a salesman. Adam put together an excellent PowerPoint presentation and a trailer, with no footage shot but instead composed of clips from other movies. He electrified the room. If he were pitching a 1972 Thunderbird, he would have sold it twelve times over that day.

Many filmmakers find it difficult to wrap their heads around new strategies like raising money for marketing and production, or shifting from a single product focus (the film) to one of relationships (the need for engagement around everything they generate). Most filmmakers don't want to think about how they are going to be responsible for releasing and marketing their films, let alone building their audiences, because the filmmakers still remember movies like *The Brothers McMullen*, which was made incredibly cheaply, sold to a distributor, and earned significant box-office business, launching Eddie Burns's career. It's funny how our big successes can later also present barriers for us and others. Adam is different, though. He is committed to these new initiatives, and he was one of many filmmakers who found the confidence and connections out of A2E to move forward. (He actually made *Car Dogs* later that year, with actors George Lopez and Oscar winner Octavia Spencer.) Sitting inside those Kabuki conference rooms, we felt as if we were catching the first performance of the Sex Pistols or the Velvet Underground. There weren't many of us, but we were inspired so much that we might just go on to make a new sound, or the cinematic equivalent. We knew we were on the brink of something exciting, something that was bigger than our own individual movies, something that could have an impact on society at large. Maybe filmmakers would start to take on full responsibility for their work, budgeting the complete process through the release of their movie and not just to festival delivery.

Only four or so out of the twenty-six film society board members came to the event. When these few who did come saw what I had been talking about all along, they became enthusiastic. They got it. Not only did they see the number of sponsors A2E brought in, the money it made, and the national press it earned, but they also recognized how the San Francisco Film Society was helping to move the culture and business of film forward. And my board president, Pat McBaine, said, "Now's the moment, Ted. This is when you can make your asks and get the board to step up."

We were supposed to have a board retreat immediately after the festival, which was really a five-hour meeting where I was to put together my first-ever PowerPoint presentation. But our festival ended in the beginning of May, when many of the members took off for their summer holidays. The dates for the retreat kept getting pushed back week after week until we found ourselves in mid-July. It wasn't ideal. Too much time had passed since the festival, and it would be difficult to capitalize on the energy that we had all felt at the A2E workshop.

After the festival, the first thing I did was try to solve the organization's cash-flow issue. We were barely getting by. Clearly, we would be a better organization if we didn't have to sweat it out every month worrying if we would meet payroll. A surplus allows you to be proactive. So I made a request: $250,000 to help us function smoothly—not as a gift but as a loan—something to allow us to weather the storm. It was less than our monthly burn, but enough to smooth out the rough edges. But one board member decided to make this request a sign of crisis. "No," I said, "I'm just saying a $250,000 loan will make us stronger." I had heard stories about boards being political hothouses where people assert power, but I didn't believe that to be the case in San Francisco. I was wrong. In that budget meeting, key players were absent, and some of the few who were there did not understand the cash-flow issues. Even though our financial director, Keith Cowling, and I demonstrated that we could be cash positive by year's end, the suggestion that we might have cash-flow concerns created fissures inside the board—fissures that would later turn into a full-fledged earthquake.

For the next six weeks, everything I tried to do was getting blocked. We needed to hire another staff member, but she required fifteen hundred dollars more than we budgeted: blocked. Consequently, our staff had to expand its workload even further for eight weeks until we found an appropriate person. Morale suffered because things weren't getting done. By the time the board retreat was going to happen, I had twenty-two issues that were being stalled. I was being micromanaged. My head was starting to pop.

At the retreat, armed with that tool of corporate-speak known as the PowerPoint, I presented my case. I talked about how the festival had gone well. I also spoke about the challenge of creating revenue without additional financial investment, and how I'd done precisely that, delivering the A2E program, which I believed could eventually generate a high six figures for the organization. I proposed a fall celebration that would solve the time disconnect between our original awards gala and the industry's major awards events, elevate the organization's Hollywood profile, and bring in significant sponsorship.

I also unveiled what I felt was my most important endeavor, a new funding initiative, which I called FIX—both an acronym for Film Innovation eXchange and a pun for what was needed. The endeavor would be based on investor subscriptions and funding forums that would capitalize on the organization's recent success at supporting Sundance prize-winners like *Fruitvale Station* (as well as my own track record). I had started working on this a year before I came to the film society and finally was ready to unveil it. We had a funder in place willing to underwrite the start-up costs, and I demonstrated that the program would generate hundreds of thousands of dollars of revenue for the film society. How could society members not jump on board? I had also put together a corporate giving program and brought in three new private sponsors for new funds. "This all rocks," I thought. Innovation was finally going to come to the film industry, and San Francisco was going to be recognized for its contributions to the film world.

But when I left the room, I'm told, people ended up squabbling over whether we had a cash-flow problem and whether my explorations into finding new ways to fund and distribute movies was a violation of the organization's core mission. Afterward, one new board member promptly resigned. Clearly, our house was not in order.

In its executive session, the board decided to block most of my initiatives. I was told yes on some things, and then I was told that the yes was not really a yes. I knew that nonprofits depend on their boards for their livelihood and boards are, by their nature, cautious, but still, I was surprised. I thought we had proven ourselves. I thought I had demonstrated that I had done exactly what I had initially told them I set out to do.

From the time the society first approached me about the job, I thought, here's a small organization, at least as it pertains to the national film culture. It has room to grow. It has a budget of seven million, which is one-tenth the size of something like Sundance. It's got a small staff and a giant board. It could change. San Francisco is a city of innovation, capital, and culture, so if change is going to happen, it's going to happen in the Bay Area. But I discovered that while the desire to fix the film industry has become a greater passion for me, it's not what most other film professionals, film societies, and film cultural organizations care most about. They love movies, and great movies still get made, so what do they have to worry about? The situation I was in felt eerily similar to me. When I was in the business of making films, I wanted to do it for the art. When I was working at the film society, whose business is preserving that art, I was more interested in advancing the art of the business. I was reminded of Sam Goldwyn's question—are you in it for the art or the business?—and the contradictions inherent in this industry of passion thundered loudly in my head.

Over the months that followed, the board and I struggled to find a common agenda. The staff and I developed proposals for the programs I wanted to launch. A few of the board members, most significantly the outgoing board president, Pat McBaine, recognized how transformative FIX, my funding initiative, could be for the film society. But it was precious to me, and its success would hinge on me. Success would require that I bring in many of my past investors. I only wanted to do it if the organization was 100 percent behind it. As much as Pat and the new board president, David Winton, tried to assure me they were committed to it, I wasn't convinced. There was just too much opposition within the organization.

Someone once told me if your spouse consistently chastises you for not putting the toothpaste cap back on, you know the relationship is over. We all need to overlook the small stuff. But the board's lack of support was becoming difficult in a big way.

At the end of the summer, I traveled back to New York to spend time with my son. He was thirteen. And it was the first year that I had ever spent apart from him, living on the opposite coast. When he was born, fatherhood helped me to recognize that passion and sincerity were necessary aspects of all my endeavors. He was now in full-blown puberty, and like all of us at that age, he experienced some unique challenges. He had learned to be passionate about his art, and it made me reflect back on my own. Was I being sincere with myself? Where were my priorities? Was it to keep my job, or was it to do what I came out to do in San Francisco—advance film culture?

When I returned to the film society, after a stopover at the Toronto International Film Festival, I spoke openly to the board about my ongoing challenges with the organization. Most everyone tried to find a way to make things work, but it became clearer to me that our priorities were not aligned. I finally chose to resign. Pat and David would not accept my resignation and asked me to give them conditions on which I would remain. The next morning, I offered them a list of twenty-seven things I felt should change with the organization. Some of these they wanted to deal with, but they would not accept entrepreneurial innovation as something just as important as exhibition, education, and filmmaker services. I soon made my resignation final, although I would finish out the year to help with the transition to a new executive director. I felt terrible that the team would have to undergo yet another major shift, although at least the curse was lifted. I had not died in office as my two predecessors had. But the experience left me disappointed, reminding me of times in the past when, while I was making films, trying to be a good person and a good collaborator, and maintaining a positive disposition, I would come face-to-face with backhanded, obstructive, stubborn, and just plain mean-spirited people. It's a struggle to maintain your youthful enthusiasm for this business after such letdowns, but keeping your spirit up is also one of the most important facets of surviving. I couldn't give up. But the only way to facilitate change, I now believed, was either through a for-profit or as a start-up.

Around this time, I started using the phrase *a complete systems reboot* to describe what was needed for the film industry. Unless this happened, we were fated to stay mired in an outdated and unsustainable model. In the 1990s, two key tactics of independent producers were to make movies for underserved audiences and to differentiate ourselves in the marketplace. Independent film used to be a business of singles, not home runs—where a producer aimed for a million-dollar box-office gross on a two hundred thousand spend. This approach allowed directors to experiment and take real risks in both form and content. And it worked because there were more newspaper film critics, art-house theaters, and foreign sales. But then *Pulp Fiction* exploded on the scene, and independent filmmaking became the business of profit margins rather than the underserved audience. You now had to make movies for everyone (be it *Little Miss Sunshine*, *Juno*, or *Crouching Tiger, Hidden Dragon*). And those movies cost a lot to market. Then along comes the Internet, giving us the opportunity to truly target audiences, and here we are full circle. Now you can make movies for those niche audiences again.

And this is essential, because it's folly to think you can still make movies for everyone, using less and less money—unless you're making low-budget horror films, that is. The producers of the *Paranormal Activity* series figured this out. They can make a movie for under three million dollars, a studio will market it for around ten million, and the movie makes a clear and specific promise to a mass audience: "This will scare you." But for all those other kinds of movies, it's time to think about going after the easy-to-find underserved audiences, not unlike the way we used to target communities with the movies of the New Queer Cinema or the Black New Wave.

We also need to shift the terms of our industry. Instead of thinking of ourselves as media makers who want to employ new technologies to distribute and market our work, maybe we should align ourselves with technologists (or at least technology collaborators) who want to use the existing media to make our work flourish. It's a fundamentally different way of structuring things, but it is based on the dictates of our time. As opposed to "I made a great story; I want people to come to it," it's more like, "This is where everyone is gathered; let me give them a great story that will encourage them to stay together." So while working with my wife Vanessa on her movie *All Eyes and Ears*, I took a new approach. Although people might still call the film a documentary, we consider it more akin to a "story world." Yes, it's a feature film, but it's also composed of twenty other short films. And this is how we've designed it, so that different people can engage with it at different times and in different ways.

When I write treatments for feature-film projects now, I'm also writing up proposals for collaborative storytelling platforms with a handful of narrative extensions and social-engagement opportunities united around consistent themes. I was inspired by *Star Wars Uncut*, a giddy marvel and shot-for-shot remake of *Star Wars*, which was 100 percent crowd-sourced. Complete with sock puppets and adults in far-out costumes and authored by a team of thousands, it was just the first ripple of a tsunami that was about to shake up the culture. And in the same way that I need to have a supportive funder, a great cast, and a talented crew, I also want to bring in an enthusiastic marketing partner or shrewd outreach coordinator on every project and ideally a community that is already primed to participate in the experience. As we take responsibility for the life cycle of our film, our responsibilities also expand.

During my days at the San Francisco Film Society, Vanessa's film became increasingly important to me. After working all day in my Presidio office, I needed to feel the passion of making something original and unique. I'd retire to the edit room across the hall. There Vanessa and I would watch cuts and restructure the film. It made me feel alive. It made me feel heard. I again felt part of something.

Great professional collaborators are hard to find, but more so in your personal life. Mixing the two can be disastrous, as I knew firsthand, but when it works, it's exhilarating. Fortunately, this time I had gotten it right. As we worked on *All Eyes and Ears* and I witnessed Vanessa's unwillingness to settle for merely good enough, it reinforced my commitment to do something significant. I wasn't going to look for a job or even just make another movie. I had to find a way to improve things, particularly for the people and communities I cared about.

The pleasure I had making Vanessa's film also clarified something I had been struggling with for some time. When we produce movies for our living, our commitment is to get movies made. Regardless of our integrity, just getting the movies made often takes precedence over making them well. We are rewarded for quantity over quality. I was determined that whatever I did next, I was going to produce films not for my own profit, but for my passion. I needed to earn my living in a new way and think of filmmaking more as a hobby.

It was fortuitous, then, that after I had resigned from the San Francisco Film Society and was thinking about how to fulfill my new goals, I had an offer from Fandor to become its new CEO. A San Francisco–based online art-film community and subscription viewing and streaming platform, Fandor had already been around for two years and built both a good platform for watching and interacting with art movies and a strong team, but it was still in a relatively nascent stage. Dan Aronson, the cofounder and CEO, was a tech guy with a great love for movies. I had first met him via Dan Cogan (who runs Impact Partners, the documentary investment initiative that I had patterned my FIX funding model on), and we had discussed the Fandor strategy: building a place that puts curation, contextualization, availability, social engagement, and other interaction all in one easy-to-use and attractively designed site. It wasn't something easy to do, but Dan and his team were almost there.

At the start of 2014, the mainstream-film industry press began to recognize that the marketplace was flooded with an abundance of movies. The press spoke of it as a problem, a glutting of the distribution channels, but the big issue is not that there are too many movies, but that we don't do a good-enough job of matching movies with the people who will like them. Companies like Amazon, Netflix, and Pandora know this very well. Historically, people pick a movie to watch on impulse, not on an educated choice. But this impulsivity was changing. And independent film could benefit from this shift. In the early days of Netflix, the company's chief content officer, Ted Sarandos, told me that the longer a customer used Netflix, the more his or her taste gravitated to art-house cinema, and the more people the customer was engaged with on the site, the faster it happened. Access and community elevate quality.

Dan Aronson also aimed to foist change with Fandor. I liked that he wanted to come up with an alternative to Netflix, Hulu, and Amazon—a complement to those services but with a strong sense of curation and community. Recognizing that creators were not being compensated fairly for their work, Dan wanted to change that. He championed an even revenue split, with 50 percent of subscription fees going to the content owners on a pro-rata basis, according to overall minutes watched, so the more a movie performs, the more the makers earn.

I first agreed to join the advisory board of Fandor when Dan and I had first met. Being on the advisory board simply meant I was available for questions. I also met Chris Kelly, who was Fandor's main funder and had been Facebook's first chief privacy officer. He was also an enthusiastic supporter of independent film. When I moved to San Francisco, Fandor was in my backyard, and I spent more time with both Dan and Chris. Our conversations frequently dealt with big picture questions such as what's wrong with indie film, and how can we make it better?

In June 2013, I asked Chris to join the San Francisco Film Society board, but he was too busy. But as we continued our dialogue, it became increasingly clear that we shared the same goals. We needed to find a solution to the "tyranny of choice"—too many movies, too many video-on-demand platforms—and bring a sense of logic to the new media universe. The idea of a systems reboot struck a chord with Dan and Chris (after all, they had come out of the tech world), and after I had resigned from the film society, they asked me if I wanted to work with them and suggested I use Fandor as the centerpiece for this reboot.

Fandor was a start-up and a fantastic place to start. Once again, I felt I was being made an offer that I could not refuse. And it was a job with a reasonable salary . . . in San Francisco . . . with people I liked. And a board of only three people, not twenty-six. I was excited to partner with a chief technology officer and bright-eyed, brilliant engineers. I had thought that I would have to raise capital to start a new company, but here was a place with the people and the tools already in place to move forward. (And unlike the San Francisco Film Society, which was located in the beautiful Presidio, with plenty of parking options but few, if any, decent food options, the Fandor offices were located in the heart of the city, near the Transamerica Pyramid building, where I could walk around Little Italy and Chinatown and sample hundreds of great restaurants—ah, the simple pleasures.)

I accepted their offer. And embarked on another major change in my life.

Way back in the mid-1990s, I had already been conceiving business plans and ways to cultivate what I thought the industry needed. In the fall of 1995, I wrote an article for *Filmmaker Magazine.* In "Indie Film Is Dead," I mapped out several of these problems: the industry's reliance on marketable concepts; the inevitable failure of smaller distributors; the dwindling of foreign sales; the decline of film reviewers; a mentality of close-to-the-chest confidentiality rather than open information flow. And I've been making lists pretty much every year since then. One of my principle concerns remains the same. Filmmakers need to take on a greater responsibility for the business of their movies.

But now, more than ever before, filmmakers have the tools at their disposal to do just that. You can reach a lot of people online—especially if you're Katy Perry (who as of this writing has more than fifty million Twitter followers). But even if indie filmmakers reach a very small percentage of that number—conventional wisdom says that 3 percent of moviegoers see art-house films—that's still a lot of people (1.5 million, to be exact). We also have to capitalize on indie films' greatest strength. They compel audiences to talk about them. Good film generates a shared emotional response among strangers. So if you combine those two things—access and community, which the Internet does—you're set. But no one has yet effectively designed a place or a platform that captures these two key elements.

There are lots of differences between watching a movie online and watching it in theaters, or even on DVD or VOD. You stop and start, you pause, get up and leave, and you don't necessarily come back to it. And we filmmakers have to take these watching habits into account. People can also record and memorialize their experience of a film watched online, whether it's through comments made alongside the film or online discussions. And the more filmmakers marry films with the ability to connect around them, the greater the experience. Boots Riley, a musician, writer, comic, and activist, told me how much fun he used to have as a kid going to the movies with the best crowds; they didn't decide where to go, on the basis of what film was showing, but on where the funniest people went. Similarly, I've always seen films as a dialogue between the audience and the screen. I love talking about movies, perhaps even more than I do watching them or making them. And now we've finally reached a point where you can provide context, engagement, and participation all in one sphere. We just need to take the next step—the call to action. Movies don't end when the credits roll. They are not over even after you leave the theater. Movies can bring people together and create shared responses among communities and cultures that endure for far longer. Harnessing that power and facilitating transformative experiences for individuals and society is the ultimate goal of mass art forms.

If that sounds a little grandiose, on the opposite end of the spectrum there's no denying that many were drawn to a career in movies because of the fantasy of it: the stars, the fame, the Academy Awards. I must admit that I'd been excited to know some of the greatest stars before they became famous, particularly when they remember me long after the fact. It was also a thrill to walk up the red carpet at Cannes or when someone has come up to me and said that one of my movies affected his or her life.

But if I had to pick my most thrilling moment, it would be the making of Hal Hartley's *The Unbelievable Truth* and working with a team of people who had little experience, but incredible desire. It was my first production that ran on people's passion, and the experience shaped so many of the later films that I was involved with. We didn't need the star system. We didn't need Hollywood. We could make heroes of everyday people—both the subjects of our stories and the dedicated filmmakers who helped get it done. That DIY spirit was embodied by the 1980s rock band the Minutemen, whose motto "We jam econo" described their no-frills all-punk attitude. They weren't looking to book stadium gigs; they were their own roadies and had day jobs. Then when rock and roll became their full-time occupation, it wasn't about glamour or ego. With *The Unbelievable Truth*, it was the same thing. We were a bunch of folks who didn't come from privileged backgrounds and who all came together to try to make something meaningful and beautiful. That you could get together with a bunch of your friends and put on a show—and over twenty people from the cast and crew went on to direct their own movies—was inspirational. These days, I'm back where I was. I may be in high tech, but I'm still on the ground floor, trying to do something new and different.

I can't deny that after making about fifty movies, though, filmmaking stopped feeling fresh. And that's probably why I adopted social media, moved to San Francisco, took the film society job, and then moved over to Fandor. This sense of novelty gives me the same kind of buzz that I felt when I was just starting to make movies. It's one of the reasons I wanted to have a child: to be able to see the world with fresh eyes. It's one of the reasons I fell in love with Vanessa: We bonded over this idea of embracing change, as people and professionals. That desire to change makes things better, whether that's a movie, the film industry, or a relationship.

When I went to film school, I also had big dreams. But as things progressed in my career and I became more established, I became more practical. For a long time, I needed to focus on movies that I could get made. Now, when I think about making movies, I want to move away from the practical project and go back to the dream project. I want to develop a script for five years or even seven years to get it truly right. Or shoot on the first draft if that is what will yield the best movie. And when a financier asks me to cast an actor who I don't think is appropriate for a movie, I want to be able to say no. I want to make movies where I don't settle and not just do what will get the movie made immediately. I want to make movies that cannot be ignored.

In the past, I have always had to sacrifice my dreams in order to earn a living. I couldn't take on dream projects, because, in truth, I couldn't afford to. Now, I hope that by earning a living in a new way, I can start to focus on my dreams more. I want to follow in the footsteps of San Francisco's great producer Saul Zaentz, who produced only ten movies over thirty years, but all of them—from *One Flew Over the Cuckoo's Nest* to *Amadeus* to *The Lord of the Rings*—embodied a sense of ambition and creativity, and three of them won the Best Picture Oscar. Those are the sorts of projects I want to make over the next twenty years. But that's just a part of what I want to accomplish.

Living in San Francisco now, I'm struck by how, in this city, you're often put in a position where you literally see things from a new perspective. The fog clears, and something is revealed. You come to the crest of yet another hill, and you see a new horizon. The metaphor is never lost on me, and it still resonates every day. It makes me remember my NYU thesis film—where I ultimately sacrificed my vision to get the teacher's support. The film was titled *Crest of a Hill*. I never could have known it at the time, but that's where I'd be decades later. But this time, no compromises.

Appendix

141 Problems *and* Opportunities
for the Independent Film World

In 2010, I wrote a blog post on "Hope for Film" about thirty-eight problems facing the independent-film community. While I always prefer to look at the opportunities and solutions before us, as opposed to the problems and concerns, I still felt compelled to come up with a list of issues that we need to solve. The following year, I added another thirty-eight concerns. And the year after that, I added another twenty-four. And I am concerned that the list will keep growing and growing.

Even blessed with my last name, I can't always be optimistic, at least if I also want to speak the truth. Sometimes, throwing a brick is an act of love. And granted, I've thrown a lot of bricks at this indie-film thing. What can I say? A great deal is wrong with our culture these days, and a hell of a lot can hurt our business.

The exciting part for me is that these lists demonstrate a tremendous opportunity for those willing to break from the status quo and take action. In fact, let's call these opportunities instead of problems. From here, we just have to work together to make it better. It is that simple.

Every deficit is an opportunity for the creative entrepreneur, right? So here (in no particular order) are one hundred opportunities for us to tackle. Maybe they are not so insurmountable after all.

1.   Too many other leisure options make it difficult for film compete for people's time.

2.   An overabundance of specialized films opening prevents word-of-mouth publicity and diminishes audience's attention for these films.

3.   An overabundance of available films being distributed prevents them from staying in one theater for very long and makes it more difficult to develop a word-of-mouth audience.

4.   There is a lack of access—outside New York City and Los Angeles—to films when they are at their highest media awareness (encourages bootlegging and limits appeal by reducing timeliness).

5.   Distributors have abandoned (and failed to develop) community-building marketing approaches for specialized releases (which reduces appeal for a group activity, that is, the theatrical experience).

6.   Distributors have failed to embrace limited streaming of features for audience building.

7.   The reliance on theatrical release model predicated on a large marketing spend restricts content to broad subjects (which decreases films' distinction in marketplace) and reduces ability to focus on already-identified and aggregated niche audiences.

8.   An emphasis on up-front compensation for star talent creates budgets that can't reasonably recoup investment.

9.   Union health, pension, and welfare (HP&W) payroll fringe

levels are too high to allow low-budget production to benefit from know-how and talent of union labor.

10. There is a lack of media literacy and education programs that help audiences recognize the superiority of deliberating on what to see over impulsive choices.

11. The collapse of the U.S. acquisition market requires reduced budgets for filmmakers and thus limits content.

12. The collapse of international-sales markets requires reduced budgets for filmmakers and thus limits content.

13. Foreign subsidies for the marketing of foreign films reduce the appetite for U.S. productions among buyers in foreign territories.

14. Foreign subsidies for foreign productions contribute greater budget percentage than U.S. tax rebates do, allowing foreign productions to have larger budgets and thus more production value and expansive content—thus making it harder for U.S. indie product to compete.

15. The recession has reduced private equity available for film investment.

16. The credit crunch has reduced filmmakers' ability to use debt financing for film investment.

17. The threat of piracy makes library value of titles unstable, which limits investment in content companies and reduces acquisition prices, which in turn reduces budgets, which then limits the options for content. As a result, everybody loses.

18. The industry has failed to develop a new business model for Internet exploitation at a level that can justify reasonable film budgets.

19. The creative and business communities of film have both failed

to embrace new creative story-expansion models that would
facilitate audience aggregation and participation (to seed, build,
and drive audiences).

20. Today's culture emphasizes single pictures for filmmakers versus an
ongoing conversation with fans has led to a neglect of content that
would help audiences bridge gaps between films and would prevent
each new film's need to reinvent the wheel for audience building.

21. The panic due to the fifteen-year promise of crystal-clear down-
loads over the Internet despite the reality that this technology
only recently developed has allowed the fear of this change to
create a business practice of inactivity.

22. Bootleggers have developed a platform that allows audiences to
simply download whatever they want, wherever and whenever they
want to do so—something that the film industry has yet to do.

23. The loss of jobs for newspaper-based film critics reduces curatorial oversight, which lessens word of mouth and people's desires
to see a film.

24. A reliance on synopsis-style reviewing fails to provide enriching
cultural context for films and thus reduces audience satisfaction.

25. The lack of marketing and distribution knowledge by filmmakers
limits DIY success.

26. Mimicking Hollywood's obsession with regurgitating past
success models, indie filmmakers are regurgitating the storylines
of past indie-festival hits or are navel-gazing. Cinema is one
hundred years old, but we still tell the same stories in the same
ways. Audiences get bored, move on, play video games.

27. American indie filmmakers are only recently starting to look
at non-U.S.-centric stories that can "travel" into international
territories.

28. Because the United States has no funding for the arts, American filmmakers have to develop material based on preexisting markets instead of forward-thinking inspiration.

29. The United States has no coproduction treaties (other than Puerto Rico's Letters of Understanding) that allow American filmmakers to access foreign soft-money subsidies.

30. The specialized distributors force exhibitors to program for full weekly runs, which prevents exhibitors from developing a local community audience or niche programs on off nights.

31. The truly independent exhibitors only recently developed into a collaborating organization that could come to allow true independent features to be easily booked nationwide.

32. There is no independent collection and disbursement agency that could allow DIY distribution to take hold.

33. Filmmakers still believe that festivals are primarily markets and not media launches.

34. The ego-driven approach to filmmaking versus one of true collaboration generally yields lower-quality films and greater dissatisfaction among all participants.

35. There is a lack of real role models who represent integrity and commitment to the craft (to inspire others).

36. Corporate hierarchy and access is driven foremost by privilege (college, connections, class), limiting diversity and new content and approaches.

37. Filmmakers are unable to influence iTunes editors to promote their work.

38. It is hard to justify a high ticket price for a movie. Consumers have too many better options at a lower price. They will not pay

a high price just to get out of the house or to watch a desired movie whose ticket is expensive because it is only playing in one place. We still think of movies as *things* people will buy. We have to think of movies as something that enhances other experiences. When movies are thought of in this way, their value increases. Film's power as a community-organizing tool extends far beyond its power to sell popcorn (and the whole exhibition industry is based on *that old popcorn* idea).

39. The industry has never tried to build a sustainable investor class. Every other industry has such a go-to funding sector, developed around a focus on the investors' concerns and standardized structures. In the film biz, each deal is different and generally stands alone, as opposed to leading to something more. The history of Hollywood is partly defined by the belief that another sucker is born every minute. Who really benefits from the limited funding options currently available, other than the funders and those who get fees for the deals? We could build something that works far more efficiently and offers far more opportunity.

40. The film business remains the virtually exclusive domain of the privileged. Although great strides have been made to diversify the industry, the numbers don't lie. The film industry is ruled by white men from middle class or better socioeconomic backgrounds. It is an expensive art form and a competitive field—but it doesn't need to be a closed-door one. Let's face it: People hire folks who remind them of themselves. These days, in order to launch their career in the film business, everyone needs to intern, and the proposition of working for free is too expensive for most. Living in New York City or Los Angeles is not affordable for most people starting out. We get more of the same and little progress without greater diversity. And the continued poor economy limits diversity even more now.

41. There is no structure or mechanism to increase the liquidity of film investments, either through clear exit strategies or secondary capital markets. The dirty secret of film investment is that it is a long recoupment cycle with little planning for an exit strategy. Without a way to get out, fewer people choose to get in. Who really wants to lock up an investment for four years? Not investors, only patrons.

42. Independent filmmakers (and their industry advisors) built business plans based on models and notions that were developed before September 15, 2008, when Lehman Brothers collapsed and the economic world changed. Filmmaking is not the same business that it was then, and we shouldn't treat it that way. Expectations have changed considerably, probably completely. Buyers' and audiences' behaviors are different (those that still remain, that is). Products are valued at different levels. We live in a new world; our strategies must change with it.

43. The film business remains a single-product industry. The product may be available on many platforms, but it is still the same thing. For such a capital-intensive enterprise to sell only one thing is a squandering of time and money. Films can be a platform to launch many other products and enterprises, some of which can also enhance the experience and build the community.

44. We have thought very little about how to make events out of our movies. The list seems to have stopped at 3D. There has only been one *Rocky Horror Picture Show*, and the first one is very, very old. Music flourishes because the live component is generally quite different from the recorded one. The film business could benefit from a greater differentiation of what utilizes different platforms.

45. We ignore film's most unique attribute. As demonstrated by how little of people's online time is spent watching content (30

percent), we know that people want connectivity and community more than anything else. In the same way that reviewers
once placed films in cultural context, we need to re-create a
community aspect to film-going. If you wonder why people
don't go to the movies more often, the answer is not as much
about the content as it is about the lack of community. Without
that, why not just stay home to watch? Film's strongest attribute is its ability to work as a community-organizing tool. Film
forces us to feel, to think, to engage—let's not ignore that.

46. Independent-film financing is still based on an antiquated
     foreign-sales model, even though all acquisition markets are
     collapsing and fee levels shrink from market to market. This old
     model is centered around stars' perceived value—an attribute
     that has been less reliable than ever before. There has got to
     be a better way than the foreign-sales-estimate model, but few
     people talk about it or even admit to needing a new model. The
     participants who get most hurt by the old model are the inves-
     tors who take the advice of the "experts" that this is the way it's
     done. Business used to be done this way, but we have to move on
     before we burn to the ground.

47. Filmmakers don't own their audiences yet (and few even attempt
     to). What will happen when agents start to cut deals for their
     clients who have one million engaged fans, people who will
     preorder their content, promote it passionately, and deliver more
     of their friends? The balance of power is about to shift, and those
     who have prepared for it and amassed their followings will be
     able to change the conversation significantly.

48. We've failed to develop fetish objects to demonstrate people's
     love of cinema. The only merchandise we sell is "fan-boy" toys.
     We need to come up with items that demonstrate their owner's
     sense of style and taste. Beyond the lavish art books of Taschen,

what do we have? We can do better. Such products manufacture desire and enhance identification with the art form. We need to streamline the transformation of leisure time into both intellectual and social capital (i.e., movie-going and its by-products). How do we identify, reward, and encourage those who appreciate our work?

49. Creators, distributors, and marketers have accepted a dividing line between art and commerce, between content and marketing. By not engaging the filmmakers in how to use marketing tools within their narrative and how to bring narrative techniques to marketing, we diminish the discovery and promotional potential of each film. We limit the scope of our art by restricting it to the flat dimensions of the ninety-minute product. Movies should find us early, lead us to new worlds, bridge us to subsequent experiences, connect us to new passions and loves, and help us embrace a more expansive definition of cinema, life, and self.

50. We don't recognize that one of film's greatest assets is its ability to generate data. Filmmakers and financiers should be insisting on owning the data their films generate. It is an incredibly valuable commodity. The VOD platform allows for tracking of the where, when, and who in terms of the distribution business, yet this data is restricted to aggregators, not creators. When you license something for a small fraction of its costs, shouldn't you receive a share of everything that it generates, including data?

51. We fail to utilize the two years from green-light to release to market our film and build our audiences. Despite having the key economic indicators (i.e., stars and concept) in place at the time of green-light, we underutilize that two-year period when we could be sourcing fans, aggregating them, and providing them with both the ramps and the bridges necessary to lead them to our work and then carry them to other new work.

52. Our industry doesn't do a good job of developing more stars. The talented actors exist, but they don't have "value." Why don't we have greater numbers of serious actors who are worth something financially? Isn't it just about giving them the roles that help them build audiences? Why don't we encourage more actors to take more risks in terms of the characters they portray? Audiences, filmmakers, and financiers would all be better served by industry-wide initiatives to launch more talent. Say what you will about the studio system of old, but they were damn good at developing new talent.

53. We need to embrace innovation and experimentation in our business models and in building better communities. We keep doing things according to the status quo long after the practice has stopped being fruitful. People are so fearful of failing publicly that new approaches are shunned. This is a perception and PR problem as much as it is a structural one. Filmmakers should have the will to fail and take risks (but be practical about it).

54. Under the present distribution system, many consumers think content should be very inexpensive or even free, even though they accept that the hardware they play the content on is very, very expensive. All the entertainment industries allow the hardware manufacturers to have policies that encourage such thinking. Hardware people get rich, and creators struggle more and more each day. People only want the devices because there is so much great stuff to play on it. Why is the balance of wealth so lopsided here?

55. None of us—neither the creators, the audiences, nor their representatives—make a stink when the aggregators get rich and the content creators live on mere pittances. Not just the product but also the services have flourished on the labor of the creators. Instead of growing angry, we have been embracing those that

gather and not those that grow. Again, we need to look at the inequity here and reevaluate how the equity is dispersed.

56. The indie-film industry doesn't insist that its artists also be entrepreneurs. It doesn't encourage direct sales to the fans. It doesn't focus on building mailing lists. These sorts of marketing activities need to be as much an accepted best practice as they need to be part of every art school curriculum. We can't keep producing artists and not prepare them to survive in the world. Passion without a plan to support it can only lead to exploitation.

57. Independent films have failed to engage constructively with other industries that we should be aligned with, most obviously, the tech world. Why are the SXSW conferences and festivals in Texas the only venues where film, music, and tech meet? Can't we do better? The music industry has The Future of Music summit, but there is nothing similar in the film world. The facilitators at the agencies rarely know who's who in terms of web and tech designers.

58. The industry offers no simple websites where consumers can get whatever they want, whenever and however they want it (other than what the bootleggers offer). Why do we let the thieves beat us at our own game? Soon it will be too late to win the people back. The fact that the one place that comes close (iTunes) is ultimately in the business of selling electronic hardware—and the industry seems okay with that—shows how we can't see the forest for the trees.

59. The industry lacks new curators—the ones with a national or an international audience. Why have we not had a more con-centrated industry- or community-wide effort to give a home to all the fired film critics? Are we afraid of the bad, just like the studios are afraid of social media and financial exchanges that could trade in futures like other commodity markets because

they are worried about negative buzz? We just need to make better movies and treat people well, and then there is no negative to spread, right? Of course, there will always be negative reviews. Nevertheless, with such a plethora of great work being made, we need to offer audiences better filters to sift through it. What's up with our collective failure to deliver more Oprahs, individuals whose support will lead to action?

60. The majority of people in the film industry are essentially luddites and technophobes, barely aware of the tools available to us to enhance, economize on, and spread our work. How can we teach our industry how to use what has already been invented (and then focus on everything else we need but don't have yet)?

61. We don't encourage (or demand) audience "builds" prior to production. Why shouldn't every filmmaker or filmmaking team be required to have five thousand fans prior to green-light?

62. We know incredibly little about our audience or its behavior. We spend so much making our films without really knowing who our audiences are, why they want our product, how to reach them, how they behave, or how they are changing. Does any other industry think so little and so late about its audience? Does any other industry do such little research into its audience? Shouldn't we all be sharing what info we have?

63. The film industry has no major visible think tank or incubator that is high-level, nonpartisan, and free-thinking enough to consider new approaches and enhance audience appeal. Moreover, such a think tank should inspire both government and private investment, develop best practices to maximize revenue and audiences, expand aesthetic methods, and facilitate the creative dialogue internationally. Independent Filmmaker Project and Film Independent do their part, as do festival institutes like Sundance but we need something that can consider problems

bigger than just those of American indie filmmakers.

64. Producers know little about preventing piracy. Where's that list on best practices for preventing your film from being pirated? Shouldn't all producers know this? I know I don't, and I can't name another producer who does.

65. The industry has little respect for producers. Granted, this might sound a tad self-serving, but producers' overhead, fees, credits, and support are under attack from all fronts. Yet it is the producers who identify and develop the material and talent, package it, structure the finance, identify the audience, and unite all the industry's disparate elements. All the producers I speak with wonder how they are to survive and remain in the business.

66. Let's face it: We are not good at providing filmmakers with long-term career planning. Whether it's financial planning, secondary professions, or just ongoing learning—we don't really get it, and that sets artists up as future prey. As an industry, and as a class, creative people get stuck in a rut quite easily and are the hardest dogs to teach new tricks.

67. With our world and industry changing daily, filmmakers need a place where they can learn the new technology or at least hear about it. Such a place must be welcoming even for the luddites. The tech sites speak their own vernacular, which is a tad intimidating for the uninitiated.

68. The industry doesn't promote the short-term release. With digital delivery here, can't we get in and get out, only to return again and offer it all over again? The week-long booking of one film per theater limits content to that which appeals to the mass market. Niche audiences are being underserved, and money is thus being left on the table and some highly appealing menus not even being considered.

69. Film festivals need to evolve a hell of a lot faster. They need to ask what value they add to both the filmmaker and the audience. One or two festivals could ask that of the industry overall, too. Now that we recognize that festivals are not a market and that filmmakers have to do a tremendous amount of work ahead of time if the festival is to be a media launch for their film, the question remains: What are festivals, and whom do they serve? The everything-to-everybody style of curating films no longer works. The run-of-the-mill panels have become dull and boring. The costs associated for filmmakers attending are rarely worth the benefits they receive. Film festivals need to be rebuilt. A lot of good ideas are out there on how to do it, but not enough have been put into practice.

70. The past ten years of digital film are going to vanish. We do little to preserve not just the works, but also the process and documents behind them. Digital is not a stable medium. We have a migration and storage problem in terms of keeping access up-to-date. The films that currently exist only in digital format won't stand the test of time. Film remains a better format for archival purposes. We need to act soon to keep our recent culture within our reach.

71. We don't encourage advocacy around the issues that affect us. How many film industry professionals could rattle off the top ten government policies that affect their trade? Why don't our various support organizations, unions, guilds, and leaders list issues and actions at the top of their websites? Are we all so afraid or so unaware?

72. People in the industry often don't go out to the movies. Okay, it's a bit like cutting off your nose to spite your face, but it seems to me that film industry folks spend less time going to the movies (and I mean seeing films in the theaters) than the average bear.

Going to the movies should be viewed as a political act. Support the culture you want with your dollars.

73. The industry itself supports bootlegging. Most of the bootlegging that I encounter comes from within the industry itself. I recently heard of a manager who asked the studio execs and his Facebook friends to send in the bootlegs of his Sundance-prizewinning client's film—and he received over seventy back; all the DVDs were, unfortunately, an early cut of the film, too. I admit I receive a lot of free DVDs from agents and managers, and I admit I make dubs for my directors so they can see actors—but I have started to donate to crowd-funding campaigns to try to balance it out. We have to come up with a uniform practice and commitment to avoid industry-supported bootlegging.

74. So few of us have determined what we love, not just in film, but also in the world in general. The more we define our tastes, the more we make good decisions based on those preferences. The more we know what we want, the greater our defenses against things we don't really enjoy. Which filmmakers can list the elements they consider necessary to make better films? If more filmmakers, distributors, and executives conversed more publicly in both the art and the business, the bar for all of us would be lifted higher.

75. The industry loves to read about, talk about, and engage in the business more than it is interested in the art. Some of this focus comes perhaps because we have more forums for the business than the aesthetics, but it is much harder to get a conversation going about creative issues than it is about financial. I'm just saying . . .

76. Filmmakers are unable to earn a living even when they consistently make successful films. Budgets have been dropping over

the years—and fees go down with them. Movies are few and far between in terms of years for their makers, and without overhead deals or teaching gigs, a creator has a hard time staying focused on film unless he or she is wealthy. And of course, net profits grow into more of a joke daily (although they don't have to).

77. The acquisition price for U.S. rights hovers around 10 percent of the total costs to create and deliver a film—and no one complains. The present situation seems like a cartel, where all buyers got together and said, "Let's just offer less." If no one breaks rank, other than occasionally, all the buyers benefit. The only thing that could turn the cartel around would be passion by one acquisition executive given reign to spend freely—and the markets are supposed to be devoid of that sort of passion. But we are above just letting a market race to the bottom. We should recognize that the health of a culture depends on those who create and innovate, and like everyone else, these creative people need a financially secure life.

78. Art film is dead. Consider that "Oops, I Farted" is the dominant "specialized" title of desire in these United States of America. Art film be damned. The gaseous (fictional) title is courtesy of producer Mike Ryan, who used it as shorthand for what he saw as most companies' acquisition strategy: the audience-friendly, falsely transgressive, youth-focused star title. Art film is dead. Distribution companies don't just aim to give people what people want. The companies also lead in terms of determining audiences' tastes, as everyone knows that people generally like what they get (the March Hare syndrome, where Alice's March Hare says people think "I like what I get" means the same thing as "I get what I like"). Where are we being led?

79. The year 2013 is the last year of celluloid. What could be a better signifier of this transformation than the fact that Kodak filed

for Chapter 11 bankruptcy protection in early 2013? People are writing sad eulogies and fond remembrances. These days, nostalgia arrives almost immediately after a passing.

80. Although just as many women direct documentaries as men do, women are not even close in narrative features. This imbalance holds true even if the Sundance competition was proportionally represented in terms of gender for the first time ever in 2012. It sure took a long time to reach this point. And how much does anyone want to bet that it slips back fast? And what of all the festivals that are not so progressive? Sure, folks say it really needs to always just be the best films, and I am not arguing for quotas anyway. But we need to acknowledge that the system does not grant the same opportunities to everyone. And further, equal opportunity has never come close to providing equal outcome. We need to further the discussion of why there are not more women, youth, and people of color in positions of power in the entertainment industry. After all, they are the top consumers; it would make sense that they know better what the people really want.

81. Great reviews—even in the most important newspaper in the world—have no effect. It used to be that indie and art film was good business because it was completely review driven. You did not need to do much advertising if the critics gave you love. Those days are dead and gone. Two films I produced in 2011, *Dark Horse* and *Starlet*, enjoyed excellent reviews in the *New York Times*, but saw no effect from it. *Dark Horse* even hit the trifecta with awesome reviews in *The New Yorker* and *New York* magazine (*Time* and the *Los Angeles Times*, too), but the review mojo did the film no good, either. Granted, many factors contribute to a film's lack of real cultural impact, but still, reviews like these were once worth their weight in gold. And now they are not. Critics were once moviegoers' guide through the cultural

landscape—and that is how folks selected what films to watch. Maybe it is time for a change, but for now, we haven't found a substitute for professional critics. Review aggregator sites let the audience know general opinion but offer little nuance. But losing these professionals' voice makes it even harder for filmmakers to distribute what once was recognized as quality.

82. The *New York Times* and others in the press are questioning and criticizing the film and television tax credits. These tax credits create jobs, spread wealth, and keep our number two national industry afloat. Film is a migratory industry, and the jobs will flee if the industry suspects that the tax policy is not stable. When the press goes after something in such a one-sided fashion, you wonder what really is afoot. The industry must combat such wrongheadedness. It needs to truly quantify the national spending in the indie-film industry.

83. People don't go to the movies anymore—particularly young people. My tale of my twelve-year-old son ("I don't like movies, although I love many that I have seen") was quoted globally. Sure, I need the statistics to back this up, and I hope you send them to me, but we all recognize that youth attendance is dropping. Isn't it time we woke up from our dream and started making films that had real youth appeal?

84. Virtual print fees (VPFs) suck (these fees are how digital projectors were financed and are supposed to be payback for the advance, but the high rate effectively shut indie films out of national chains). My colleagues and I had to turn down dates for *Dark Horse*, because of VPFs. Sure, we have a digital master (in a DCP, or digital cinema package), but between the traditional-film rentals you a pay an exhibitor and the VPF, most indie films can't expect to make money. Let's say you pay 60 percent to the exhibitor and anticipate only a two-thousand-dollar gross. That

leaves you with eight hundred dollars. And guess how much the VPF generally is? So you get nothing. And it is not just in the United States that the structure does not work. Ditto for the United Kingdom.

85. Even worse than the lack of transparency in video-on-demand (VOD) numbers is the lack of any outcry about this problem. How can we make all of this public?

86. VOD is still treated as a second-class citizen, as VOD premieres are not currently reviewed in major media outlets. I am thankful we have *On Demand Weekly*, but when will the major media publications get wise to it? And why is this not happening now? Is it that they fear they would then lose the advertising for the movies? Would they not be opening up a new advertising revenue source? What's wrong with this picture?

87. The U.S. industry reports box-office revenue figures but not attendance. How do we know how our business and culture are doing if we can't get access to the numbers? When will we truly have transparency in all things? I thought information wanted to be free. We were promised jet packs.

88. We have yet to begin a real effort to quantify the spending on indie films, both directly and indirectly. If we don't harvest the data that our work generates, we don't control the power that is rightfully ours. Since the only thing that talks in this town is money, we need to speak accurately about how we create jobs, benefit communities, and generate wealth.

89. A digital disaster is looming in the wings. It has many aspects, but we particularly bury our heads in the sand when it comes to the preservation of digital works. Recommended best practices for digital data is to migrate it from your drives every three months. If you don't do that, you cannot be assured you will

have an archival-quality copy. By 2008, very few cinema makers were finishing their work on celluloid—which could preserve work for over one hundred years. So in the race for technology to save us, we traded one hundred-plus years for three months. Hooray, right?

90. To quote A. O. Scott of *The New York Times*: "By the end of this year, *The New York Times* will have reviewed more than 800 movies, establishing 2012, at least by one measure, as a new benchmark in the annals of cinematic abundance." Grand abundance is not a bad thing; choices are wonderful when you know they are there. I even argue that from a cultural point of view, this abundance is splendid. The problem is, we still haven't evolved our culture or business infrastructure to adapt to this change. We still rely on the methods of promotion, discovery, consumption, and participation that were built in the era of scarcity and control. Without pivoting our methods toward this new reality, people don't see more movies, so the movies don't recoup, and more frustration abounds in the industry. Many items on this list are a direct result of this overabundance.

91. The industry undermines the possibility of creating a sustainable investor class. We all know about the *Harry Potter* net profits. I have to admit, though, *Napoleon Dynamite* was a surprise; how did the creators only get 12.88 percent? Even if it was legal, it's not right. The best thing any of us can do for our industry, culture, and community is to make sure that those who create, as well as those who support the creators, are rewarded for the work they create. Despite our being so far away from making this a reality, I see and hear little discussion about this issue. Equitable compensation should be an urgent matter on all of our leaders' lips.

92. There is not enough money to teach media literacy in the

schools. We are bombarding kids with content, and yet we don't give them tools to decipher it, let alone defend themselves against it. All the conversation that *Zero Dark Thirty* stirred up is great, but it only underscores the support we must give our children.

93. Blog commenting burn-out is the law of the land. Comments were my favorite things on blogs. I used to get a lot on my blog "Hope for Film." Now we get "likes" and tweets. I started blogging because it seemed like a community-building tool. When it is one-sided, it is not community. Maybe it is me. Maybe I am writing in a style that no longer encourages commenting. Or maybe it is the community itself. Or maybe all the comments just end up on the Facebook page. Whatever it is, blogging is more vibrant when people participate.

94. There is so little that reads as truthful in the press. It was so refreshing to read an interview with Terry Zwigoff on *The Playlist* at the end of 2013 because he told it as he sees it. And that is so rare. It is a shame. Imagine a world where people recognized it was okay to share how they felt—oh what a wonderful world that would be.

95. We limit culture by the limits of what we support. I got to make movies because a few folks recognized that although they didn't personally like my films, other people did and my films were furthering the cultural discussions. The success—and now necessity—of the various film support labs for screenwriters, fiction directors, and documentary directors are invaluable, but also limiting. American documentaries are generally about social issues, personal triumph, and pop culture, because these are what our support structures encourage. Ditto on the fiction tale of triumph over adversity. And I love all those forms, but so much more out there is still being overlooked. And we even neglect

the commercial forms. Where are the labs for horror films
or thrillers, the genres that actually work in the marketplace?
Where are those that really are trying to advance the cultural
dialogue? How can we start to widen our reach? This may sound
like a minor point, but I do think we are doing our culture
and community a disservice by not supporting more of what
the audience wants. Can this be a symptom of the gatekeepers
thinking they know best? How can we give the community a
bigger say in which films get advanced?

96. The bifurcation of the haves and have-nots, I mean the
Hollywood tent poles and their franchise story worlds versus
the indie side's passionate amateurs, has created a possibility
gap. Indie film was once a farm team for the studios. David
O. Russell, Ang Lee, Quentin Tarantino, Spike Lee, Kathryn
Bigelow, and many, many, more of our current greats all came
through true indie work. The next wave is being deprived
of access to all the colors on the palate. The drop-out of the
midrange picture means that some of our greatest hopes for the
future will never get to explore the greatest technological tools or
the most expansive or immersive story structures. We are going
to limit our dreams of the future by not giving new waves of
artists access to all the experimental tools that are available.

97. Narrative film, despite firmly embracing microbudget limits,
has not yet implemented staged financing, that is, financing
that occurs in steps rather than requiring that the full amount
be raised before the project even starts. Although I firmly
advocate some sort of staged financing, filmmakers have very
few financing options other than raising all their money up
front. Many people may argue that is irresponsible to shoot a
film without full financing in place, but you need only look at
the documentary world to see the positive results from staged
financing. Documentary films have proportional representation

in terms of gender in the directorial ranks; could this be related to staged financing? Since indie will always be an execution dependent art form, wouldn't it make sense to have a structure that allows for proof of principal?

98. Investors have nowhere to turn to get better information regarding nontraditional film investment. When they can only turn to the agencies for "expert" advice, the investors only get one side of the story. Yes, they can hire high-priced consultants, armed with all sorts of numbers, but where do the investors usually find these consultants? Why, from the agencies of course! The agencies have tremendous insight, for sure, just as these consultants do, but it is hard for change to take hold when all the advice comes from the same source. Imagine if we had a real investors' summit, led by folks outside the business or by power centers? Imagine if we had services in place to train new investors in specific areas of what might become their expertise. Imagine if we had in place the structures that allowed these same investors to collaborate across projects.

99. There are few leaders in indie film. I was very inspired by both Joana Vicente's and Keri Putnam's move into not-for-profit commitment. Without them taking a first step, I probably would not have been willing to put down my project-producing magic wand and focus on rebuilding infrastructure for a time. But frankly, I expected many more people at this point to be committed to giving more back. Those who have made a lifetime of nonprofit have counterbalanced this deficit of people a bit, but I expected more. I started the blog because I thought if I spoke up, others would too. There have been many positive contributions to the blog, and yes, new leaders have emerged to some degree, but frankly, I would have expected more producers, directors, executives, and screenwriters to step up and say that we have a tremendous opportunity before us and we'd better act on it or

else that window will close. I still believe it to be true: If you are not part of the solution, you are part of the problem. There may be "99 Problems," but you need to make certain that you are not one of them.

100. The film business lives in *Bizarro World*, thinking we do something for the love of it, but in fact creating something incredibly far from what we actually love—and thus making it so much harder to do what we love in the process. We have turned our strengths into our weaknesses. Even worse, we now assume that this wrongheaded view of the business is correct and needs to be this way. It's not and it doesn't, but I don't hear a whole lot of folks saying we need a complete systems reboot of the whole film ecosystem (see number 102).

101. It's not enough to just think outside the box. As the expression implies, the box is a trap. But the box, which usually represents the status quo of the real world, represents, in the film industry, a false reality. We have to break the box, probably smash it to bits, and then build a better box together. The red pill or the blue? We have chosen the wrong one, and we fail to recognize the cultural factors weighing on film culture and to build for that. Recognize the false construct, and see through the matrix. This is the reality. (In April 2013, I blogged 50 cultural "realities" that should shift one's creative practice and approach to business—search for it!) And we are now poised to be slaves to the false construct forever, instead of living in a far preferable world where we would use these truths that I previously defined to deliver a better world.

102. The corporate suits see *no* business in art. Only Sony's division Sony Pictures Classics, which releases foreign and art films, is left. The others have all given up. They have determined that blockbusters are the safest bet, even if that yields a *Lone Ranger*

regularly. Studios will make films for the world, and what translates well into many languages is not beautiful. Expect more loud, fast, dumb.

103. Film is no longer the ultimate pop culture art form. Be it video games, television or social media, the new big guy in pop culture has beaten cinema, both critically and commercially. Sure, there is plenty of good stuff to watch on TV, great games to play, and we all are addicted to our phones, but we are allowing the next generation of auteurs to get recruited into other fields before they even have a chance to experiment or blossom within a field that was once the first stop of all pop culture fanatics.

104. Successful artists cannot support themselves through their work. We've known for a long time that most of us can't. But we did believe that once someone had made it, the person was safe. Those days are over, too. We have our poster boy in David Byrne saying that "the internet will suck all creative content out of the world." What we have now does not work for anyone but the global corporate powerhouses. Our culture is threatened. We can no longer permit the wholesale exploitation of our creative classes. There needs to be a global action.

105. The interests of the artists and the "stores" that sell our work are no longer aligned. The largest distributors and stores have no real incentive to actually sell good work, yet the best way for artists to survive and create a regular supply of great work is to be fairly compensated for it. This misalignment of artist and business may be far more problematic in the music business, but music experiences everything the film biz does, only a few years ahead. And in the music industry, the business is either to sell computer products or gain an audience base so you can flip it and make a mint.

106. Superabundance applies not only to content but also to platforms. Today, more than five hundred VOD services available in the European Union are dedicated mainly or wholly to feature film. Choice is generally a good thing, but it can also lead people to shut down and not take action. Ultimately, people need to know where to go to get what they want. We need to create the promise of a good experience and not further confusion of the what, where, and when.

107. The long tail—or the idea that a large number of smaller film titles could collectively lead to profitability down the road—no longer exists, if it ever had. Or if it did, it was crushed by both the tsunami of the new and the last battalions of the corporate-funded superstars. Good luck getting noticed when the 1 percent buy a louder scream than what the rest can yell combined. Artists struggle to survive in the era of the blockbusters' total domination.

108. We are enduring a digital recession. We know it is hard to get work, any work. And we know that it is hard to make film-making a sustainable profession. But it also goes beyond that. Technological advances increasingly reduce the value of basic filmmaking skills.

109. Indie film is not about community or culture—it is more about business and success than ever before. This is where I let my gray hair (what's left of it) show. The folks in this business generally forget that we are first and foremost a community. We could be lifting indie film up all together, but no. When those in the business know you, but see no business in you, they generally don't bother with a personal touch. If they pass on your film or your script, they rarely call or write a personal letter. I have seen the biggest of film festivals do this to some of the most successful of filmmakers. I have seen agents ignore

former clients. I rarely see people in the business do that extra something unless there is something in it for them. Everyone asks, and few offer. I have witnessed this firsthand, and seen and heard of it with my collaborators. It is a shame, a downright dirty shame.

110. We don't budget—let alone train people to budget—for the full life cycle of the film, and thus we lose most of the value for our work without receiving proper compensation. Film schools generally train people only halfway, focusing on just getting the film to the festivals and market. We have to learn to schedule, project revenues, and budget for the longest of hauls. Without this training, we will never truly recognize the value of our work. What's more, we won't be prepared to extract or maximize revenue from our work—and if we don't improve this careless financial approach, the creator class won't survive. Fixing this was the motive behind the A2E (Artist To Entrepreneur) program I launched during my tenure at the San Francisco Film Society (and something I would still do if I found the proper host).

111. It's as if the industry wants all independent films to fail. There are numerous educational initiatives that our leaders and institutions could (and should) undertake that could help indie films succeed, but no one has yet begun such a move. We have no marketing checklist for bringing a film to release. We need a map to run this race. It's a simple fix, not yet executed. Although I am no expert in this arena, I have been working on such a map. That is just one, of many examples I could cite, that the industry, including our support organizations, have failed to launch.

112. The exhibition calendar remains overcrowded with too much of the same—particularly when it comes to summer (for

blockbusters) and winter (for Oscar bait). Why can't we have a balanced or logical release schedule? Films cannibalize each other. New York City has over twenty-five films opening on any given weekend. In 2013, over 900 features opened there.

113. Print media continues to die—and with it the film biz's key way to market to the masses and allow quality work to be discovered. *Newsweek* is no more. In 2010, it sold for one dollar, signaling the state of the business. The 2013 "magazine of the year," *New York*, will go biweekly. So much for such accolades. Newspapers were wonderful things: people bought them generally to read the horoscope, but discovered wonderful things turning the pages, like revolutions in far-off lands and auteur films playing around the corner.

114. Digital viewing offers no uniform reporting, clarity, or transparency of data that would allow the business and culture to advance. This situation has been at play for a while, and I have mentioned it in my annual list of problems posted on my *Hope for Film* blog. However, the establishment's present call for it gives the idea of transparency new prominence, both in the United Kingdom and in the States. The European Union even has a film body dedicated to it: The European Audiovisual Observatory, whose motto is "Transparency through information" (www.obs.coe.int). Wow. Imagine if the United States had a film entity that could say the same. Maybe it will start to get better here, too.

115. The creative community is completely confused by the pros and cons of copyright. On one hand, there appears to be no evidence supporting a reduction in revenue from infringement of individual copyright. On the other hand, we can't afford to lose anything and are desperate to hold on to any possible way to make money. If we had an independently minded media think

tank, it would be great terrain for a white paper. As much as I dislike panel discussions, I could stomach a few more on this subject, but it just does not seem sexy enough for the festival circuit.

116. The creative class has allowed itself to become corrupt and settle for getting a film made, thinking that this is enough. Compromise is the name of the game, and quality suffers as a result. Quantity is encouraged over quality, and the corporate structure promotes playing well with others as the most valued quality.

117. The creative community does not know what to do next—in terms of not getting totally wiped out by the glories of the Internet. We can look at the music industry, and know the indie film business is next. Ouch.

118. Hollywood and the Motion Picture Association of America (MPAA) have enacted a cunnilingus censorship. Evan Rachel Wood has thankfully made this a cause to rally against. It seems pretty evident that there are more challenging censorship issues in this world, but it is also evident that to feature this particular sex act in the U.S. leads to an R rating from the MPAA. It is up to filmmakers to normalize oral sex. As *The Guardian* points out, "The more film-makers that feature oral sex as normal and non-symbolic, the less hostile it becomes for the MPAA—and the more it'll be embraced by culture more generally. There's surely a silent majority of adults who would rather see two characters love one another than a piranha choking up a penis."

119. In the United States, we continue to rely on a rating system that does the opposite of what it intends—another proof that the film business is *Bizarro World*. Sure, the MPAA ratings system generally has kept local censors at bay, but as Peter Travers pointed out at the end of 2013, "Not only are kids not

being protected, but films are still not reaching their intended audiences." The ratings system should help match people with the appropriate content, not drive them away or make it more difficult to book.

120. We do not have institutionalized, "staged" financing in the narrative-film business. We are forced to seek all our financing up front. Not only does this restriction limit an artist's ability to change his or her work in response to social, economic, or political change—or even just a better idea—but it also reduces investors' ability to predict future success. Most importantly, though, tends to reward those who can most confidently boast of their future intent rather than allowing a meritocracy. We see the benefits of "staged" financing in the documentary field, where not only is this structure beginning to take hold among funding institutions, but there is also equal gender representation amongst nonfiction directors, whereas only 6% of Hollywood narratives are directed by women.

121. Money rules everything, and above all, it rules politics. As a result, certain political topics are verboten in movies. Once maybe the media shaped politics, but now power has shifted and clearly in the United States today, money controls our politics, which in turn controls our media. Nowadays, big-money politics can kill projects about politicians, regardless of the political figure's point of view. This unfortunate situation is a disgrace for democracy—and a stab in the side of free film culture. It was a sad day when both CNN and NBC abandoned their Hillary Clinton projects.

122. Hamilton Nolan aptly describes how artistic integrity has become a thing of the past: "There is no longer a penalty for selling out. There is no longer a public censure that accompanies it. There is no longer an outcry within an artistic subculture

when one of its members is fully subsumed by corporate America. The idea that an artist should preserve the sanctity of their work—that they should not allow it to be manipulated by commerce—is no longer considered a mainstream opinion." (See Hamilton Nolan, "What 'Sellouts' Were," *Gawker*, September 30, 2013, gawker.com/what-sellouts-were-1426892512.)

123. Polarization—the gap between the corporate studio's blockbusters and everything else—grows by the day. For every *Mud* or *Fruitvale Station*, most indies rarely travel far or wide. We start to resemble the music industry, depending on a few name brands, while all the unwashed hordes never get to peak above the festival blanket or to be discovered beyond New York or Los Angeles.

124. Artists cannot afford to live in our cultural centers. It's a real Catch-22. Artists make cultural centers, but these places become too pricey for their creators to live in. If you are in the middle class, you can only afford 14 percent of the currently available homes in San Francisco. The number drops to only 2.5 percent in New York City. I love both cities, but can't see my future in either of them as a result. And I don't really want to move to Akron, Ohio, either (no offense intended, Akron!).

125. Producers are not valued—be it via compensation or credit—for some of their most valuable work: script development. I understand a producer's sharing credit with a financier, in light of the work they will do, but how do we show proper respect for the work that got them all to agree to sit down together in the first place? America needs a credit for those who move the script to the first key stage that attaches the talent and the shrewd financiers. How can we say the story is king when we aren't willing to acknowledge all that goes into getting it right? A credit would be the first step, but budgeting a development fee outside of the regular producer fee makes equal sense too.

126. There are virtually no studio overhead deals for producers of ambitious content. Without an overhead deal—when a studio or other deep-pocketed company covers your operational costs— you have to be prepared to earn your next paycheck on your next film. You cannot afford to just keep making work better. You have to focus on what can get made now. The lack of security influences your choices of material and how long you can spend to get things right. Without an overhead deal, there is no way you can pursue quality. You get drawn into the crap . . . uh . . . the makeable-now projects. You can't hold out. You have to compromise. Now granted, most overhead deals were probably not great for business, but they sure allowed producers to chase after great projects. And better movies were made as a result. It's all connected, isn't it?

127. The American video store is pretty much dead and gone. Sure, there are holdouts and some stores that will never go away, but they are virtually a fetish object. Maybe in the future, video stores will be what makes a neighborhood vibrant, but I wouldn't bet on it. Granted, Blockbuster was my least favorite of the bunch—and now it is gone—but the video-store giant pretty much symbolized the collective embrace of the pleasure of deciding what to watch. You could wander in and change your mind. A leisurely path to discovery. The best stores always boasted someone who knew more about cinema than you could ever dream of. Matt Singer offers a eulogy for the video store: "We live in a world where immediacy and instantaneous access is the fundamental driver of commerce. Convenience certainly has its place, but expertise should still have one too." (See Matt Singer, "Why We Still Need Video Stores," *The Dissolve*, November 6, 2013, http://tinyurl.com/pd33rp2.) Right on.

128. Access to much of our greatest film history is becoming more limited. Netflix's innovative model, along with the ease of kiosk

DVD dispensers, crushed the local video stores. Streaming cemented the stores forever in the grave. The physical DVD business died, taking not just the midrange title with it, but also much of our cinema history. Of the top fifteen titles on the American Film Institute's 2007 list of the best American movies, none are currently streaming on Netflix. We have enjoyed the rise of the video-store-educated-auteur, but the next generation will be shaped by the now-available-for-streaming canon. Face it: the assertion that you can now watch whatever you want, whenever you want, and wherever you want is just not true. Maybe you want to pay for twenty-five different services so that you can feel like you have that privilege, but most people are going to watch what's on, and it won't be the greatest films of all time. And besides, don't you miss that stoned, pimply-faced clerk who really did know everything there was to know about a certain type of movie?

129. We confuse censorship with business when it comes to foreign lands (China, particularly). Caving to government pressure is not the same as caving to a studio's notes. Frequently we see the comparison made when cuts are made to get a film released in China. This form of censorship, however, is not the same as acquiescing to a financier's control of content; a Western filmmaker can choose where his or her financing comes from. But the independent filmmakers working in China don't have a choice. Even local film festivals get shut down in China. Our filmmakers in the West do not help their Eastern friends when the Westerners make it seem like no big deal to alter their work. The independent filmmakers in the East are never given the opportunity to even show their work as a result.

130. We indie folks try to bring people *to* our work, instead of taking our work to where the people are. We spend all our money and effort to get people together around existing content. We try

to make them *want* to go to the movies, to make them *want* to watch that specific thing. Don't pull, push. Take your film to the places, both online and off, where groups are already gathered, and then we could simply provide them with the sort of thing they are interested in. Sometimes screen it or bundle it or gift it or just promote it, but perhaps what we have to offer is better than it is, and instead of changing people's behavior and making them come to us, we should go to them more often.

131. We recognize the unfair advantages that wealth and society create, but we don't do anything about it. This is most prevalent and obvious in the film industry's continual reliance on the unpaid-internship structure for career advancement. Most film jobs are in New York City and L.A., two truly expensive cities to live in. We ask those who are accumulating vast amounts of debt through our education system not only to live in these cities, but also to work for free, so that they too can have the privilege of working in the entertainment industry. We need to have a way to pay for our interns, or the only folks who will ever work in the film business will be those born with a silver spoon in their mouths.

132. The winners-take-all blockbuster model has stomped the "long tail" flat. And as much as I hoped people would try to resist and not just dream of a world where diversity, quality, and ambition caused the worthy to surface, that world doesn't exist. Those who speak the loudest (thanks to the largest marketing budgets) not only win, but also shut out the little guys.

133. The majority of U.S. citizens prefer to watch movies at home. A Harris poll at the end of 2013 showed that the scales had tipped. Two-thirds went to the theaters less often in 2013 than previously. Obnoxious patrons and high-priced concessions seemingly scared moviegoers away.

134. Media consolidation feels inevitable. As I write this, I have no idea where it will go, but the fact that a merger between Comcast and Time Warner is even considered indicates how far wrong we have gone. What are our values? Does business trump democracy as a matter of course? Can a line even be drawn? The cable industry is one of many virtual monopolies, and the movement toward further mergers gives the industry incredible leverage over the creative community.

135. Net neutrality is not recognized as an absolute necessity. With the cable business far from being a free zone, the last hope of a level playing field is the Internet. Somehow, the commitment to preserve it as such has been lost. The fight does go on. And it grows forever more complicated. First we really just focused on the *last mile*, the infrastructure (wire or fiber) that physically connects your home to your Internet service provider. Now we are looking at the content-delivery networks that provide the web's backbone. Hopefully we will also place our attention on the walled gardens of commerce that provide the direct interaction with audience and consumers, and on that note, let's move on to number 136.

136. The Internet is becoming less free. As users of mobile devices outpace users of desktop computers, people rely more and more on applications rather than the Internet for obtaining information. To use these apps, you have to first know of these apps, and the platforms that host them control how you find them and how they surface on their sites. Unfortunately for the cause of open, free access to information, the apps are dominated by just two providers, Google and Apple. These companies are walled eco-systems, and their authority is definitive. (See, for example, Jim Edwards, "Mobile Apps Are Killing the Free Web, Handing a Censored Duopoly to Google and Apple," *Business Insider*, April 7, 2014, www.businessinsider.com/mobile-web-vs-app-usage-statistics-2014-4.)

137. The problem of orphan works persists. Orphan works are those for which the legal chain of title and copyright is no longer clear. But now at least two of our film-support organizations (Film Independent and the International Documentary Association) are doing something about the problem. Without a legal process to keep them in the conversation, orphan works fall out of circulation, and their contribution to culture can be lost to the public forever.

138. Netflix and iTunes drop titles that don't have closed captions. Granted, the government-required closed captioning has made many titles available to a community that had previously been deprived of this material. Many filmmakers nevertheless witnessed their work being removed from the platforms, even when the film wasn't yet legally required to have closed captioning. For this reason, smart filmmakers have started budgeting for closed captioning.

139. Pop culture now builds many audiences of elite specialists, losing the common generalists in the process. As Frank Bruni wrote in the *New York Times*, we now have a vast myriad of choices of what to watch and engage in, transforming us all from generalists with common knowledge to specialists stuck in our area of expertise. In the mid-1970s, America's top-rated television series, *All in the Family*, drew more than 50 million people per episode. That was in a country of about 215 million. *NCI*, the number one television series in 2012–2013, typically drew fewer than 22 million people, even counting those who watched a recording of it within a week of its broadcast. There are nearly 318 million Americans now. We don't use pop culture to bring us together anymore, but use it to separate us still further.

140. Although all the big Internet platforms are producing "content," at least one of them is bound to fail in a big way. Consider Netflix, Amazon, Hulu, Microsoft, Yahoo, and others. In the search for another *House of Cards*, will one mistake cause the whole building to fall? Why does it seem so precarious when tech players become media companies? It's worth plumbing this question further, but when any big entity does a major misstep, everyone proceeds cautiously. I wrote this point only one-quarter of the way into 2014, and I will be surprised if we reach the end of the year without a major rethink.

141. Lists like this make the foolish despair.

Filmography

Double Hope Films

All Eyes and Ears (2014)

China in Three Words (2013)

Starlet (2012)

Dark Horse (2011)

This Is That Corporation

Pandemic 41.410806, -75.654259 (2011)

Collaborator (2011)

Martha Marcy May Marlene (2011)

Super (2010)

Adventureland (2009)

The Savages (2007)

Towelhead (2007)

The Ex (2006)

Fay Grim (2006)

The Hawk Is Dying (2006)

Friends with Money (2006)

Thumbsucker (2005)

The Devil and Daniel Johnston (2005)

A Dirty Shame (2004)

The Door in the Floor (2004)

21 Grams (2003)

Good Machine

American Splendor (2003)

The Laramie Project (2002)

Lovely and Amazing (2001)

Human Nature (2001)

Storytelling (2001)

In the Bedroom (2001)

The Tao of Steve (2000)

Ride with the Devil (1999)

The Lifestyle (1999)

Luminous Motion (1998)

Happiness (1998)

No Looking Back (1998)

Fuzzy Logic (1998)

The Sticky Fingers of Time (1997)

Wonderland (1997)

Love God (1997)

The Myth of Fingerprints (1997)

Office Killer (1997)

The Ice Storm (1997)

Arresting Gena (1997)

Monsters (1997)

She's the One (1996)

Greetings from Africa (1996)

Walking and Talking (1996)

What About Me? (1996)

Flirt (1995)

Safe (1995)

The Brothers McMullen (1995)

Roy Cohn/Jack Smith (1994)

Amateur (1994)

Eat Drink Man Woman (1994)

Auf Wiedersehen Amerika (1994)

What Happened Was . . . (1994)

Surviving Desire (1993)

The Wedding Banquet (1993)

Punch and Judy Got Divorced (1992)

Simple Men (1992)

I Was on Mars (1992)

Pushing Hands (1992)

Theory of Achievement (1991)

Ambition (1991)

Angry (1991)

Chicken Delight (1991)

Keep It for Yourself (1991)

Surviving Desire (1991)

Trust (1990)

An Unremarkable Life (1989)

The Unbelievable Truth (1989)

Tiger Warsaw (1988)

Doom Asylum (1987)

Index